Social Memory and War Narratives

Palgrave Studies in Cultural Heritage and Conflict

Series Editors: Ihab Saloul, Rob van der Laarse, and Britt Baillie

This book series explores the relationship between cultural heritage and conflict. The key themes of the series are the heritage and memory of war and conflict, contested heritage, and competing memories. The series editors seek books that analyze the dynamics of the past from the perspective of tangible and intangible remnants, spaces, and traces as well as heritage appropriations and restitutions, significations, musealizations, and mediatizations in the present. Books in the series should address topics such as the politics of heritage and conflict, identity and trauma, mourning and reconciliation, nationalism and ethnicity, diaspora and intergenerational memories, painful heritage and terrorscapes, as well as the mediated reenactments of conflicted pasts.

Dr. Ihab Saloul is assistant professor of cultural studies, and academic coordinator of Heritage and Memory Studies at the University of Amsterdam. Saloul's interests include cultural memory and identity politics, narrative theory and visual analysis, conflict and trauma, diaspora and migration as well as contemporary cultural thought in the Middle East.

Professor Rob van der Laarse is research director of the Amsterdam School for Heritage and Memory Studies (ASHMS) and Westerbork Professor of Heritage of Conflict and War at VU University Amsterdam. Van der Laarse's research focuses on (early) modern European elite and intellectual cultures, cultural landscape, heritage and identity politics, and the cultural roots and postwar memory of the Holocaust and other forms of mass violence.

Dr. Britt Baillie is a founding member of the Centre for Urban Conflict Studies at the University of Cambridge, and a research fellow at the University of Pretoria. Baillie's interests include the politicization of cultural heritage, heritage and the city, memory and identity, religion and conflict, theories of destruction, heritage as commons, contested heritage, and urban resistance.

Also in the series:

Social Memory and War Narratives: Transmitted Trauma among Children of Vietnam War Veterans
by Christina D. Weber

Social Memory and War Narratives

Transmitted Trauma among Children of Vietnam War Veterans

Christina D. Weber

SOCIAL MEMORY AND WAR NARRATIVES
Copyright © Christina D. Weber, 2015.

All rights reserved.

First published in 2015 by
PALGRAVE MACMILLAN®
in the United States—a division of St. Martin's Press LLC,
175 Fifth Avenue, New York, NY 10010.

Where this book is distributed in the UK, Europe and the rest of the world, this is by Palgrave Macmillan, a division of Macmillan Publishers Limited, registered in England, company number 785998, of Houndmills, Basingstoke, Hampshire RG21 6XS.

Palgrave Macmillan is the global academic imprint of the above companies and has companies and representatives throughout the world.

Palgrave® and Macmillan® are registered trademarks in the United States, the United Kingdom, Europe and other countries.

ISBN: 978–1–137–50151–6

Library of Congress Cataloging-in-Publication Data

Weber, Christina D., 1971–
　Social memory and war narratives : transmitted trauma among children of Vietnam War veterans / Christina D. Weber.
　　　pages cm.—(Palgrave studies in cultural heritage and conflict)
　　Includes bibliographical references and index.
　　ISBN 978–1–137–50151–6 (alk. paper)
　　1. Vietnam War, 1961–1975—Social aspects—United States.
　2. Vietnam War, 1961–1975—United States—Psychological aspects.
　3. Veterans—Mental health—United States 4. Veterans—United States—Family relationships. 5. Veterans' families—United States.
　6. Memory—Social aspects—United States. 7. Collective memory—United States. 8. Post-traumatic stress disorder—United States.
　9. Vietnam War, 1961–1975—Influence. I. Title.

DS559.8.S6W43 2015
362.86'30973—dc23   2014043780

A catalogue record of the book is available from the British Library.

Design by Newgen Knowledge Works (P) Ltd., Chennai, India.

First edition: April 2015

10 9 8 7 6 5 4 3 2 1

Library
University of Texas
at San Antonio

This book is dedicated to the men and women who participated in this study along with their families. Thank you for sharing your lives and experiences

CONTENTS

List of Illustrations		ix
Introduction	The Traffic in Memories	1
One	Exploring Trauma and Memory through the Social Monad	25
Two	Conceptualizing the Vietnam Veteran Narrative as a Narrative of Trauma	47
Three	Exploring the Social Monad through the Crisis of Articulation	83
Four	The Vietnam Veteran Father: Reconfiguring Hegemonic Discourses of Masculine Subjectivity	121
Five	Narrative Disruptions of the Dominant Fiction	153
Thoughts and Conclusions	Stretching toward and beyond the Horizon	193
Methodological Appendix		201
Notes		205
Bibliography		213
Index		219

ILLUSTRATIONS

Figures

0.1　Father and Daughter, circa 1981　　　3
0.2　War Locker—The Gift　　　18

Table

A.1　Interviewee details　　　203

INTRODUCTION

The Traffic in Memories

Memory, Trauma, and a Constitutive Theory of Subjectivity

Early in my research for this book I was sitting in a coffee shop absorbed in my thoughts on how to write about the trauma of the Vietnam War through the eyes of the second generation—children of Vietnam Veterans (COVV). As I struggled with these thoughts, I was interrupted by a conversation between two men. Their conversation, initially, held nothing of interest to me. They were complaining about their jobs and local politics and gossiping about their mutual friends. They captured my attention, though, when I heard one of the men say, "He'd have to of been in Vietnam—nutty as he is." His friend tacitly agreed. Actually, it was not a tacit agreement: he laughed. I wanted to ask the man what he meant by his remark, but did not feel comfortable intruding on their conversation. So I silently reveled in the serendipity of this interruption. The resonance of the man's comment and his friend's response exemplifies the innocuous way social memory infiltrates our everyday lives and expressions. His remark is an example of how we can read the social meanings at work in the subject position of the Vietnam Veteran and how they are inscribed onto our hearts and minds. And in relation to my research, it exemplifies the complex traffic at work in memories of a historically traumatic event such as the Vietnam War.

Most of the women and men I interviewed for this research regarded the interview as a platform to repair the image of their fathers as Vietnam Veterans. This is not an easy process for them. They struggle to articulate to me who their fathers are, and I struggle to mediate between their personal narratives and the cultural and historical narratives working within their descriptions and assessments. Understanding the meanings beneath *He'd have to of been in Vietnam—nutty as he is* hinges on our transitory reliance on public representations of the Vietnam War generally and the Vietnam Veteran specifically. The remark makes sense to the friend, to me, and to most of you because there is something we all envision—whether we believe it to be true or not—when such a comment is made. Interrogating the meaning-making process involved in the Vietnam Veteran symbolizing an assumed set of behaviors that include *nutty* or crazy actions requires me to delve into the way both the symbolic and enacted aspects of society work together to shape implied meanings of social subjects.

As a child of a Vietnam Veteran, I hear comments like those made by the man at the coffee shop with a mixture of irritation and pride. At times I have experienced my own father as the *nutty* Vietnam Veteran, but can anybody who has not lived with that craziness know the density implied by that word? Where does the tacit agreement of the relationship between Vietnam Veteran and nutty come from? Is it from social images such as films and high-profile news events, or maybe an interaction with a homeless person who says he is a Vietnam Veteran? What has made this connection so easily accessible in our social imaginary? And how does it go on to shape the construction of self in a Vietnam Veteran's child? I, too, watch the movies, read the news, and see the homeless men, but I also lived with a man who cried and became violent when watching those movies and who angrily insisted the homeless man "wasn't in Vietnam, he's a liar looking for sympathy." Although my memories and repertoire of meanings are tarnished, infected, and affected by my life as a child of a Vietnam Veteran, I mention this not to privilege my position but to emphasize the way personal experiences are deeply enmeshed in cultural memory and narratives. How do I even begin to distinguish the cultural from the personal, between one person's story and another's? Ultimately, that should not be my question. Rather than isolating and separating cultural memories and narratives from personal ones, my interests in this book revolve around understanding the ways they rely on each other for meaning and legitimacy. This moves me away from focusing on cold, hard facts and into searching through the warm and pulsing realities caught in a perplexing tangle of ineffable ideologies, shadowy memories, and dynamic lived experiences. The myriad public representations at work in our society surrounding the Vietnam Veteran and Vietnam War weigh on the COVV as they make sense of their fathers, themselves, and their

Introduction

Figure 0.1 Father and Daughter, circa 1981.

relationships. It also affected me as I conducted my research and write these words.

Interpreting these narratives means I must tell a story that acknowledges that lived experiences are greater than the sum of each piece of the story; our memories are told through history and society. Thus, it is important to think through the relationships developing in narrative construction instead of generating a catalogue of expressions that serve to epitomize the segments, never quite reaching the critical intersections that make the whole greater than the sum of its parts. By studying intersections between personal experience and social history, it is possible to analyze and articulate the process without diminishing the vitality of the lives that are the life force beneath our work.

"So you don't always say Vietnam but you know it's the reason he is the way he is." Much like the comment made in the coffee shop, this comment by one of the men I interviewed (Stan) contains a dense, obfuscated understanding of Vietnam. As difficult as it is to give voice to the word *crazy*, Vietnam is an even more contradictory social concept—inarticulable by virtue of its overarticulation in society. Vietnam is an unspoken presence in Stan's life, which he understands through his father's struggle with post-traumatic stress disorder (PTSD) and depression, along with a host of other health problems. It also infects Stan's ability to comprehend his and his father's place as a man in America.

Vietnam is full of tension for both Stan and his brother Greg. Greg identifies the presence of Vietnam in his life as one of "awkward anxiety." This term underscores the innocuous way in which the event of the Vietnam War becomes part of Stan and Greg's relationship with their father.[1] It epitomizes how difficult it is to understand the war's presence in their lives. It also strikes me how flippant comments such as the one made by the man in the coffee shop contribute to my subjects' anxiety about the meanings of their fathers' status as Vietnam Veterans. Greg commented,

> You know, here's all the wars. Stick Vietnam on at the end. And it's almost like the whole country was ashamed. It wasn't talked about. It was just kind of stuck on there and so even then I felt—it made me feel awkward about it. Okay, so Vietnam. So my dad's a Vietnam Vet. So that's a bad thing? Or is it a good thing? What does that mean? I never knew what it meant.

And he still doesn't. Neither Greg nor Stan settles on an answer to these questions. They navigate through societal confusion that, ultimately, becomes their confusion. The stories inscribed on this palimpsest are at times impossible to read without the multiple dynamics that filter through the larger social (hi)story, each piece feeding into the other, contributing to the confusing historical moment of Vietnam. It also contributes to the tensions Greg and Stan feel exist between themselves and their father. Vietnam is an awkward specter that these men grew up with—one of immense confusion and anxiety.

The fragmented stories of their father's service in Vietnam are punctuated by the war's silent presence within their family. This has generated the eruptions of multiple layers of meaning, which coexist uncomfortably in Greg and Stan's interpretation of the war, their father, and themselves. Questions they had about the war and its effects on their father plagued both men's interviews and were deeply connected to questions about their own life position and the vast generational differences they felt existed between them and their father. Their intersubjective relationship with their father along with knowledge of the Vietnam War and their own individual life experiences merge, creating a great deal of disquiet about the war and who they are as men. In particular, a significant undercurrent within Greg and Stan's narratives is their attempts to connect Vietnam to their strained relationship with their father. Stan continually expressed anger toward and disappointment in his father. At the same time, this created a great deal of guilt, because he was not entirely sure why he felt so much anger toward him. "Geez, why am I mad at him? It's not his fault. I should, you know—he's a sympathetic character. Why would I be mad at him? He's done everything for me. And, I mean, I should be thankful." Stan's awkwardness and feeling that he cannot blame his father for his behaviors intersect with his father's status as a Vietnam Veteran and his struggle with the trauma he experienced in Vietnam.

Watching their father struggle with PTSD, depression, and alcoholism leaves both men hesitant about where to locate the source of their difficult relationship with their father. Is it because of their father's individual fallibilities? Is it because their father is a Vietnam Veteran with PTSD? Is it because America has not been able to deal with the Vietnam War in a healthy and constructive way? *So my dad's a Vietnam Vet. So that's a bad thing? Or is it a good thing? What does that mean. I never knew what it meant.* These are the questions that Greg and Stan imply in their anxieties and to which they were unable to find a definitive answer. These are also questions that I have to ask as I analyze my interviewees' comments. By engaging with these questions, we do not find answers so much as greater insight into the complex way that social memory intersects with personal experiences.

While the Vietnam War is a significant part of these men's lives, they have a somewhat indirect and removed relationship to it. They are the second generation who must navigate the gift of traumatic presence in their lives with their fathers. They may not always *say Vietnam* to explain their struggles with their father but it is a distinct presence that tangles into their unease about the prescriptions for masculine subjectivity in American society. Greg and Stan's uncertainty about the meaning of the presence of Vietnam in their lives leaves them using the event to underscore their descriptions about how their lives and relationships are irresolute and in-formation. Social presence reminds us of the active negotiation of public representations and intersubjective relationships that constitute lived experience. The inscriptions on this palimpsest halt and start up again in different places, complicating attempts to link cultural memory and history to the lives of individuals. As a document that has been inscribed several times, the palimpsest is where the remnants of earlier, imperfectly erased scripting is still detectable (Gordon, 1997, 146). The narratives of COVV demonstrate how layers of stories bump into each other, reflecting and refracting lines of sight and comprehension that take them through the rough terrain of history and subjectivity. It reminds us that both lives and histories are documents in process: never finalized, never complete. These men's ambiguous relationships with both their father and the Vietnam War remind us of the density of lived experience. While I work through more layers over the course of this book, delving into Greg and Stan's narratives in more depth, the irresolution is interminable. Hence this is an introduction that must pick up and start in another locale in order to continue on in the process of reading narratives of trauma.

In this book, I pursue a line of thought that explores the role trauma and memory play in a constitutive theory of subjectivity. What Marianne Hirsch calls postmemory,[2] I expand into an active and generative concept, which I identify as the social monad. The traumatic event of the Vietnam War is the case study—the social monad—I use in this research and it stands as the sheath of this book. As an exploration of a history of the present, this book is much more than a history of the Vietnam War. The war is the starting point from which I explore the way individuals negotiate traumatic memory as they develop a sense of self within specific historical and social positions. More importantly, the process of telling the stories of our lives requires continual negotiation between personal memories, intersubjective relationships, social memory, and the stories we hear others tell, all of which occur in tangent with the social monad. In this respect, we start to understand the complex ways in which cultural narratives and personal relationships, together, affect the way the next generation knows and experiences history in the present. In particular, we start to understand how a social monad manifests in the subjects living out the tightly bound network of social relations housed within what American society calls the Vietnam War. The social monad ceases to appear as some social abstraction. Instead, it is a visceral and embodied reality that the next generation must traverse in its own social context. In and through affective relationships they have with the subject of trauma (the Vietnam Veteran), COVV come to know the trauma of the Vietnam War through their father.

In a recent class discussion on the impact of war on social change, a student made an astute observation. She said that she is living in a generation that has never *not* known war. This struck me as significant to the work of this book and the ongoing relevance to examining and understanding the impact of war on culture. I am telling the story of COVV some 30 years after the war's end. How will the war efforts in the United States impact future generations? If we take some of the experiences of my interviewees in this book seriously, this will be an ongoing and significant question for us in the years and decades to come. One of the underlying goals of this book is to initiate conversations and develop preliminary tools that can help us find answers to this question. Therefore, the focus of this book is twofold: (1) to use the Vietnam War as a case study to develop my epistemological approach through the concepts of the social monad and the traumatic subject and (2) to draw out a nuanced analysis of how later generations come to terms with the Vietnam War through their relationships with their Vietnam Veteran fathers. The social monad and traumatic subject are analytical tools that could be applicable to the analyses of other conflicts and wars, albeit with different focal points, outcomes, and emphases. It is my intention to develop and use these concepts to address some of the more intangible ways in which trauma and memory move through social relationships, shaping the transmission and understanding of sociohistorical events such as war and conflict.

The Gift

Walter Benjamin, via Shoshona Felman's analysis, invites us to ponder the residue of a traumatic history.

> What Benjamin attempts, in other words, is to transmit the story that cannot be told and to become himself the storyteller that cannot be one but that is one—the last narrator or the *post-narrator.* The trauma—or the breakdown of the story and of memory, the fragmentation of remembrance and the rupture of the chain or of the "web of stories"—is itself passed on to the next generation as a testament, a final *gift.* (2002, 46—my emphases)

The *ruptures* emerging from the breakdown of articulation is what makes trauma visible; the pieces being the *gift* handed to the next generation. For COVV, piecing together the fragments of remembrance is fraught with uncertainty; yet, it is the process of piecing together that transforms trauma into a space of insight, creating meaning in the crevices between what is known and unknown. This is demonstrated by Montana, one of my interviewees:

> I think there has been a lot more that I've had to piece together about my life on my own than maybe some of my friends growing up that didn't have a father, veteran for a father. There's been a lot of silence. There's been a lot of—I don't know how else to describe it except holes that are just these gaps in my experience that no one explains. That no one is willing to explain. And I've been trying to do the tying together myself. There haven't been stories. When there have been stories, they haven't been happy, there's just... [sigh]. Absence is the only way I know how to describe it. Just these gaps that I've had to fill in for myself.

Tim O'Brien's daughter is also left to piece things together.

> When she was nine, my daughter Kathleen asked if I had ever killed anyone. She knew about the war; she knew I'd been a soldier. "You keep writing these war stories," she said, "so I guess you must've killed somebody." It was a difficult moment, but I did what seemed right, which was to say, "Of course not," and then to take her on my lap and hold her for awhile. Someday, I hope, she'll ask again. But here I want to pretend she's grown up. I want to tell her exactly what happened, or what I remember happening, and then, I want to say to her that as a little girl she was absolutely right. This is why I keep writing war stories. (O'Brien, 1990, 131)

O'Brien's book, *The Things They Carried*, evocatively captures the articulation of traumatic memory through the *way* he tells the story. The book consists of numerous short stories that are disjointed and meandering. At times he lies to us so he can tell us the truth. For O'Brien, there is a distinction to be made between *happening-truth* and *story-truth*. He is, using Shoshona Felman's words, a *post-narrator who wants to reestablish the transmissability of his experience, and to transmit the happening that cannot be told*. Story-truth enables O'Brien to do this. But the story is not whole. Its presence is defined by holes, gaps, silences—absence. As Kathleen observes her father's struggle with his memories of the war through the books and stories he writes, she ponders the truth, making a naïve (yet astute) observation that opens up very difficult questions about the war and participating in it. O'Brien answers her with a simple truth that in his mind is not the whole truth—can never be the whole truth. The silence following her father's response becomes another piece of an extraordinarily complicated puzzle. Like Montana, Kathleen is left to fill in the gaps and unsettled spaces between what she knows and what she comprehends. She has to try to understand how the stories fit into what she knows (and can never know) about her father and the war. Sometimes the stories do not even seem like stories. They can be abbreviated comments or sarcastic jokes as well as defensive silences and ambiguous gestures.

When Renee, another one of my interviewees, asked her father if he killed anybody in Vietnam, she explained that "there was this glazed look, and it was, like, don't go there." She continues: "There was just this blankness that came over his face. And, you know, he never answered me. He never responded." When I reiterated what she said to me, she corrected herself by saying "It was very evasive." She explained to me that he said "'You don't know what they did to us over there. [...] I watched friends be killed by, you know, 5-year-olds and 6-year-olds.' And so it wasn't 'yes I did' nor 'no I didn't'" (my emphasis). How can a father help his child feel what he felt in that moment of trauma? And would he really want to do that in light of the pain those feelings conjure? The gift, moving between father and child, is never a simple handing down of history like a baton in a relay race. There is an incredible amount of emotional life traffic moving between the traumatic subject and the second generation.

Traumatic memories move intersubjectively between father and child, extending beyond the language of the stories that my interviewees hear and into the way they interpret those stories in light of the interactions they have with their fathers. The truth of the past, to draw on Jeffrey Prager's work, "can be discovered, by the person who experienced it, only through witnessing how the past is inscribed affectively in experiences and fantasies and then acted on in engagement with others and with the world" (1998, 164). Here it is expressed through a Vietnam Veteran's relationship with his daughter. This is also true for O'Brien. Time and again his stories reflect back on his daughter's questions and demonstrate his struggle to mediate his past as a soldier with his present as a father. He writes in the short piece, "Good Form,"

> I want you to feel what I felt. I want you to know why story-truth is truer sometimes than happening-truth. Here is happening-truth. I was once a soldier. There were many bodies, real bodies

with real faces, but I was young then and I was afraid to look. And now, twenty years later, I'm left with faceless responsibility and faceless grief.

Here is the story-truth. He was a slim, dead, almost dainty young man of about twenty. He lay in the center of a red clay trail near the village of My Khe. His jaw was in his throat. His one eye was shut, the other eye was a star shaped hole. I killed him. (O'Brien, 1990,180)

By explicitly juxtaposing happening-truth with story-truth, he asks us to reconsider our quest for Truth. At the end of the story, he returns to the question his daughter asked, writing "'Daddy, tell the truth,' Kathleen *can* say, 'did you ever kill anybody?' And I *can* say, honestly, 'Of course not.' Or I *can* say, honestly, 'Yes'" (O'Brien, 1990, 180). He could say yes *or* he could say no. Both possibilities are true. When placed together, these responses tell us something about narrating trauma and the complexities of the truth of traumatic experience. This does not mean that there is no truth to the war or the war experience; what it does mean is that truths are often found in the process of piecing together, shaping a narrative that is unfinished, in-formation. Thus, there is an ongoing attempt to retrieve the irretrievable, articulate the inarticulable, as COVV receive the gift of the Vietnam War. O'Brien hands Kathleen (and us) pieces. Just as Renee is left to contemplate the meaning of her father's response, Kathleen must do the same. I wonder, as she sat on her father's lap, just what was tacitly exchanged between them. The truth Kathleen and Renee were looking for may involve more than the truth of their fathers' acts; their search may be for the men who were/are their fathers and the gift of history they are starting to recognize themselves within.

The Things They Carried focuses on one of the greatest hurdles in the process of remembering: putting traumatic memories to words. The quagmire of a lost past full of contradictory emotions, and the irresolution it carries, can (and often does) leave one paralyzed into silence. O'Brien counters that silence through his disjointed stories that attempt to make sense of the things *he* carries. The book opens with a laundry list of things Lieutenant Cross and his men carried on their combat missions. As we read the list of items, it soon grows apparent that there is a complex mixture of tangibles and intangibles. With the guns, malaria tablets, and P-38 can openers, "they carried all the emotional baggage of men who might die. Grief, terror, love, longing— these were intangibles, but the intangibles had their own mass and specific gravity, they had tangible weight." (O'Brien, 1990, 21). Thus, while language is necessary to express memories of the past, the stories of the past carry weight that goes beyond words. Included in the stories O'Brien tells us are the interactions he has with his daughter. Kathleen has more than words to make sense of; she carries the weight of her own memories with her father. Enmeshed in those memories are the love and turmoil found in their relationship. Language provides a skeleton, but the meaning, the flesh filling out the structure within it, comes from something beyond the words themselves.

> The thing about a story is that you dream it as you tell it, hoping that others might then dream along with you, and in this way memory and imagination and language combine to make spirits in the head. There is the illusion of aliveness. (O'Brien, 1990, 230)

The stories O'Brien writes can provide comfort to other Vietnam Veterans, who cannot find words for their experiences. But through my own experiences of reading O'Brien's work, the stories help COVV (well, at least one—me) find answers to questions that are as impossible to ask as they are to answer. And the stories may hold even more intimate meanings for Kathleen. We dream along with O'Brien but the spirits that come to life in our heads are different for each of us. The process of remembering is affected by our relationships in the world; it carries weight, because how we remember is interconnected with who we are and how we know one another. The process of remembering relies on a variety of spirits and fantasies that stem from the official and cultural documentation of the past, as well as our own affectual relationships. The second generation of a war *is* handed a gift. This gift is the social monad, an in-formation presence that leaves the second generation navigating an unresolved past; they struggle to secure meaning in this past by working between solidified social forms and fluid, embryonic, forms of affective lived experience that disrupts preconceived notions of social life. From this ruptured gift—emerges the concern for opening an oppressed past, which is part of Walter Benjamin's theory of history as trauma. Felman explains that this concern implies "a correlative theory of the historical conversion of trauma into *insight*" (2002, 33—my emphasis).

Locating the Enunciative Site of the Social Monad

Like the bundle of nerves that meet at the end of the body's spine, the network of stories found in a social monad is a source of intense feeling and activity. Walter Benjamin reminds us that, "memory creates a chain of tradition which passes a happening on from generation to generation.... It starts the web which all stories together form in the end. One ties on to the next...as the great storytellers have shown" (1968, 98). The social monad generates meaning from which the social body interprets and negotiates a historically traumatic event such as the Vietnam War. It also *creates a chain of tradition* from which individuals develop their own stories, which then feeds back into the dense site that is the social monad. This network of stories moves from generation to generation, not as a cohesive nugget the second generation is forced to carry, but as a complex set of fragments that the second generation must traverse in order to shape their subjectivities.

Tom Bissell does just that in his article, "War Wounds: A Father and Son Return to Vietnam." Providing insight into the texture of trauma's residue on the second generation's subjectivity, the title of his article implies, perhaps unintentionally, that he must *return* to the site of trauma—Vietnam—in order to better understand his father and himself. Yet the son was never in Vietnam—at least not physically. Instead, the trauma came home with his father and Bissell experienced it through him. "Despite it's remoteness, the war's aftereffects were inescapably intimate. At every meal Vietnam sat down, invisibly, with our families."(Bissell, 2004, 57). Vietnam became part of the daily lives of Vietnam Veterans, which then became part of the lives of their families, loved ones, and children. It became part of America but in ways that stammer and fumble for expression in a world where war often is viewed—by those uninitiated to its darker realities—as a distant visage without referent. So when Bissell tells us *Vietnam sat down at every meal* with his family, he is trying to tell us how trauma is lived out and through the life his father lives—and the life he has lived with him. The Vietnam War, as a social monad, has a peculiar weight and density in the lives of COVV.

From a surface glance, the social monad is a carapace protectively defining and shaping the perimeters of social understanding of the Vietnam War. Invoking Walter Benjamin, the (social) monad is the crystallized solidification of a traumatic event. As he explains, "Where thinking stops in a configuration pregnant with tensions, it gives that configuration a shock, by which it crystallizes into a *monad*" (Benjamin, 1968, 262; my emphasis). The event temporally passed but its effects, bound in the social monad, continue to haunt present life because the event has been passed *on* as a dense site of social activity.

This dense site reveals a far more complex system of social enterprise than the hardened carapace implies. The inner workings of the social monad—to look at it from the inside out—reveal a complicated tangle of personal memories and intersubjective relationships that are at once attached to the crystallized social frame, yet have distinct lives of their own. Relying on the social narrative of the Vietnam Veteran, the man at the coffee shop reinforces the social monad as he incorporates it into his own story. The men and women in this book rely on crystallized narratives of the Vietnam Veteran and the Vietnam War as they simultaneously transform them into stories that apply to their own experiences with their fathers. Each enliven the complex underbelly of the social monad, actively reminding us of the presence of the Vietnam War in our society.

Stammered articulations such as those expressed by Bissell and my interviewees alert us to the presence of the gift that Felman invokes in her work. "The rupture of the chain of stories or of the 'web of stories'—is itself passed on to the next generation as a testament, a final gift" (Felman, 2002, 46). Bissell grew up with a *web of stories* his father told him of the war, but the stories were filled with gaps and seeped into his own memories in ways that are in tension with his father's memories of war—the memories of war having a different utility for son than for father. The *chain of tradition* is tainted by numerous glitches in our ability to communicate and translate lived experience into social narratives. As Bissell remembers, "Sometimes it feels as though Vietnam is all my father and I have ever talked about; sometimes it feels as though we have never really talked about it" (2004, 57). In those myriad stories that seamlessly entered his memories of his father, the gift of trauma emerges as something even more intangible, discrete, and incomprehensible than his father's stories of his experiences in Vietnam.

> When I was a boy, I would dread the evenings my father had too much to drink, stole into my bedroom, woke me up, and for an hour at a time would try to explain to me, his ten-year-old son, why the decisions he made—decisions, he would mercilessly remind himself, that got his best friend killed—were the only decisions he could have made. (2004, 57)

But what becomes of such information in the mind of a ten-year-old? It is through exchanges such as these that we can locate the Vietnam Veteran as the site of the enunciation of trauma. It is through remembering these stories that Bissell understands how his own life has been structured around the event of the Vietnam War. It is because of these stories that Bissell decided to go with his father to Vietnam. He wanted to find his father—the man he was before Vietnam. "I believed I could find him in Vietnam, where he had been made and unmade, killed and resurrected" (2004, 58). What he found, though, was that the trauma of the war is indelibly linked to his father. They could not be disconnected—his father is the man resurrected in Vietnam. While he deeply desires to separate his father from Vietnam, he cannot. Bissell discovers that the stories of his father rest upon the stories of his father's service in Vietnam. They are part of the man who is Bissell's father.

The traffic in memories and their chaotic movement in the stories of our lives can be discerned in Bissell's own process of misremembering the story of his father's war injuries. Since he was a boy, Bissell believed that his father was shot in the line of duty and then saved by a black soldier. This story provided a frame for him to identify his father as a "passive hero" as well as explain his father's racial tolerance. But the story is a falsity; it never happened. During their trip to Vietnam, his father recounts the story of how he was injured. Bissell tells his father that the story is "not the story you told me" (2004, 64). In truth, his father had never told Bissell about the circumstances of his injuries. The story of his father being saved by a black soldier was a creation on Bissell's part to make sense of war stories that seemed to make no sense: stories that were told to him in confusing ways and without narrative coherency. He is handed garbled and painful memories of the past that were without context in his own mind. This gift of the story that cannot be told is received by Bissell as "a fragmentation of remembrance" (Felman, 2002, 46).

> I remember telling that story to myself, but I don't remember being told that story. At some point the story simply appears in my mind. Why did I create this story? Because it made my father heroic? In the emergency of growing up we all need heroes. But the father I grew up with was no hero, not then. He was too wounded in the head, too endlessly and terribly sad. Too funny, too explosive, too confusing. Heroes are uncomplicated. *This* makes them do *that*. The active heroism of my imaginary black Marine made a passive hero of my father; they huddled together, alongside a road in the Vietnam of my mind, shrouded in nitroglycerin, the cordite of gallantry. (Bissell, 2004, 64)

What Bissell tells us is important. We begin to understand how trauma becomes part of a larger story: the story of America and the story of masculine subjectivity project heroic certainties—certainties Bissell felt he needed in his life. Certainties his father could not *give* him. In his desire to make his father a hero, Bissell's narrative blends fact and fiction in order to find certitude where there was none—would always be none. He takes imaginative license with the past in order to reconcile the pain and suffering he witnessed in his father with the fabric of his father's larger social existence. Bissell's construction of his father emerges out of happening- and story-truth.

"The story made sense of the senseless," Bissell tells us. "But war does not make sense" (2004, 64). In the aftermath of the chaos of war, relationships between fathers and sons, fathers and daughters, struggle to generate a bridge between the stammered articulations of something that is unspeakable in his lived experiences. COVV fumble for a way of speaking about how trauma is made manifest in their daily lives. But how can one be sure that what she is seeing and hearing is fact, fiction, or the presence of story-truth told to them in the face of her father's attempt to articulate trauma? Trauma's presence can be difficult to discern amid the myriad experiences daily life generates. Part of the difficulty in analyzing the social monad of the Vietnam War is finding a way to clarify trauma's stammered echoes in order to understand how the past is part of the present. Articulating presence is hard enough, but how does one speak of a presence intruded upon by experiences that are beyond normal human experiences—when the present must address the presence of an imperfect (traumatic) past? The translucent and shadowy parts of social life demand our attention. The demands are often innocuous, other times they suffocate with their all-consuming presence. Trauma—or more precisely, its articulation—is slippery and frequently eludes our linguistic conventions. This is why we rely on images of the past in its most tangible forms. Within the historically traumatic event of the Vietnam War, trauma can be seen and heard in the image of the Vietnam Veteran. He is the enunciative site of trauma. He is the symbol of a history that America struggles to reconcile. He is the one we look to when we need to speak about the effects of trauma and its lingering presence and where we encounter uncertainty and doubt as well as clarity and assurance.

The Vietnam Veteran Narrative underscores the centrality of the Vietnam Veteran in our confrontation with trauma. His narrative is one of trauma and is the site where we start to understand the crisis of truth and crisis of survival that takes place for a survivor of trauma. O'Brien is an ideal example of these points, yet his story is not the only possible manifestation of this narrative. Vietnam Veterans such as Oliver Stone, Mark Baker, Ron Kovic, Philip Caputo, and the fathers of my interviewees contribute further to the Vietnam Veteran Narrative. Each speaks of trauma in his own way, but their stories, when woven together, comprise a larger story of the Vietnam Veteran that has been injected into the cultural imaginary. The Vietnam Veteran Narrative takes for granted the position of the masculine subject in American society. The narrator dreams about the masculine virtues and ideals that he took to Vietnam. In the wake of trauma, these ideals are shattered, becoming nostalgic promises as well as testaments to his (and/or society's) failures. In the end, the narrator has to pick up these pieces and try to rebuild his beliefs—that is, he has to recreate his story. He needs to make sense of himself and society in order to function as a social subject; he needs to find a means of survival. Part of that story includes his existence as a traumatized subject. Although this trauma is particular to combat and the Vietnam War experience, the Vietnam Veteran Narrative is instructive about the way trauma becomes part of one's subjective sense of self, extending beyond events (and their chronological stasis) in unpredictable and lasting ways.

In this book, I consider the insights the trauma of the Vietnam War brings to COVV; how meanings of that traumatic event are both diffused and fortified as the focus of articulation shifts from event to subject. For the children, their fathers are more than Vietnam Veterans; they are fathers with a present physical and social existence. They are men who create an exigent set of meanings about the Vietnam War that enable them to recognize its presence even as it appears in intangible and inarticulable fragments and pieces. Although I do not claim COVV hold the key to unlocking the complexities of this contentious historical moment, they do tell us much about ourselves in the present and how history is at once distant and intimate in our articulations of who we are and what gives our lives meaning. The stories of the Vietnam War are found in histories of strategies and policies, literary works such as O'Brien's, and films such as *Platoon*. But they are also found in a father telling his daughter, in a moment of emotional pain, that we are living in hell here on earth. They are found in the psychological records a father hands to his daughter to read. They all matter to history. The trauma of war does not end when the troops come home, nor does it end with cathartic memoirs or therapy. The person carries the trauma home with (and in) them, and children—young and old—feel the weight. So, attention needs to be given to how this gift filters into the daily life of individuals. O'Brien tells us that the thing about remembering is that you don't forget. Thus, my research is about the way history gets under our skins and how we carry it into our daily lives; how we don't forget.

INTRODUCTION 17

Organization of Book

The book's organization follows the dynamic movement within the social monad. Consisting of two primary co-constitutive layers of data, I weave together interviews I conducted with COVV and social artifacts considering the Vietnam War and Vietnam Veteran. Specifically, I analyze Oliver Stone's films on the Vietnam War (*Platoon*, *Born on the Fourth of July*, and *Heaven and Earth*), autobiographies of Vietnam Veterans, and media images of the Vietnam Veterans in current history. Because the Vietnam Veteran is the locus of social meanings of the trauma of the Vietnam War, I contain my data to social artifacts portraying Vietnam Veterans. The dynamics of the social monad emerge out of the integration of these two layers of data.

For the narratives of COVV, I relied on an interview schedule that consisted of semi-structured questions, which focused on different thematic points of the subject's knowledge of Vietnam and his/her relationship with his/her father. The men and women I interviewed came from two rounds of data collection: October 2001 to April 2002 and August 2002 to May 2003. The first round of interviews was generated from my contact with a Vietnam Veteran organization (which I call VVO in order to maintain confidentiality) in Western New York. The second round of interviews developed out of my contacts at VVO and snowballed into a variety of different contacts with community and university organizations. This resulted in 25 narratives.[3]

The chapters of this book are organized around these different data sources in order to integrate the analysis between individual and social forms. I explore this issue in greater depth in chapter one. In chapters two and four, I approach the social monad from the outside in, examining the crystallized social narratives and representations of the Vietnam War and Vietnam Veteran. In chapters three and five, I approach the monad from the inside out, disrupting (and at times reifying) these social narratives with the narratives of COVV.

The Vietnam Veteran: The Epicenter of the Social Monad

One point that I cannot overstress is that the Vietnam War, as a social monad, is expressed through the subject of the Vietnam Veteran. It is *a configuration pregnant with tensions*. This is a point that Tim O'Brien expressed about ten years after his return from Vietnam.

> The nation seems too comfortable with—even dependent on— the image of a suffering and deeply troubled veteran. Rather than

face our own culpabilities, we shove them off onto ex-GIs and let them suffer for us. Rather than relive old tragedies, rather than confront our own frustrations and puzzlements about the war, we take comfort in the image of the bleary-eyed veteran carrying all that emotional baggage for us. (1979, 100)

The *emotional baggage* the Vietnam Veteran carries consists of the historical tensions generated from the trauma of the Vietnam War.

As a result, the story of the Vietnam War is usually told through the image of the Vietnam Veteran, and that image has a number of manifestations in American society. I explore several of them in chapter two and revisit them again in chapter four. In particular, I look at how the Vietnam Veteran is the storyteller (narrator) of the Vietnam Veteran Narrative (discussed in chapter two). This narrative is part of the outer shell of the social monad. Although the Vietnam Veteran Narrative materializes out of the myriad autobiographies, novels, and films by Vietnam Veterans, the story it tells is much more expansive

Figure 0.2 War Locker—The Gift.

in scope: "For autobiography has to do with time, with sequence and what makes up the continuous flow of life. Here, I am talking of a space, of moments and discontinuities" (Benjamin, 1968, 28). The Vietnam Veteran Narrative is not simply autobiography; it is a *space* where the flows of life rupture chronological narratives, focusing on disruptions, breaks, and tensions that reveal the trauma of the Vietnam War—exposing the way individual and social memory and experience intersect. "Where there is experience in the strict sense of the word, certain contents of the individual past combine with material of the collective past.... In this way, voluntary and involuntary recollection lose their mutual exclusivity" (Benjamin, 1968, 159–60).

The story the Vietnam Veteran Narrative tells is both personal and social. It attempts to articulate the disparate pieces of the past and their effects on the present. The narrator tells the story not just of the war, but of loss of belief in America and the world he knew before entering into war. He also explores the nuances of masculine subjectivity and how what it meant to be a man shifted as he moved into the combat zone, then back into a society within which he could no longer recognize himself. Tangled within the COVV's narratives are these types of stories and silences told to them by their fathers and society. The Vietnam Veteran Narrative and the imagery of the Vietnam Veteran in social images intervene with, and hence, complicate my interviewees' narratives of their father. The layered story lines reveal a palimpsest of historical comprehension that renders any single moment in the articulation of this traumatic event fraught with uncertainty and ambiguity that is impossible to alleviate. By rendering *the bleary-eyed veteran* as the repository of social anxieties about America's political actions and values, public discourses cannot seriously ask questions (or engage in meaningful public debate) about the dangerous repercussions of war on society.

COVV and the Social Monad: Articulating Presence

In most description and analysis, culture and society are expressed in an habitual past tense. The strongest barrier to the recognition of human cultural activity is this immediate and regular conversion of experience into finished products. (Raymond Williams, 1977, 128)

Raymond Williams was concerned with the way non-fixed forms of knowing were often muted by the analysis of the world in *an habitual past tense*. Involved in developing a method that writes against the frame of habit, which turns narratives into *finished products*, is the challenge of facing our own incapacities to articulate presence—unfinished social formations. COVV's narratives are unfinished. The men and women I interviewed were searching for their own place, not only in the story of the Vietnam War, but also in their present lives. Sometimes Vietnam was part of that story, sometimes it was not. Nevertheless, I cannot do justice to their narratives without making clear my intense desire to leave their narratives *unfinished*. Whether I succeed or not at articulating their presence in this book is up to you—the reader—but it is an effort that needs both to be stated upfront and an explanation. Without the logic behind some of my underlying efforts and struggles, the significance of the social monad may disappear behind theoretical abstraction.

Our necessary reliance on the hardened tools of language can quickly ossify our interpretations of the dense and sinuous site where "history and subjectivity make social life" (Gordon, 1997, 8). But the truth is that life is fluid and in motion, even when ostensibly stuck in analytical forms of social expression. This can make hearing what lay beyond preconceived social forms a formidable task. To analyze a text for what it is saying in-between words and within historical breaks can make sociologists nervous and speculative about the veracity of one's analysis. But it is vital to look at what may not be fully articulate *yet*—that glimmer of recognition where feeling and thinking are in an "embryonic phase before it can be fully [an] articulate and defined exchange." At the same time, though, "its relations with the already articulate and defined are...exceptionally complex" (Williams, 1977, 131). What is important, then, is that once an embryonic presence has made itself known to us, we allow ourselves to become acquainted with it, understanding "that much is at stake in our recognition of *engagement* with ghostly matters, in our ability to stop fleeing from the recognition of something more" (Gordon, 1997, 206; my emphasis). This means that it is important not to turn away when we come in contact with the lingering effects of history—the trauma of the past; nor should we brush those effects aside, minimizing their meaning upon our lives or their relevance to larger social systems.

Avery Gordon's book, *Ghostly Matters*, explores the perimeters of "sensuous knowledge" through the theoretical concepts of haunting and ghosts. In her book, she explores how seemingly invisible social structures seep into individual and social life. Gordon saw the way literary writers such as Toni Morrison and Luisa Valenzuela opened that door. And she, in turn, walks through those doors, discovering alternative ways of knowing, seeing, and expressing the world.

> Morrison and Valenzuela see with remarkable clarity and with an extraordinary generosity of apprehension the haunting way systematic compulsions work on and through people in everyday life. They see into the abstractions: they comprehend the elusive concreteness of ghostly matter. They capture those singular and yet repetitive instances when homes become unfamiliar, when your bearings on the world lose direction, when things are animated, when the over and done with comes alive, when the blind field comes into view, when your own or another's shadow shines brightly. (Gordon, 1997, 197)

Morrison and Valenzuela do this through historically informed literature; Gordon does this through sociological research.

"Sensuous knowledge is a different kind of materialism" generated from affectual relationships (such as those between father and child). "It is neither idealistic nor alienated.... Sensuous knowledge is receptive, close, perceptual, embodied, incarnate. It tells and it transports at the same time." Sensuous knowledge also moves and motivates. It is what provokes the mind to see what is not entirely manifest. "To experience a profane illumination is to experience the sensate quality of a knowledge meaningfully affecting you. To experience a profane illumination is to experience something to be done" (Gordon, 1997, 205). It is the seemingly indirect affectual tie to history that provoked my work on this project and brought me to the door where I could see the worth in doing research that equally values intellectual and emotional ways of knowing, ultimately engaging with their points of intersection. To articulate presence—the presence of history in our mundane existence—I emphasize the importance of affectual life on our everyday understanding of the world. Through their discussions of their fathers and their intersubjective relationships, my interviewees articulate a way of knowing the Vietnam Veteran—the sensuous knowledge of the Vietnam War—that undermines our society's attempts to deny the deep and ongoing effects of war. Such denials run deep in the United States because it is a country whose primary physical remembrance of modern war (prior to the attacks on the World Trade Center) lies in the bodies of returning war veterans and all that they carry. In such cases, it is easier to marginalize and thereby isolate the effects of war by identifying ramifications at the purely individual anecdotal level. *Rather than relive old tragedies, rather than confront our own frustrations and puzzlements about the war, we take comfort in the image of the bleary-eyed veteran carrying all that emotional baggage for us.* As COVV speak of the war and their fathers, the objectified and externalized memories articulated through complex social discourses of the war demonstrate that far more is going on than isolated anecdotal events, transforming the bleary-eyed veteran's presence into something dangerous and urgently in need of public address.

Conducting a history of the present of the Vietnam War came from my personal process of recognizing and engaging with this social monad. Examining the memoirs of Vietnam Veterans in my previous research (Weber, 2001) led to questions about how their experiences of trauma went on to affect the second generation—their children. Being a child of a Vietnam Veteran, I struggled with the motivations of my interest. For me, this project is as much about the possibilities that could be culled out of my theoretical questions about memory and trauma, as it is a personal endeavor to look into the gaps and fragments of my own life. Recognizing my own relationship to the effects of historical and social structures revealed my own relationship to the Vietnam War as a social monad. Knowing both Benjamin's and Gordon's work, I came to realize that my personal convictions in this topic were neither coincidental nor isolated to my personal experiences. I still struggle with the personal nature of this project, but there are numerous insights to gain from not fleeing from my own position of recognition.

As such, my analysis of COVV's narratives relies not only on the interviews I conducted and the deeper societal discourses at work within their narratives. It also depends on the dynamics of my own particular way of knowing that cannot be objectified or erased from this work. The metaphor of the palimpsest is useful in this analytical frame because it provides a visual image of the difficulty of trying to read and interpret the multiple scripting that exists on a single piece of paper—that exists within the social monad. Erasures, attempts at erasure, and new scripting encourages the diffusion of lines; a few lines venture out on their own tangents only to move back into the shadowy erasures of the past. The palimpsest reminds us of the presence of manifold stories and narratives inscribed into the larger story of our (social) lives, evoking a feeling of incompleteness, contradiction, and uncertainty. It also helps us comprehend how one person's story works with another's to engender a more inclusive narrative of social experience. But what does this scripting rely upon? How do we discern these lines in order to find legibility (and, in effect, social legitimacy)? Where do individuals' stories overlap with the stories contained in our social memory? Seeing the way individual memories fuse with social memory is not an easy task. The words blur together and can lead us down unknown paths where we lose a sense of the larger piece of parchment upon which we work—in my research that parchment constitutes the social monad of the Vietnam War.

CHAPTER ONE

Exploring Trauma and Memory through the Social Monad

Tensions in Theories of Memory and Trauma

Ted, an interviewee I discuss in more detail in chapter five, attempts to separate his father from the image of the prototypical Vietnam Veteran throughout the interview, explaining, "There was that stigma that everybody over there [in Vietnam] got attached with. And even, you'd see those reports in the media, 'former Vietnam Veteran opens fire at a McDonalds restaurant' or whatever, then it brings back that stigma that's so prevalent." Similarly, Samantha, another interviewee, made the comment that when Vietnam Veterans were finally acknowledged by society in the media they were portrayed as men who had a lot of problems, leading people to assume "that half the street bums on the corner are probably old Vietnam Veterans." In Ted and Samantha's minds these types of assumptions generate the negative undertones constituting the image of the Vietnam Veteran. This is not a benign image; rather, it is one that actively interjects into their personal relationships. They and my other interviewees seek to generate a different view of their fathers—Vietnam Veterans.

Actively working with and against the social image of the Vietnam Veteran, Ted and Samantha highlight the juxtaposition of individual and social memory. Jeffrey Olick has developed the tension between these forms of memory, making it clear that social memory is a tangle between individual and collective memory processes. "There is no individual memory without social experience nor is there any collective memory without individuals participating in communal life. Thinking about remembering in this way demands that we overcome our inculcated tendency... to see individual and society, in the words of Norbert Elias, as separate things, 'like pots and pans'" (Olick, 1999, 346). The course of exploring sensual knowledge within memory and trauma studies necessarily leads to the corruption of the lines demarcating individual and collective forms of experience and remembering. The social monad hinges on the intersection between (and corruption of) individual and society in the process of narration. The tensions residing in the in-between and in-formation narratives are the very sites from which the social monad becomes visible.

To a large degree, my research relies on the assumption that one person's story overlaps with another's story—especially if we speak about the lives of fathers and their children. Taking this point further, my use of the social monad necessarily leads to seeing how one story ends and another begins. This does not mean that I cannot work with each narrative as a cohesive entity but it does mean that the stories each interviewee tells are fraught with a host of tensions as I look in and between individual and social histories. The story of America is a story imbricated with official national history and the peculiar ways individuals understand themselves as social subjects within that history. This is a key point of my analysis because many of my subjects utilize hegemonic forms of the Father and Vietnam Veteran as they talk about intimate specificities of their fathers. They also rely upon an active knowledge of the Vietnam War's tumultuous position in American history. This knowledge weighs heavily upon my interviewees as they retrieve their fathers from the hardened stereotypes at work in the Vietnam Veteran Narrative. Ted and Samantha continually work to separate their fathers from the image of the Vietnam Veteran that pervades social imagery, telling me how their fathers live and breathe within that structured story they assume I—and the rest of America—know about the Vietnam War.

Throughout the book, I use the concepts individual (or personal) memory and cultural (along with social and collective) memory[1] when I make the distinction between my interviewees' narratives (and other personal narratives I use) and those that focus on social subjects (Vietnam Veteran Narratives and the Father), the meanings of commemorative sites (such as the Vietnam Veterans Memorial), films (such as *Platoon*), and historical and political texts. Still, it is necessary to reiterate that these two forms of memory have a precarious existence. One cannot exist without the other. The meanings generated from cultural memories assume that "all remembering is in some sense social, whether it occurs in dreams or in pageants, in reminiscences or in textbooks" (Olick, 1999, 346). Because my interests lay with the social monad as a complex integration of individual and collective memory, this distinction begins to dissipate in my analysis. Although I rely on the autonomy of their existence, I ultimately want to break down that autonomy and interrogate their interrelationship.

For Olick, trauma is a fruitful example of how memory defies the purely individual or collective through the ways they are externalized and objectified in family relationships.

> While we might speak of the residue of individual traumas, insofar as parents or grandparents imparted to their offspring stories of their experiences, psychological traumas cannot be passed down through generations like bad genes. In the first place, the fact that the memory of personally traumatic experiences is *externalized* and *objectified* as narrative means it is no longer a purely individual psychological matter. And in the second place, discussing the ongoing nature of trauma in terms of such transmitted personal narratives does not capture what we really mean—that is, an unassimilable breach in the collective narrative. (1999, 345—my emphasis)

The expressions of personal narratives *do* capture what we mean—but not alone. As we move deeper into this exploration of the social monad though the juxtaposition of children of Vietnam Veterans' (COVV's) narratives with the cultural narratives of the Vietnam Veteran and the Vietnam War, the ruptures and gaps in the web of stories surrounding masculine subjectivity are exposed and propelled into discourses surrounding the event and a variety of social identities. Traumatic events are more than the sum of personal traumatic experiences; yet it is those experiences, which *externalize* and *objectify* traumatic experiences, and their memories, that provide a means of social recognition. On this point I proceed, analyzing two texts that open up the relationship between cultural and individual memories.

Trauma and the Tangle of Social Memory

Individual and collective memory are tangled up in the process of remembering traumatic events. The act of remembering an event like the Vietnam War exposes emotional investments in the cultural meanings and representations of the war. Each theorist in the two texts I analyze provides useful insights into the complexities of social engagement with the difficult moments of the past, drawing out the struggle involved in giving and taking meaning from those events.

Marita Sturken provides a provocative analysis of the Vietnam Veterans Memorial (The Wall) in her book, *Tangled Memories: The Vietnam War, The AIDS Epidemic, and the Politics of Remembering*. Sturken analyzes cultural memories and their intervention in official historical discourses. By drawing out the confusing array of meanings that are projected onto The Wall, Sturken demonstrates how memory is a narrative rather than a replica of an event. "I am primarily concerned with questions of the popularization of history, specifically how histories are told through popular culture, the media, public images, and public memorials—how cultural memory engages with historical narratives in the public sphere" (Sturken, 1997, 5). Ultimately, she is concerned with the power struggles going on in the making of official historical discourses. She clearly distinguishes between cultural and individual memories, stressing that she is not interested in personal memories insofar as they remain personal. But it is the tangle of individual and cultural memories that *together* intervene in official historical discourses. Personal acts of remembering at a public memorial are what give The Wall its powerful cultural statement.

Sturken cannot express the power of The Wall without evoking the personal stakes involved. Yet, the personal stakes cannot remain individual isolated events. This list of names creates an expanse of cultural memory, one that could be seen as alternately subverting, rescripting, and contributing to the history of the Vietnam War as it is being written. The histories these names evoke and the responses they generate are necessarily multiple and filled with complex personal stakes. These narratives concern the effect of the war on the Americans who survived it and whose lives were irrevocably altered by it (Sturken, 1997, 59).

She discusses the practice of leaving objects and letters at The Wall as replete with personal and cultural meanings.[2] The Wall may provide a rescripting of the meanings of the war, but it also carries the weight of emotions that cannot be relegated to either the personal or cultural sphere. The memories and emotions a visitor brings to the memorial do not leave him/her when s/he returns home. There is a sharing of meaning taking place; each affects the other. This shared meaning is the tangle of social memory, which participates in expressing the social monad.

Dear Michael: Your name is here but you are not. I made a rubbing of it, thinking that if I rubbed hard enough I would rub your name off the wall and you would come back to me. I miss you so.
   We did what we could but it was not enough because I found you here. You are not just a name on this wall. You are alive. You are blood on my hands. You are screams in my ears. You are my eyes and soul. I told you you'd be all right, but I lied, and please forgive me. I see your face in my son. I can't bear the thought. You told me about your wife, your kids, your girl, your mother. And then you died. Your pain is mine. I'll never forget your face. I can't. You are still alive. (quoted in Sturken, 1997, 77)

Sturken makes the following assessment of the letters: "Many of the letters are addressed not to visitors but to the dead. They are messages for the dead that are intended to be shared as cultural memory" (Sturken, 1997, 78). We see how the traumatic subject underlies Sturken's analysis, consisting of an amalgam of trauma's individual and social manifestations. To analyze the meanings of personal and cultural loss and grief is to understand what the individual and culture provide to one another. The intense personal emotions expressed in the letters never leave the individual behind. The emotions fluidly move between the individual and the cultural site. The letter writers come to this memorial and leave their letters. They do not leave the letters at an individual grave (if there is one). They share their grief at this memorial, which socially legitimates their losses. The acts of individuals feed into the emotional intensity of the memorial. At the same time, the memorial gives a tangibility to an individual's grief. In the context of the social monad, we can assert that meanings of the trauma of the Vietnam War are found in the cultural physicality of The Wall *and* the aggregated acts of individuals visiting it.
   Using the social monad as a frame of analysis reminds us that individual memory cannot exist without cultural memory (and vice versa). Sturken recognizes this: "Personal memory, cultural memory, and history do not exist within neatly defined boundaries. Rather, memories and memory objects can move from one realm to another, shifting meaning and context" (1997, 5).
   Approaching the Vietnam War as a social monad, individual and social expressions cannot be isolated to separate realms of meaning. Holly, one of my interviewees, exemplifies how individual and collective memory are infused into and inform one another.

It was—the [Vietnam Veterans] Memorial was—my dad doesn't talk about his experiences in the war very much and it's kind of just not really a part of how he expresses himself. And then when we were there at the Memorial and I saw him get, you know, really emotional—he didn't want to talk about it but he was crying. As a child it kind of startled me a bit 'cause I wasn't used to seeing my dad cry. I think that was one of the first times where I've had a full grasp of probably how painful it was for him. Because we've talked about it before. I knew my dad served during the war and I knew he didn't want to talk about it and I knew it wasn't a fun time for him but it [...] didn't really hit me until I saw him crying.

What did not *hit* her was the depth of the impact of the trauma of war on her father. Seeing him in the context of the memorial opened up her understanding of the war and *"probably* how painful it was for him." It is not simply The Wall that impacted her; Holly's father's reaction to the memorial and her being a part of that experience with him served as a fundamental source of knowledge even though he did not really talk about what he was going through. Sensual knowledge emerges as a vital response to reading individual and the collective memories together. At the same time, the meaning of The Wall has distinctively separate meanings for the Vietnam Veteran and the child of a living Vietnam Veteran. Yet, Holly and her father share the moment, even if they both receive very different meanings from it. To say a memory has this meaning here and that meaning there elides the more dynamic processes of memory engagement. Maintaining such separations also has the potential to silence individuals and marginalize and isolate individual experiences of trauma, missing the links between personal suffering and historical events.

Analyzing the *intersubjectivity* of remembering is integral to analyzing the Vietnam War as a social monad. Prager develops this concept in his analysis of a woman's process of memory recovery, which plays a crucial role in her narrative of self.[3] Prager explains that

> what appears to be simply an impersonal account of one's past to one's present... actually represents a social process through which the self identifies itself interpersonally in a world of others and the past becomes not only organized and detailed but also *experienced*. (1998, 65—my emphasis)

That is, the past plays a crucial role in how we experience ourselves in the world in the present. This is precisely what was happening to Holly.

The past remains something that informs the present. But how does this happen? The traumatic subject becomes dislodged from the chronological passing of time by virtue of the continuation of social life. The traumatic event, therefore, moves through time within the subject who experienced it. "And so this past is not actually past in the sense of 'over,' since it continues as an animating absence in the presence..." (Butler, 2003, 468). This is by no means the only way a social monad moves from one generation to another, but it is a significant way to garner an understanding about how a traumatic past *continues as an animating absence*. The fathers of my interviewees embody the trauma of the Vietnam War, yet they live their lives as husbands, fathers, workers, and men; their status as a Vietnam Veteran is an absent presence to my interviewees, because they know that their fathers were affected by the war even if he rarely talks about it to them. Part of interrogating the social monad is trying to understand how my interviewees create meaning from the gaps and silences between their fathers and his status as a Vietnam Veteran.

We live in the present and remember in the present, not alone but through our relationships with others and the social world. "Remembering occurs not in the individual, but intersubjectively through the social environment the individual is embedded." That is,

> by emphasizing the relation between the individual and others, intersubjectivity offers an alternative to a conception of memory in which the present is understood exclusively in relation to a determinative past. The process of remembering is now appreciated for its relation to the social world in which it occurs, and making its own independent contribution to what is remembered, distinctive from past events or experiences. (Prager, 1998, 97)

The intersubjective process of remembering is deeply imbricated in the social monad. Because the event of trauma becomes part of the person experiencing it, it logically follows that the event, for the next generation, can only be known through the interactions with that person, the subject of trauma.

Analyzing a traumatic event intersubjectively provides an entryway into seeing the absent presence of trauma in the dynamics between fathers and children. O'Brien does not remember what happened to him in Vietnam enclosed in a vacuum. He remembers as he lies in bed next to his wife; he remembers as his daughter asks him if he killed anybody; he remembers as he takes a trip to Vietnam with his daughter 25 years after he left there; he remembers as he finds out a war buddy committed suicide ten years after returning home. Nor does he remember as a blank slate. He remembers as a white man growing up in the Midwest. He remembers the war as he remembers losing his first girlfriend at the age of eight to Leukemia. He remembers as a man who almost went to Canada to avoid the draft. He remembers as a man who came home and went to college. He remembers as a writer, a father, a husband, a friend. He remembers as one who survived.

If we are to listen to the departure from the event, we need to be able to hear the way accounts of the past are told in the context of the world in which the survivor lives. In my case, as a child of a Vietnam Veteran, the departure is heard almost exclusively within the context of the father-child relationship. COVV understand their fathers' experiences as sons and daughters; so within the telling of what they understand of their fathers' experiences, they speak of their relationships with their fathers. The *original* trauma is never tangible to them; it is only real through their relationship to their father. It is impure pieces of the past that they know is real to their fathers, but they are less certain of how that fits into their own lives. An intersubjective analysis is helpful, then, because it relies not only on examining the visible parts of the father-child relationship, but also the affective parts of the relationship that are more difficult to see. The emotional bonds between the father and child deeply impact the way my interviewees put the pieces together of their fathers' experiences with trauma. But there are always gaps in their understanding.

As the second focal text, Ann Cvetkovich's book, *Archive of Feeling*,[4] provides further insights into these relationships. By analyzing Lisa Kron's[5] performance piece, *2.5 Minute Ride*, she emphasizes the intersubjectivity of remembering a historically traumatic event, paying attention to the ways highly affective relationships come to bear meaning for both the person and the historical moment, uncovering the silence underlying it. In the process, both Kron and Cvetkovich transgress the individual/society (personal/cultural) arguments by analyzing the emotional dynamism of our remembering processes. Rather than conflating these binaries, they allude to the significance of the traumatic subject, which enables them to focus their attention on how our affective relationships move more fluidly between the tidy categorizations of individual/society, public/private. Their look at the way affective experiences and expressions exist in both political activism and in highly personal experiences, such as sexual and love relationships, provide the possibility of accessing the silence, uncovering the complexities of the remembering process.

Kron directly addresses the difficulty of articulating her relationship to the social monad of the Nazi Holocaust. As a child of a Holocaust survivor, she uses performance as a way to speak about witnessing her father's life as a survivor, her visit with him to Auschwitz, and her life experiences as a lesbian. She uses her personal memories of these experiences to articulate something for herself, while trying to convey the emotions within those experiences to others. Feeling that the visit to Auschwitz would be something too structured to feel anything real and fearing having to witness her father's reactions to revisiting the concentration camp, she is completely taken aback by her reactions:

> But when I entered the crematorium for the first time in my life I feel horror. Physical repulsion. I can feel my face contort, my lips pull back. In the gas chamber, my father stops to take his 2:00 pill. This breaks my heart. I stand aside and cry. Hard. I can feel...I can feel the bottom. It's clear to me now that everything in my life before has been a shadow. This is the only reality—what happened to my father and his parents fifty years ago. (Kron, quoted in Cvetkovich, 2003, 22)

The poignancy of this scene is not just in engaging with the horrors of the past. Visiting this highly charged cultural space in the presence of witnessing her father, a traumatic subject, go on with his everyday survival—taking his medicine—evokes an engagement that provides her with an insight into the painful past her father embodies. It is not the brutal experiences of the concentration camp that she tells us about, yet they are all that matter. What she tells us about is how life—hers and her father's—comes to bear witness on the irretrievable past. The poignancy that exists between the past and the present surfaces through witnessing her father take medication in a place where he and so many others faced unnameable horrors. Her life is entangled with her father's ongoing fight for survival. Cathy Caruth explains that in the telling of trauma, "it is the inextricability of the story of one's life from the story of a death, an impossible and necessary double telling, that constitute their historical witness" (1996, 8). To witness the trauma of the past is to witness the death and life that brought Kron to the present moment of standing in the crematorium with her father. To witness the trauma of the past is to recognize how the Nazi Holocaust is a part of her father.

Kron's testament to her witnessing of history is not done through easily accessed representations of the Holocaust. In fact, she struggles against them. She states,

> You know what this looks like already. I don't know why I'm telling you this. Everybody's seen these images. I'm sure you've seen *Sophie's Choice* and *Schindler's List* and the pictures of the bodies and the bulldozers on PBS. It's on every fifteen minutes practically. I don't know why I'm telling you this. I don't need to describe this to you. I feel like a cliché. Ugh. (Kron, in Cvetkovich, 2003, 23)

I feel like a cliché. Yet throughout Kron's performance she utilizes numerous emotions to convey why she is not a cliché. Through the *gift* of a fractured history she converts trauma into insight. In particular, the clichés—the hegemonic and structured forms of remembering—surrounding the Nazi Holocaust dominate the way we remember that event. They infect Kron's memories to the point that she feels numb to its meanings in much of her own life. The gift of the second generation concerns our ability to speak against those hardened and enclosed frames of memory that constitute the social monad, even as they rely on them to tell their stories. To speak against it means to see the way life is still moving through that traumatic event. Converting trauma into insight alters our historical knowledge of the Nazi Holocaust; it transforms historical knowledge into a visceral present, animated by her interactions with her father. She expresses life—her life—through the seemingly unrepresentable and over-told landscape of the Nazi Holocaust. As Cvetkovich comments,

> Kron wants to jolt her audience out of its customary responses... in order to confront them with other *affects* such as humor, the poignancy of everyday life, and the moral uncertainty of her father's claim that he was lucky to have been born a Jew so that he couldn't possibly become a Nazi. *2.5 Minute Ride* offers unrepresentability not as awe-inspiring but as *material necessity*. Indeed, the challenge it addresses is *how to make room for another kind of story* in the face of the hyperrepresentation of the Holocaust and its saturation of the cultural landscape by a proliferation of horrific images. (2003, 23—my emphases)

Cvetkovich continues, "The daughter of the Holocaust survivor faces a dilemma in attempting to document her father's life: *'When I try to tell his stories I begin to hyperventilate and I don't know why'*" (23). The claustrophobic feelings found in her narrative are the result of the dense permeation of the Nazi Holocaust narratives in our cultural memory. With the saturation of those images, it can feel like there is no room for alternative narratives of the Nazi Holocaust, especially ones without clearly framed articulations.

This is not unlike the dilemma that COVV face. Compelled to defend their fathers against what they feel are inaccurate or incomplete images of Vietnam Veterans, COVV work in tense relation to the social narrative of the Vietnam Veteran in order to explore the meanings of the Vietnam War and trauma in more depth. Samantha and Ted both felt the presence of a deeply rooted social narrative as they worked through their own narratives of their fathers. This echoes Greg's sentiments from the Introduction: "Okay, so Vietnam. So my dad's a Vietnam Vet. So, that's a bad thing? Or is it a good thing? What does that mean? I never knew what it meant." Although he did not know precisely what it meant, he did feel the weight of the Vietnam War upon his conceptions of his father—and himself.

Kron transgresses personal and cultural memory by relying on the strength of intersubjective expressions of their experiences. Yes, Kron struggles with cultural memory in her personal attempts at articulating and documenting her father's life—and her own. But the point is not to discern between the two; it is to understand the affective play both have in our understanding of the event and our own individual lives. We are tangled in the social monad, which contains the narratives of cultural memory and individual memory. Both are integral to the way we make meaning out of our lives and historical events; we cannot isolate the cultural from the personal. The difficulty of expressing experiences that are connected to a historical moment so socially and culturally overloaded with meaning leaves numbed gaps laden with silence and inarticulable feelings and emotions that fumble toward audibility.

Silence and the Inarticulable: Trauma and the Social Monad

Doris Lessing, a child of a World War I Veteran, reminds us that "we are all of us made by war, twisted and warped by war, but we seem to forget it" (1994, 20). Tightly imbricated, trauma and memory studies at times appear as a singular body of research. Yet, I want to take some time to focus a little more closely on the work done in trauma studies in order to further set up my examination of the social monad. Specifically, the work done on trauma draws out the importance of the silent and inarticulable nature of traumatic experiences. This silence affects the process of remembering, often causing breakdowns in articulations of the traumatic event. These breakdowns are the result of experiences that our outside-of-normal experiences and narratives do not abide by expected forms of articulation; that is, the collective narrative. In the contested spaces of such traumatic moments, how do we make room for a different way of speaking about those moments? How do we address breaches in the collective narrative? And, how do we engage with silence? Here, I delve into why these traumatic moments and experiences may require different ways of listening and questioning. Silence and inarticulability leave the truth of the past continually beyond reach, embryonic in form, because it is continually open for working and reworking our understanding of the social world. These inarticulable and numbed experiences and expressions deeply affect processes of remembering, as well as material life, relationships, and cultural understandings of historical events. This is why the social monad is such a dense site. The struggle to be heard, to articulate an intense experience in a way others can understand, strengthens the presence of the social monad through continual reexamination and rearticulation that defy space and time.

The Gift of Silence: Historical Amnesia and Intergenerational Expressions of Trauma

Post-traumatic stress disorder (PTSD) officially came into being in the third edition of *The Diagnostic and Statistical Manual of Mental Disorders* (DSM-III) in 1980. Largely a result of the great number of combat veterans from the Vietnam War seeking assistance from Veterans Affairs (VA) in their readjustment to civilian life, the inclusion of PTSD in the DSM-III legitimated a psychological condition, which had, until then, a contentious existence in the field of psychology. To say that PTSD came into being in 1980, though, tells us nothing of the historically ambivalent relationship western societies have had with trauma studies over the last century. As Judith Herman comments,

> the study of psychological trauma has a curious history—one of episodic amnesia. Periods of active investigation have alternated

with periods of oblivion.... This intermittent amnesia is not the result of the ordinary changes in fashion that affect any intellectual pursuit. The study of psychological trauma does not languish for lack of interest. Rather, the subject provokes such intense controversy that it periodically becomes anathema. (1992, 7)

Trauma, then, is much more than a psychological malady; it is a deeply cultural phenomenon that forces us, as Herman goes on to write, to come "face to face with both human vulnerability in the natural world and with the capacity for evil in human nature. To study psychological trauma means bearing witness to horrible events." These events are not natural disasters. When "the traumatic events are of human design, those who bear witness are caught in the conflict between victim and perpetrator. It is morally impossible to remain neutral in this conflict" (Herman, 1992, 7). Thus, our ambivalence with trauma studies often reflects our ambivalence with historical moments and events that cause breaches in our collective narratives—dominant fictions as I continue to call them throughout this book (and which is discussed in greater depth in chapter three).

Traumatic events can cause stammered articulations of what was once easily enunciated in the social world. Such a breach ruptures the chain of stories, leaving us without a way of fully grasping what happened. As Cathy Caruth points out, "For history to be a history of trauma means that it is referential precisely to the extent that it is not fully perceived as it occurs; or to put it differently, that a history can be grasped only in the very inaccessibility of its occurrence" (1995, 8). There is, then, ambivalence precisely because it is *not fully perceived as it occurs*; and in a sense, the future is the space where it comes to be perceived in shifting and unpredictable ways. This is due to the way the traumatic event becomes part of the person who experiences it. As such, it requires reconsideration of what trauma implies as it leaves behind episodic amnesia and breaches in our collective narratives. Within the context of this book, American society's ambivalence with the Vietnam War alerts us to the Vietnam War's traumatic nature in our hearts and minds.

The language of trauma, then, is an attempt to retrieve the traumatic event, to repair the breach, and to restore the memories of that event, processes that take place individually and socially. But I am not so much interested in retrieving and restoring the event (if that is even possible) than I am in understanding the breach and its effects—something that ultimately constitutes the social monad. What breaches in our collective narratives are found in the context of the Vietnam War? In particular, the trauma of the Vietnam War stammers on the break that occurred in the enunciation of masculine subjectivity.[6] The men who felt the effects of the war firsthand embody the anxieties generated by this break, taking it into their lives as fathers. COVV take in this anxiety around masculine subjectivity through their relationship with their fathers and society. This means my interest in trauma extends beyond the language of pathology and recovery, reaching into the narratives of individuals who are sorting out its meaning in their everyday lives. While it is in clinical psychological literature that we find core discussions about the effects of trauma on the psyche, the analyses do not address how sociohistorical structures intervene on the psyche.

The clinical psychological literature stands in contradistinction to the work done on trauma in literary criticism and psychoanalytical theory; yet it is important to touch on this body of work, because it reminds us of the deeply personal ramifications involved in facing the traumas of war. Setting the clinical research beside cultural analyses of trauma highlights the tensions that exist within trauma studies: personal confrontations with war atrocities and their social effects. The socially traumatic nature of the Vietnam War should not take awaythe very real experiences individuals had in their confrontations with those war atrocities; not everybody alive during the Vietnam War has symptoms of PTSD. There is an important need for the existence of research on the damage trauma does to the individual psyche, but it would be naïve to assume a person's individual experiences with trauma are nothing more than isolated experiences of suffering. In fact, it is such naïve assumptions that isolate social and psychic symptoms, exacerbating the effects of trauma.

In particular, when we look at the mechanism of *silence* in trauma, we begin to see how personal experiences are beholden to societal meanings of an event such as the Vietnam War. Silence, as one particular way in which trauma is isolated and objectified, provides insight into the complex relationship between the cultural and individual experiences and expressions of trauma. Delving into the complexities between personal and social struggles with trauma is the impetus behind my interest in the way trauma is passed down to the next generation. Looking at a traumatic event as a social monad problematizes any attempt to make a clear line of demarcation between individual and cultural experiences, because it ceases to remain contained (if it ever was) in the individual's psyche and insistently asserts itself into the traumatic subject's position in the social world.

While there is a plethora of work on trauma experienced by World War I, World War II, Korean, and Vietnam Veterans and survivors, as well as cultural manifestations of trauma in literature, film, media, and other societal expressions, work on its intersubjective dynamics is minimal. Only recently has there been an interest in such studies, most of which focuses on children of holocaust survivors. As Yael Danieli comments in the introduction to the *International Handbook of Multigenerational Legacies of Trauma*, "The multigenerational legacies of the growing numbers of 'forgotten generations' that appear in this book have not previously received adequate exploration within the field of traumatic stress" (1998, 5). One must wonder if this gap in trauma literature is related to the *episodic amnesia* that has permeated its history. I make this point because there is something to be said for our obsessive interest in the damage of war, yet we continually ignore, or perhaps, cannot hear, the more lasting echoes of war on the homes and families of the soldiers and other survivors. As Doris Lessing notes,

> I used to joke that it was the war that had given birth to me, as a defence when weary with the talk about the war that went on—and on. But it was no joke. I used to feel there was something like a dark grey cloud, like poison gas, over my early childhood. Later I found people who had the same experience. Perhaps it was from that war that I first felt the struggling panicky need to escape, with a nervous aversion to where I have just stood, as if something there might blow up or drag me down by the heel. (1994, 10)

It is with an intense hope for the future that we, as a culture, try to put the atrocities of the past behind us; we do not want our actions and beings defined by those events. We do not want to reside in the darker spaces of the past that implicate us in violence. Yet, what does that do to the participants in those events and their families, people who may not so easily be able to put the event behind them? How do they narrate their lives under such intermittent moments of amnesia and come to make sense of their subjectivity—their sense of being in the world? If we listen to Lessing, there is something there, whether they know (or like) it or not, haunting them, the next generation, in some inexplicable way (*a dark grey cloud?*)—*a nervous aversion to where they had just stood, as if something there might blow up or drag them down by the heel.* Does the next generation hold a *nervous aversion* to the past, a past that society ambiguously locks away in the recesses of its consciousness? Or are our own voices marginalized at the expense of a singular (over-told) narrative of trauma? Can that history come to the next generation at moments that are, as of yet, inarticulable, to remind them (and us all) of that history *dragging us down by the heel?* Is that part of the fear and amnesia in our memories of and relationship with trauma? *The struggling panicky need to escape* from history?

The gaps between clinical psychological research and cultural analyses of trauma (via literary criticism and psychoanalytical theory) intersect with their emphases on the role of silence. Silence is the problem of the second generation, another facet of the gift of trauma that must be deciphered and acted upon. As the point of convergence and divergence within the two bodies of literature, silence is a mechanism for the transmission of trauma. What becomes clear, though, is that silence, as a latent effect of trauma, does not provide an escape from the history of trauma; oftentimes it is what ensnares us in the social monad, even if we were not alive to experience its initial social and psychic impact.

Ultimately, PTSD plays an ambiguous role in my interviewees' narratives. "If PTSD must be understood as a pathological symptom, then it is not so much a symptom of the unconscious, as it is a symptom of history. The traumatized, we might say, carry an impossible history within them, or they become themselves the symptom of a history that they cannot entirely possess" (Caruth, 1995, 5). The personal narratives of the men and women I interviewed moved back and forth between articulating PTSD as a pathological symptom within their fathers' behaviors and questioning its presence as a social phenomenon.

Uncertain about the way PTSD manifests in individuals, many were uncertain if their father expressed official medical symptoms. Less than half of the men and women discussed in this book claimed that their fathers were diagnosed with PTSD. Trauma and PTSD were an enigma for many of these men and women. Some were not sure if their fathers had been diagnosed while several believed that their fathers have PTSD but have not bothered to go to a mental health facility to be diagnosed and treated. As Samantha commented,

> I never knew whether or not he was diagnosed with Post-Traumatic Stress Syndrome [*sic*] and he said no. But he was—he has never been in such a clinical environment where he would have been diagnosed with that. I'm sure my father— [breaks off...]. So even if he had [PTSD] he probably wouldn't have sought [psychological assistance] out.

Other discussions my interviewees engaged in regarding PTSD included Mark's uncertainty about the manifestation of PTSD in people, asking me to explain what constitutes a flashback. Greg, who had watched his father experience a flashback, reflected on how much he disliked the term because it did not encompass the full spectrum of pain, sadness, and suffering a person experiences in the moment that a traumatic memory flashes into the present. I asked the question about whether or not my subjects witnessed a flashback in order to gain a sense of the depth of knowledge they had of PTSD and trauma. But, similar to their feelings of being removed from and unable to understand the original moment of trauma their fathers may have experienced, most subjects did not necessarily have firsthand knowledge of their fathers' psychological health and did not feel comfortable making assumptions about it. This created uncertainty in my subjects' minds as they tried to explain the effects of trauma on their fathers. This diagnostic term is, to some degree, symptomatic of the ambiguity that the silent structures of trauma's articulation leave to the second generation.

Ultimately, silence, as a thematic structure of intergenerational trauma, reveals a number of tensions in trauma studies. To address the silence of trauma is to dredge up sociohistorical issues that extend beyond the event (the Vietnam War in my research) itself. It also requires us to delve into emotionally charged intersubjective dynamics, such as the father-child relationship. Addressing the silence has required me to ask questions, not only about the war, but also about social meanings of fatherhood and masculinity. It also demonstrates that the intergenerational transmission of trauma is linked to more than individual behaviors, alerting us to the larger structural questions that traumatic events incite. In particular, it leads us to look at how one's subjectivity takes on the traumatic event and psychological maladies, shaping the way the traumatic subject interacts in the social world. At this point, though, I want to go into more depth about the structures of silence working within the social monad.

Structures of the Social Monad: The Crisis of Articulation

The attempts at articulation (both spoken and emotive) are what enliven the social monad. Surviving a traumatic moment, with its variety of expressions, informs a society's current understanding of the traumatic event. In particular, family discussions, with their silences and gaps in normative activities, articulate the continuing trauma of war for the veteran and embody that trauma as a living, breathing aspect of family life. In turn, this affects the way the men and women in this book make sense of the meaning of the war and gender. The *structures of silence,* which permeate both the individual and sociohistorical levels of trauma, enable a way of analyzing trauma that is not limited to pathologies in interpersonal relationships. What emerges from theories on traumatic memory is a concept I call the *crisis of articulation.* As I have been implying throughout this chapter, the structure of the social monad contains a dense site of social activity that includes repeated and continual attempts to articulate the traumatic event. These can be conscious and unconscious, verbal and emotive, expressions. Nevertheless, each attempt at articulation contributes to the intense intersubjective and societal dynamics that enliven the social monad.

This concept was born out of the work by Cathy Caruth and her delineation of the concepts the *crisis of truth* and the *crisis of survival.* "What trauma has to tell us—the historical and personal truth it transmits—is intricately bound up with its refusal of historical boundaries;...its truth is bound up with its crisis of truth" (Caruth, 1995, 8).Caruth has led the way in developing these aspects of trauma theory through her analyses of a variety of cultural expressions, including social theory, literature, and films. For example, her readings of Freud's *Moses and Monotheism* and the film *Hiroshima mon amour* (by Alain Resnais and Marguerite Duras) in her book *Unclaimed Experience* conceptualize trauma within and beyond individual experience, expanding it into a methodology of reading history through trauma.

Conducting and writing a history outside the margins of our *immediate understanding* requires an alternative way of thinking about historical analysis. This means I am not searching for causal links between historical events and effects, nor am I simply looking for signs of pathology in individual behavior.

> I would propose that it is here, in the equally widespread and bewildering encounter with trauma—both in its occurrence and in the attempt to understand it—that we can begin to recognize the possibility of a history that is no longer straightforwardly referential (that is, no longer based on simple models of experience and reference). (Caruth, 1996, 11)

Theorizing trauma in this fashion shifts our attention from the symptoms of individuals in isolation to the symptoms of the social subject in historical context. This shift in no way marginalizes the pain and suffering of the individual (nor does it defer responsibility from individuals); what it does is implicate such suffering in the discourses of history itself (encouraging a shared responsibility). Neither does such theorizing continue to debate whether or not the original traumatic event was real or fantasy, whether it took place inside or outside the psyche. It is the temporal delay of events that define the traumatic experience, ultimately leaving us without direct access to the events themselves.

> It is always the story of the wound that cries out, that addresses us in the attempt to tell us of a reality or truth that is not otherwise available. This truth, in its delayed appearance and its belated address, cannot be linked only to what is known, but also to what remains unknown in our very actions and our language. (Caruth, 1996, 4)

Thus, our inability to access the event—the truth of the event—produces a *crisis of truth* (a concept Caruth draws from Shoshona Felman's work). The traumatic event can only be known and understood through its aftershocks, because they permeate a variety of expressions, ever-struggling to retrieve the original event. The point, though, is not that there is no truth to the events that caused somebody such as Tim O'Brien to continue to feel the residue of guilt and horror 25 years after his experiences in the Vietnam War. The point is that those experiences are not symptoms isolated in his mind alone, for him and us to understand solely within the context of individual suffering; rather, the stories O'Brien and other Vietnam Veterans tell, *carry an impossible history within them* and they are the *symptom of a history that they cannot entirely possess*. They are the potential post-narrators of trauma, handing their children, specifically, and the second generation, generally, the gift of an historical conundrum. That is, within their personal witnessing of trauma, those who experience trauma (should) alert society to the traumatic nature of the historical moment itself, leading us to questions about the social implications such insights reveal, and our responsibility in these historical events. But articulations of this trauma are seemingly impossible.

O'Brien's work, which I discussed in the introduction, provides a salient example. His ability to find truth in answering both yes *and* no to if he killed somebody while in Vietnam captures an aspect of the *crisis of truth*. Although O'Brien did not physically kill anybody, he is uncertain of his responsibility in the events of the war itself, a concern that could only appear after the moment itself. The question of whether or not he killed another person inquires into more than if he did the act of violence; it ignites his deeper concern with how his (and our country's) very presence in Vietnam and the war was itself an act of violence. As a commanding officer, he led his men into battles. His mistakes cost lives; his orders cost lives. Running events over and over in his head, he lives with the uncertainty and guilt of being present in Vietnam and witnessing the death of many people—Vietnamese and American—all around him.

Yet, he survived. And in that survival the crisis of truth is ever present along with what Caruth terms the *crisis of survival.* Coming to terms with the event; coming to terms with survival. Caruth and the other researchers she includes in her edited volume, *Trauma: Explorations in Memory,* understand that

> by turning away...from a notion of traumatic experience as neurotic distortion, the authors of these essays bring us back continually to the ever-surprising fact that trauma is not experienced as a mere repression or defense, but as a *temporal delay* that carries the individual beyond the shock of the first moment. The trauma is a repeated suffering of the event, but it is also a continual leaving of the site. (1995, 10—my emphasis)

This means that the repeated expressions of the first moment, *the continual leaving of the site,* carry insights into the way the personal and the social struggle together to make sense of the social world. The gift post-narrators give to the next generation is more than a personal story of their trauma; it is an impossible and fragmented history we, the next generation, need to listen to if we want to gain any insight into the ramifications of war in our society. To be able to hear and recognize those insights requires, as Caruth emphasizes, a way of listening to the departure from the site of trauma. To depart from trauma, to survive trauma, means that the experience becomes part of the person who went through it. To understand O'Brien's work is not simply to listen to the brutality of what he saw in Vietnam—it is to hear the way he must tell the story through his daughter's inquiries. It is to hear his desire for her (and us) to understand, not the trauma itself, but him and the events of his life. He wants his daughter to understand how that experience of trauma impacted his life as a man. This effort reinforces his position as a traumatic subject.

The *crisis of articulation,* which I explore in greater depth in chapter four, is a concept that I develop from Caruth's work as a way of describing the impossibility of resolving the crises of truth and survival that constitute the traumatic subject. This comes out in my interviewees' narratives in the struggle to make sense of the irresolution between the men who are their fathers and the men who served in Vietnam. They continually work between their personal relationships with their fathers and their awareness of the negative images of the Vietnam Veteran that seem to be prevalent in society. In this sense, they struggle, not with articulating the event, but with articulating their fathers as masculine *and* traumatic subjects. History, trauma, and self are tangled up with one another.

The interplay between cultural and personal memory that COVV draw on alerts me to the complex way in which we draw on personal and cultural realms of life in order to articulate the social memory of the Vietnam War. The stories these men and women tell weave together many different narratives to begin to build a story of their subjective being and that being within the context of the Vietnam War. The way they speak about the Vietnam War leads us to a way of seeing history as part of the social monad, which can provide insight into the ways we think about the Vietnam War in the present. It can draw together the effects of the war with the way we understand manhood and fatherhood, particularly in the context of American culture.

Conclusion: *Stretching toward the Horizon*

With these numerous concepts in mind, we return our focus to the process of writing a history of the present. "To write a history of the present requires stretching toward the horizon of what cannot be seen with ordinary clarity yet. And to stretch toward and beyond a horizon requires a particular perception where the transparent and the shadowy confront each other" (Gordon, 1997, 195). Key to this process is discovering a way to articulate presence. This means grappling with hegemonic social forms within which we recognize ourselves (or *want* to recognize ourselves) and their intersection with not-yet-articulated (embryonic) forms of social life that are consummated through the life we live in and through our bodies. Articulating presence through an examination of the social monad of the Vietnam War allows me to maintain a historical focal point as I (and my interviewees) navigate the peculiarities of individual life intruding on us and being intruded upon by us. Following the monad—the traumatic event—opens another door into the historical event—a door that lies beyond (even as it is initiated by) our preconceived notions of the Vietnam War.

Yet, "grappling with the difficulty of imagining the limits of what is already understandable" (Gordon, 1996, 195) requires us to face the limitations of what we know. Conducting a history of the present centered around the Vietnam War compels us to question what the myriad historiographies, memoirs, films, documentaries, and photographs, which construct the basis of our knowledge of the war, tell us about the beyond. The gross amount of information still coming out about the Vietnam War, 30 years after its irresolute end, speaks to the continuing presence of the social monad. That impact grows murky, though, when we try to identify the manifestation of those effects. There are numerous battles over the inaccuracies of facts and representations of the Vietnam War and Vietnam Veteran. My concern here, though, is not with reproducing the struggles in representation and meaning; I do not intend to stake a claim on that knowledge base, as this only adds to what is understandable about the war.

What I am interested in is that such battles still take place; people—theorists, historians, veterans, activists, reporters, politicians—still hold vested interests in the meanings procured from that event. And more importantly, those meanings and events return under current social events such as the war in Iraq. Comparisons between the Iraq War and the Vietnam War[7] conjure meaningful analogies for those alive during the Vietnam War and create a new relationship between the Vietnam War and the present. What also strikes me is the feeling that there will never be enough knowledge of the event to create a consensus of meaning. A full recovery of the event is impossible. The more transparent and cumulative the knowledge around the war becomes, the longer the shadow that is cast over what is really at stake in the struggle to uncover its meaning. The hope that exists in reaching that fractured horizon lies in the belief that it will somehow unlock the key to our current suffering and current problems, the belief that we could find (and finally identify) that which was lost, individually and as a society. But the horizon always escapes us. My pursuit here is beyond the horizon; it is the confrontation between the transparent and the shadowy that unfolds as we reach for that horizon. I want to know what is recovered and achieved by engaging with the irrecoverable. This is the very core of the palimpsest: an incomplete—never-to-be-completed—document of social life. It is through such a reading of my data, the interviewees' narratives, as a palimpsest that a history of the present begins to emerge as a space to articulate presence. Let us now move deeper into the social monad of the Vietnam War.

CHAPTER TWO

Conceptualizing the Vietnam Veteran Narrative as a Narrative of Trauma

Using Oliver Stone's Vietnam War films (*Platoon, Born on the Fourth of July,* and *Heaven and Earth*) as a prototypical example of the Vietnam Veteran Narrative, I read the Vietnam Veteran Narrative as a narrative of trauma.

> I think [*Born on the Fourth of July*] is about America. I think it takes America from the 1950s to the '60s and into the '70s.... What we tried to do is—the boy and America are linked. It's my generation. The way we grew up. We bought certain beliefs in the 1950s; they were tested—hard. In the 1960s losses were incurred and I think a sense of wisdom we learned in the '70s and we're still, obviously, trying to apply it to our lives. We're still struggling. It's our generation (Stone, film commentary).

Specifically, it provides the plot structure around which the story of America's break with the dominant fiction is told. Telling the story about the way the boy—that is, America—came into intimate relation with lack, the Vietnam Veteran Narrative constitutes the bones upon which individual Vietnam Veterans narrate their personal stories of loss and suffering. Individual Vietnam Veteran narratives (with a lower case *n*) give shape and contours to the historically traumatic event of the Vietnam War, but it is the Vietnam Veteran Narrative (with a capital *N*) that freezes social thought into a *configuration pregnant with tensions, it gives that configuration a shock by which it crystallizes into a monad* (to re-invoke Benjamin). By focusing on the *pregnant tensions* at work in the event of the Vietnam War, we can see how the Vietnam Veteran Narrative invokes the social monad that tells the story of the break America experienced with the dominant fiction. As I further elaborate below, the dominant fiction is a societal story told as a way to contain the structures of belief constituting a society. Through the Narrator, who is a white and typically middle-class man, a story of the American masculine subject and his claim on phallic identification—social power—takes shape. In particular, I focus my attention on the way the story moves from the Narrator's belief in a dominant fiction, which places him at the helm of social power, through the breakdown of that belief due to the trauma of war, and into his return to America where he tries to reestablish that belief. Ultimately, my analysis of this narrative reveals how the Narrator takes on a traumatic identification that disrupts his ability to establish belief in the dominant fiction through normative routes. As a result, the Vietnam Veteran Narrative, what I am identifying as a social monad, becomes an alternative dominant fiction through which the Narrator reconfigures his belief in America in ways that remind us that *we're still, obviously, trying to apply [what we've learned] to our lives. We're still struggling*; that is, the Vietnam Veteran Narrative demonstrates how America is still trying to come to terms with the break that occurred in its belief structures, particularly around gendered subjectivity.

The structure of the Vietnam Veteran Narrative follows three important movements that shape the way individual Vietnam Veterans negotiate their personal stories of their experiences in Vietnam and their return home. There is a continual tension between the disparate worlds of Vietnam and America in the Vietnam Veteran Narrative. The experience of combat and reentry into the domestic world of America leave the Narrator struggling to resolve the breakdown in his belief in the dominant fiction. The expression of trauma emerges through the narrator's dislocation as the masculine subject. In particular, the Vietnam Veteran, as Narrator, never seems capable of regaining a position in the family that facilitates phallic identification. Instead, the Vietnam Veteran Narrative takes the traumatic break as a central theme, which disallows the story to proceed beyond the compulsion to articulate the moment of trauma.

Susan Faludi reiterates the domination of the social formation of the Vietnam Veteran in her analysis of what she calls the "Vietnam War Story." In it she refers to the social form of the "good son" who served in Vietnam. She emphasizes the existence of a concretized binary between the "good" and "prodigal" sons of America, which would be "etched into the popular imagination," depicting a "gulf between the patriotic duty-bound, underappreciated working-class sons of the Silent Majority and the privileged hippie flouters of authority whose long hair challenged gender conventions and whose disregard for their country undermined the nation's self-image" (Faludi, 1999, 298–9). In varying ways, the Narrator of the Vietnam Veteran Narrative supports the image of the "good son." This is an image, though, that is tangled together with negative images of the Vietnam Veteran in American society, which I discuss in more depth in chapter five. D. Michael Shafer, in his article, "The Vietnam Combat Experience," explains that "powerful and pervasive stereotypes dominate most Americans' understanding of the Vietnam War and Vietnam veterans" (1990, 80). He goes on to assert that these stereotypes "obscure our understanding of both the Vietnam War and its human legacy. No less important, they blind us to how badly we as a nation have dealt with the war and, in particular, with those who bear the Vietnam legacy most directly, the Vietnam Veterans" (Shafer, 1990, 81). As such, these congealed images of the Vietnam Veteran in society work with the Vietnam Veteran Narrative to generate a crystallized story of trauma upon which individual Vietnam Veterans narrate their own stories of the combat experience; *both* of these narrative layers, ultimately, impact the way American society understands not only the Vietnam Veteran but the Vietnam War as well.

Reading Stone's films with published memoirs by Vietnam Veterans illuminates the way the psychic breakdown of the trauma of combat induced in many Vietnam Veterans is deeply interconnected with the socially traumatic event of the Vietnam War. Analytically, these two realms of social and individual trauma converge in the Vietnam Veteran Narrative because it is through the Vietnam Veteran that individuals and society articulate the trauma of the Vietnam War. Specifically, it emerges in the Vietnam Veteran's inability to insert himself into the position of social power by claiming phallic identification. This disrupts society's ability to maintain belief in America's ideals. Stone nicely summarizes the concern of the Vietnam Veteran Narrative in his quote at the beginning of this chapter. The story of the masculine subject facing a break in his belief system—both in terms of American idealism and masculine expectations—is the story of America. *The boy and America are linked.* But, I must emphasize, this narrative is not necessarily representative of the reality that all men experienced in Vietnam or upon their return home. The Vietnam Veteran Narrative is a social *story* of trauma that has emerged through an imbrication of the stories that are told both socially and individually. This has shaped a prototypical narrative of the Vietnam Veteran's struggles with trauma that has permeated through the social imaginary—particularly the assumption of the Vietnam Veteran's violent and antisocial behavior. I want to make it clear that this does *not* mean that *all* men who served in Vietnam held these beliefs to the same degree as the prototypical Narrator I describe here. My argument is that this plot dominates the societal stories of the Vietnam Veteran. In fact, I assert that the Vietnam Veteran Narrative belies the lived reality of Vietnam Veterans and elicits the assumption that his experiences in Vietnam are mutually exclusive of his domestic life since the war. It also assumes social forms precede and dominate the dynamic content of lived experience—something I contest throughout this book.

In particular, the tension *between* the crystallized social narrative I identify as the Vietnam Veteran Narrative *and* the myriad individual Vietnam Veteran narratives breathes life into the bones of the plot, producing a complex and layered story of the social monad of the Vietnam War that cannot be simply told as a social story or an individual story. My analysis moves between these levels and at times tells the story as both, a complex of personal and social, aspects of which cannot be entirely extracted from one another. This generates a complicated starting point for my analysis of the narratives of children of Vietnam Veterans. In particular, this and the following chapter focus on the intricate narrative layers that are inscribed on the palimpsest of the social monad of the Vietnam War. As my analysis looks toward the transitions that take place as the monad moves into the second generation, a vital third layer of this palimpsest emerges in the way my interviewees tell their stories. In particular, the focus of the narratives of the second generation shifts from the event of trauma to the subject of trauma: the survivor, the Vietnam Veteran. Children of Vietnam Veterans' narratives do not develop around how the combat experience and the Vietnam War fractured the survivor's belief in the dominant fiction; *their* narratives develop around the aftereffects. This means that in their narratives my interviewees struggle to align the survivor—their father—to phallic masculine subjectivity, thereby establishing their own belief in the dominant fiction. As such, the narrative(s) of the traumatic event of the Vietnam War are complicated intermeshing of levels of social experience that take us in and between the most intimate and fluid intersubjective relationships and the most deeply inscribed social forms that defy erasure.

Articulating and Rearticulating the Experience of Trauma: The Vietnam Veteran Narrative

Al Santoli, in his preface to the anthology, *Everything We Had: An Oral History of the Vietnam War by Thirty-three American Soldiers Who Fought It*, describes the efforts and necessities of narrating the experiences of the nameless soldier.

> We have tried to put into honest words the raw experience of what happened to us. We have reflected upon that experience, recalling, among other things, that we were once idealistic young people confronted by the awesomeness of fighting other human beings. Now as parents and as citizens we feel an obligation, for the sake of our children if for no one else, to say what we could not or did not say in the past (1981, xi).

Providing an image of war for the "uninitiated" is simultaneously a personal and social endeavor. Santoli identifies himself as an individual Vietnam Veteran, yet part of the collective Vietnam Veteran Narrative. Transgressing the boundary between *I* and *we* in his description of this oral history project, Santoli reiterates the intermingled relationship between the Vietnam Veteran Narrative and individual Vietnam Veteran narratives, which constitute the narrative layers of the palimpsest of the Vietnam War. "To encompass those realities in a book, *one* veteran traveled around the country and spent countless hours talking, crying and laughing with other veterans and their families. *I* was that veteran, and *we* present *our* story" (Santoli, 1980, xii—my emphases). Stone engages in this effort in filmic fashion through his films *Platoon*, *Born on the Fourth of July*, and *Heaven and Earth*; that is, *he* tells his *and* their story. I analyze these films (primarily *Platoon* and *Born on the Fourth of July*) under the rubric of the Vietnam Veteran Narrative, paying attention to the traumatic aspects of the narrative. With this analytical focus, I interrogate the traumatic breaks working within the social and individual levels of the social monad of the Vietnam War.[1]

I focus on Stone's films for three reasons. First, his films exemplify the way the Vietnam Veteran Narrative moves fluidly between personal and social accounts of the war experience, emphasizing that the narrative cannot easily be identified as *either* personal accounts *or* cultural forms. As a document of his experiences in Vietnam, Stone wrote the screenplay for *Platoon* a few years after he returned from Vietnam.

Several years later he wrote the screenplay for *Born on the Fourth of July* with Ron Kovic (based on Kovic's memoir of the same name). These films personalize the combat experience (centering on an individual soldier) while simultaneously generating a universal story of the combat experience. In Stone's films, *I* and *we* are dramatically blurred.

The second reason for focusing on Stone's films is because they speak to a broader audience (as well as the film format being more accessible to a large number of people) than the myriad written narratives published since the war's end. His films visually enlarge the Narrative. Lastly, and perhaps most significantly, Stone's style of filming reflects the desire to *faithfully* convey the reality of the combat experience. In *Platoon* he obsessively reconstructed the aura of the jungle and combat, even putting the actors through a rigorous military bootcamp in preparation for filming.[2] In terms of the visual narration, Stone located his camera within the soldier, addressing history and politics through the narrative position of Vietnam Veteran as masculine subject. All of this was done in order to help the *uninitiated feel what the nameless combat soldier felt*.

The desire to produce an authentic account of the war experience draws on the crisis of truth discussed in the previous chapters. In this understanding, the impossibility of the survivor of trauma knowing the truth of the event leads to an obsessive desire to provide a faithful account of that moment. Because the original event can never be articulated in its pure form, the Narrator continually tries to describe and redescribe the experience in order to find a way to convey (to himself and others) what happened—an impossible task. The moment of trauma shapes the entire narrative, becoming a continual point of reference as he discusses the events in his life prior to and after his combat experience. It is the place where the ideals he held prior to war broke down, leading to his difficult return home.

This story can be broken down into three core thematic movements: the ideals that led the boy to war, the combat experience, and homecoming.[3] Through these thematic movements, the Narrator of the Vietnam Veteran Narrative conveys the feeling that something vital was lost forever—the innocent idealism he held—within the masculine subject and that he must continue living his life under the shadow of that loss. In this context, the Narrator is a masculine subject trying to reclaim phallic identification; he forever negotiates the traumatic event (to varying degrees and effects) within his subject position as an American man. As Stone explains, the beliefs he, Kovic, and other men held as they went into service, *were tested—hard*: and it is trying to assess what was lost and learned from that traumatic moment that reverberates throughout the Vietnam Veteran Narrative. The narrative reinforces my assertion that trauma extends beyond the psyche and into one's social location—a reminder of the way trauma transgresses the boundary between individual and social.

Homecoming is the final part of the narrative and is often referred to as the second war the Vietnam Veteran experienced. As Tim O'Brien explains, "You can tell a true war story by the way it never seems to end" (1990, 76). And the story of the return home is never-ending, because the Narrator must continually work to bridge the gap between the war experience and his reintegration into civilian life. This is what compresses the event into a social monad—the continual telling and retelling and its seemingly unending presence. In the narrative, the Vietnam Veteran never seems to move beyond the traumatic event. In both *Platoon* and *Born on the Fourth of July*, the story ends on the threshold of the Narrator finding resolution. We are left without a clear view of the form recovery takes, conveying an image of recovery that is yet-to-be-understood. The trauma of the past is never over and done; it becomes a point of return in our negotiation of the present.

The First Movement: America and the Masculine Subject

When Stone comments that *the boy and America are linked*, he is referring to the dominant beliefs in American society as he and other Vietnam Veterans were coming of age. Faludi, in the opening to her popular book on masculinity, *Stiffed: The Betrayal of the American Man*, talks of this linkage through the centrality of the boy in the discourses of America. "To grow up a girl in this era was to look on with envy, and to see the boy as being automatically entitled and powerful. Surely when we were grown, he would have control. He would dispense gifts. The boys believed that too" (Faludi, 1999, 25). The boy's link with America is vital to the construction of the Vietnam Veteran Narrative, constituting the idealism not only of the boy going to war, but the values America took to Vietnam.

The Narrator's focus on the loss of innocence develops out of his belief in his social position of power as a masculine subject. The feeling of *loss* erupts out of his realization that going to war, serving in this rite of passage into manhood, is the very act that caused the break in his ability to claim phallic identification. This leads to his inability to maintain belief in the dominant fiction. The loss of innocence that is a continual theme in the narrative means that the Narrator believed in his position as a boy and the social power—in its myriad manifestations—that he would receive upon entry into manhood. The war was, as Faludi explained, "Vietnam would become a defining event of American masculinity, the bridge that collapsed just as the nation's sons thought they were crossing to manhood" (1999, 298).The belief in the ideals of America was synonymous with the belief in the inherency of the masculine subject's (i.e., the boy's) social power; they rely on one another for meaning and legitimacy.

In this section I take a broad look at the idealism ingrained in the Vietnam Veteran Narrative, focusing on its connections with the dominant fiction of American society and why the war became such a significant moment for Vietnam Veterans specifically and the nation more generally. Relying on Kaja Silverman's use of the concept *dominant fiction* in her book *Masculinity at the Margins*, we can understand the ways in which the masculine subject and America are intimately connected. Specifically, the correlation of phallic identification with the masculine subject constitutes much of our ability to believe in the dominant fiction. Simply stated, the dominant fiction consists of a system of beliefs and desires that the whole of society (and the individuals within it) rely upon for social cohesion. It is a contained, yet fluid, boundary that provides guiding structures for self and society. The meaningfulness of the American dream and American manhood are secured in *America*, as dominant fiction, defining less a story of factual events and circumstances than a series of stories that tell us about the beliefs and desires that drive social (inter)action. The stories that the dominant fiction tell are not only of ideological systems of belief; they are stories informed by a will to neutralize our differences into a totalizing set of stories, which demand our collective belief (Silverman, 1992, 54).

The alignment of the masculine subject with phallic masculinity (the holder of social power) secures our belief in the dominant fiction. Claiming the identity of the masculine subject means the dominant fiction must command belief in sexual difference and the gender order so as to prevent interruptions—and a crisis—in masculinity (and potentially the social formations constituting society).[4] My analysis focuses on the significance of the Father's position in the American family and how that is an important part of the masculine subject's claim to social power.

The traumatic event of the Vietnam War, in part, is defined by the break that occurred in gender and familial order. As the men returned home from Vietnam, it became difficult to maintain the correlation between masculine subjectivity and phallic identification, thereby threatening the belief in America as dominant fiction. It also became difficult to reinsert themselves into traditional family life. The Vietnam Veteran Narrative tells this story from the position of the broken masculine subject, enabling us to see both the break and sutures taking place in the Narrator's attempts to reestablish a connection with phallic identification and American idealism. The Vietnam Veteran Narrative is a project that extends beyond individual experiences and navigates between individual and collective structures of belief.

Ron Kovic's autobiography, *Born on the Fourth of July* (and the subsequent film), exemplifies the Vietnam Veteran Narrative's reliance on America as dominant fiction. In his book, as well as in the film, Kovic recounts his belief in America and the disillusion that takes place as result of his war experiences. As he sets up the story of his beliefs and values, he alludes to the promises made to him by America and the nation's betrayal of those promises. He, taking on the position of the Narrator, does this by detailing his memories of the launch of the *Sputnik*. He explains how this moment touched him as a boy and man, confirming the work prescribed to him for America (fighting Communism) through a shared moment with his father.

> On a cold October night Dad and I watched the first satellite, called *Sputnik*, moving across the sky above our house like a tiny bright star. I still remember standing out there with Dad looking up in amazement at that thing moving in the sky above Massapequa.... Dad put is hand on my shoulder that night and without saying anything I quietly walked back inside to my room thinking that the Russians had beaten America into space and wondering why we couldn't even get a rocket off the pad. (Kovic, 1976, 57)

Kovic's account of growing up in the 1950s in Massapequa, New York, describe what those *certain beliefs* (Stone) looked and felt like to those living during this era. The story Kovic, as the Narrator of the Vietnam Veteran Narrative, tells of watching the *Sputnik* with his father is the same story that Faludi conjures over 20 years later, when she describes the prototypical boy (the Narrator) of the 1950s watching the launch of the American satellite, *Echo*, with his father. She opens her book by telling the story of the boy Kovic saw in himself. Faludi produces a compelling account of the promises made to the men of Kovic's and Stone's generation, one that touches the hearts and minds of many Americans. As she writes, "I knew this boy. Like everyone growing up in the late 1950s and early 1960s, I knew dozens of him.... Even if he wasn't brought out into the backyard and shown an American satellite glinting in the sky, he was introduced to the same promise and the same vision, and by such a father" (Faludi, 1999, 5).

Within the dominant fiction of America that the Narrator of the Vietnam Veteran Narrative utilizes, the Father is considered the purveyor of social ideologies. It is the Father who passes on the social power to his son. In *Born on the Fourth of July*, we watch Kovic, after returning home paralyzed, ask the doctor if he will ever be able to have children. The devastation he expresses when the doctor tells him *no* is palpable. In that response he felt all the possibilities of his life, of seeing himself at the helm of the story of America, vanquished. His reactions convey the deeply imbricated nature of social constructions of the family and the Father with phallic identification and belief in the structures of the dominant fiction of America. As Judith Stacey asserts,

> the family is not an institution, but an ideological, symbolic construct that has a history and a politics. In the United States [...] this concept has been employed primarily to signify heterosexual, conjugal, nuclear, domestic unit, ideally one with a male primary breadwinner, a female primary homemaker, and their dependent offspring. (1993, 545)

As I discuss in chapter five, the position of male reproduction and breadwinning are two central components to phallic identification for the masculine subject. It is a normative structure in which Kovic, the Narrator, deeply believed. This is why the loss of his body's ability to procreate signified the deeper losses of his ability to feel like a man in society. He *bought certain beliefs* and they consisted of the idyllic life painted by the dominant fiction. While Stacey argues that "the nostalgia for the family that [the family values crowd] peddle is singularly unhelpful to children or to a social policy arena that has been criminally slow to respond to profound family transformations," the stress and strain of normative ideals of the family also deeply affect the way men and women understand themselves as legitimate social subjects. Kovic articulates this strain at the intersection of the Narrator and narrator, expressing both the social narrative that tells the story of the break the Vietnam Veteran experienced with phallic identification and belief in the dominant fiction, as well as how the individual narrator relies on this narrative to tell his own story of struggle and recovery from the trauma of his war experiences. As such, the Narrators have a hard time trying to find a viable social position—and social narrative—that can allow them to feel a part of the social world.

At the same time, Faludi and Kovic tell a story of not just the family values held in the 1950s but also of the values of the nation, which are deeply interconnected with ideals of masculine virtue. By Faludi's account, these boys were to be part of "the era of manhood *after* victory.... The men of the fathers' generation had 'won' the world and now they were giving it to their sons" (Faludi, 1999, 5). It is from this narrative position that Kovic tells his story. As Kovic worried about America catching up with the Russians, he and his friends dreamed about going into space, believing he and America were destined for great things—whether they be in space, on the baseball field, or winning the battle against Russia and Communism in Vietnam. This is explicitly shown in the film. He and his friends talk about the war that was starting in Vietnam. Kovic tells his friends, "If we don't sign up soon, we're gonna miss it. I already decided. I'm goin' in. I'm not waitin'. I'm goin' in now.... Our dad's got to go to WWII. This is our chance to do somethin', to be part of history guys...." When his friend Stevie questions his choice to volunteer, Kovic says to him, "You don't think you need to serve your country?" He follows this comment with a discussion of the fear of the spread of Communism. "When are we gonna stop 'em?" It ain't a theory, Communism is movin' in everywhere...." When Stevie replies, "Yeah, sure Ronnie, where? I don't see 'em," Kovic tells him, "That's okay, Stevie, someone's gotta stay home with the women and children while the men go do the fightin'!" For Kovic (and the more general narrator of the Vietnam Veteran Narrative), fighting (and winning) the war against Communism would secure phallic identification and establish his position as masculine subject in America.

Philip Caputo, as Narrator, makes a similar connection, attributing the Vietnam soldier with a unique brand of American idealism in his memoir, *A Rumor of War*. He writes,

> A few generalizations can be made about all of [the soldiers]. They were to a man thoroughly American, in their virtues as well as their flaws: idealistic, insolent, generous, direct, violent, and provincial in the sense that they believed the ground they stood on was now forever a part of the United States simply because they stood on it. (1977, 26)

According to the Narrator of the Vietnam Veteran Narrative, the boy was America.

This vision included an idealistic view of the hero that came from stories of the benevolent World War II Veteran. The Narrator of the Vietnam Veteran Narrative looked to figures such as Audie Murphy and John Wayne for models of masculine virtue. In a section Lewis titled "The 'John Wayne Wet Dream,'" he explains the impact of John Wayne and World War II symbolism in the films the narrator watched as a boy. "First, and foremost, Wayne signified heroism in his role as exemplary warrior in World War II combat films. That heroism was held up as genuine, admirable, and replicable" (Lewis, 1985, 22). As Baker comments in his memoir, "With all my terror of going into the Army...there was something seductive about it. I was seduced by WWII and John Wayne movies" (1981, 233). Kovic also emphasizes that when Marine recruiters came to his high school, seeing them "was like all the movies and all the books and all the dreams of becoming a hero come true" (1976, 73). For Kovic and individual narrators, John Wayne also exemplified a view of good versus evil, which is why Kovic emphasizes how deeply he believed in the rightness of America's actions in Vietnam as he was making his decision to join the Marines. Participating in the fight for freedom and progress—for America—was an important stop on the road to manhood.

Progress and belief in America's indisputable moral strength were handed to these boys like a torch of social power, securing in their minds the inherency of their inheritance of power. It is within this narrative that the story Faludi describes saliently rests. Both Ron Kovic in *Born on the Fourth of July* and Chris Taylor (i.e., Stone) in *Platoon* are the Narrators (masculine subject) of the Vietnam Veteran Narrative who, variably, carry these beliefs to Vietnam. The title of Kovic's book and the film, *Born on the Fourth of July* (*Born*), emphasizes the connection he makes between himself and America, in part, because his birthday is on July fourth, the nation's day of independence. He also asserts this poetically (both in his book and in his public appearances): "I am your yankee doodle dandy, your john wayne come home." This is another instance where the Narrator and narrator's stories converge. Kovic continually identifies himself as the symbol of these collective images and beliefs in America. Stone also does this through the character of Chris Taylor in *Platoon*. Although the story in *Platoon* is told by Stone, an individual narrator, he overlaps his narrative into the Vietnam Veteran Narrative, expressing how his dreams and hopes were not just his, but belonged to the other men, soldiers, Vietnam Veterans.

This correlation between the masculine subject and the ideals of America are part of the process of maintaining alignment between the masculine body (the penis) and the symbolic form of social power (the phallus). The phallus ultimately becomes indicative of masculine subjectivity. As Susan Bordo explains in her book, *The Male Body*,

> The phallus stands for a superiority that is distinctively connected with maleness. But... the phallus stands, not for the superior fitness of an individual male over other men, but for *generic male superiority*—not only over females but also over other species... [T]he phallus stands for a superiority that is not just biological, but partakes of an authority beyond (and often in contest with) the power, needs, desires of the body.... The phallus... proclaims its kinship with higher values—with the values of "civilization" rather than "nature," with Man who is made in God's image, not Homo sapiens, the human primate. (1999, 89—my emphasis)

There is a mutual interdependency between the images of the physically strong and potent masculine subject and phallic identification that supports patriarchal social structures. The trauma of the Vietnam War threatens this correlation, leading to the Narrator's continual struggle to maintain phallic identification.

While the penis and phallus cannot be conflated or used interchangeably, they are deeply intertwined in our sociolinguistic imaginings. This creates an internally vulnerable relationship, because the equation of the penis with the phallus is continually under threat of dislocation. Silverman explains that

> it is imperative that belief in the penis/phallus equation be fortified... for it represents the most vulnerable component of the dominant fiction. The male subject's identification with power and privilege is threatened from many directions. It is under siege, first of all, from the Law of Language, to which no fully constituted subject is immune. (1992, 47)

The Law of Language is what ultimately strips the male subject from power, just as it does the female subject. Language produces a "universal castration" (Silverman, 1992, 42) because all beings must submit themselves to language and discourse in order to become an intelligible social subject. Derek Sayer emphasizes this point in his theoretical essay, "In Search of a Subject," by writing, "For it is not that there was an already existent I who decided to enter language.... The subject is only created in the act of objectification—of 'losing oneself' in language—itself. It is found(ed), we might say, in this original loss" (2004, 144). Men's social power does not come by virtue of simply possessing a penis; it comes through relinquishing the self to the discourses of masculinity, which is invested in phallic social power. It is a power achieved only through a loss of self, along with the belief in his subject position within the dominant fiction. The trauma of the Vietnam War threatens this relationship, because it uncovers the reality that the masculine subject is as *subject* to the Law of Language and society as his feminine counterpart.

While the purveyor of the dominant fiction is the masculine subject (with his possession of the phallus), men (individuals born with a penis, who have a stake in the claim of that subject position) are not inherently possessors of the phallic space of power. Yet, men feel entitled to possess that social space of power, because the dominant fiction requires an "imaginary resolution" (Silverman, 1992, 42) between the male body and social power. That is, it requires our belief that the masculine subject does inherently constitute that space of power. It requires the boy to see himself at the helm of the story of America, *dispensing the gifts* and moving into an empowered and emboldened future. As Faludi explained, to watch the boy coming of age in this era was *to see the boy as being automatically entitled and powerful.*

As such, we cannot diminish the historical significance of the image of social power being contained in the phallus, because it reveals the deeply constituted nature of sexual difference within the dominant fiction. As Bordo reminds us,

> I certainly agree with Lacan that the phallus belongs to the realm of ideas, not biology; it's a symbol, not a body part. But the symbol emerged historically... out of forms of reverence that did have reference to biology, and these references themselves have analogues in the morphology and behavior of other male animals. The meanings that we have attached to the phallus, moreover, no matter how abstract and attenuated they have become... are grounded in the bodily image of the erect penis and ideas humans have attached to it. (2000, 94)

This tension between the phallus and penis underscores the way the dominant fiction works within social structures to create a belief in the inherency of this gendered order, which is deeply ingrained, yet vulnerable to dislocation. Such an assessment is a continual reminder of the way sexual difference is imbricated in the development of society and social power. To use the phallus as the signifier of power and believe it can be dislodged from bodily difference is to linguistically believe that the phallus is a purely empty signifier (like the *I* Sayer describes) in which *anything* can enter. The signifier is not a blank slate because the phallus carries the connotations of its erect bodily counterpart. It is grounded in bodily difference. Although the phallus privileges men, it is a privilege *subjected* to constraints. This means that not *all* men can fill this position, even as they hold the expectation and assumption that they *will* fill it. This is a tension continually affecting the construction of masculine subjectivity; the false belief in sameness of the penis and phallus puts the masculine subject in a vulnerable state, because of the societal obstacles that are continually threatening and undermining phallic identification (e.g., racial, class, and bodily differences).

While conflating the penis with the phallus secures a degree of belief in the dominant fiction, we recognize that they are not the same. The contrariness of the masculine subject's position is what makes him a significant, albeit vulnerable, focal point of the dominant fiction. As a historically traumatic event, the Vietnam War causes a disruption in the boy's inheritance of social power. But because *the boy and America are linked*, the break in the boy's inheritance is much more than his: it represents a breakdown in the national ability to claim phallic identification and America's belief in the dominant fiction. The discourses that established belief in this subject position are worked and reworked in the Vietnam Veteran Narrative, as the boy tries to reclaim his inheritance. The continual transgression of *I* and *we* demonstrates the way the individual narrator seeks to linguistically insert himself back into the space of power by overlapping his individual voice with the Narrator's.

Together, the films *Platoon* and *Born* constitute the prototypical Vietnam Veteran Narrative. In Stone's view of these two films, *Born* begins where *Platoon* leaves off. At the end of *Platoon*, we are suspended above the jungles of Vietnam with Taylor, who is assessing his experiences in Vietnam. All the action of the film takes place within the literal space of Vietnam. In *Born*, emphasis is placed on homecoming. Both films tell the story of how Vietnam *was where belief was tested—hard*. For protagonists like Kovic and Taylor/Stone, as well as other Narrator/narrators, the war forces these men to see the limits of the possibilities they were promised as boys of the 1950s; their dreams of manhood are derailed. The Vietnam War is the stark impetus behind the masculine subject's need to reevaluate his beliefs. Kovic's broken body literally expresses the limits of those promises. All his hopes and dreams to be a man are washed away by his paralysis—castration, as he calls it. Dealing with that castration haunts the Vietnam Veteran Narrative. But what caused this loss?

The Second Movement: Breaks and Sutures in the War Experience

The Vietnam Veteran Narrative emphasizes a break between values of the world the Vietnam Veteran left behind in America and the reality of combat experience. Often referring to the United States as *the world*, the Narrator isolates Vietnam and combat to an alternate reality where "the only certainty is overwhelming ambiguity" (O'Brien, 1990, 82). As Lewis remarks,

> the participants viewed the war as shapeless, disjointed, fragmented—a reality wholly other than any they had known or were prepared to meet. It seemed to many as though they had been ripped out of one world in which the familiar order of cause-effect, means-end, premises-conclusion operated and had been transported to another planet for their thirteen-month duty. (1985, 72)[5]

This distinction reveals cracks in the story of the boy and America. The experience of combat is beyond anything the boy thought he would experience in war, leaving him out of control of the story and disconnected from America. In other words, the dominant fiction breaks down as the boy, now soldier, starts to see the ways in which he is subject to the discursive structures of masculinity, revealing the tense and fragile connection between the penis and phallus.

Chris Taylor, the narrator in *Platoon*, experiences these breaks over the course of the film and his indoctrination into combat. The film focuses on the masculine subject who starts to see the limits of his own power and who tries to reclaim that illusory position of power, as he becomes a stronger and more capable soldier. Representative of the Vietnam Veteran Narrative, *Platoon* centers on the fragmentation of meaning experienced by the combat soldier. I focus my analysis of the film on the ways in which this breakdown leads Taylor into seeing (and experiencing) the fallacious relationship between masculine subjectivity and phallic identification. This is most salient in the ways in which the soldiers see the break between the beliefs they held prior to the war and their deconstruction over the course of the war experience. As Mark Baker reflects in his memoir, *Nam*, "That war shattered my whole image of the U.S., of freedom and democracy, of the world we live in, all the ideals I had gone into Vietnam with" (1981, 310); and with that, their understanding of what it meant to be men—masculine subjects—all but fell apart over the course of their service in Vietnam. The illusory relationship between masculine subjectivity and phallic identification evolves into a continual struggle to align the images of the masculine subject as the physical embodiment of masculine strength with his capacity to claim himself as the purveyor of social ideals. I turn now to Taylor to help us understand some of the ways in which this breakdown takes form.

As the Narrator, Taylor enters Vietnam with all the values and beliefs described in the first movement of the Vietnam Veteran Narrative. We watch Taylor's transition from a fresh-faced boy to a seasoned soldier. We initially see Taylor walking off of a plane, stepping on to the tarmac in Vietnam. Exuding a clean and new aura, he rubs his eyes as they adjust to the light and dust of this new place. Once his eyes have adjusted, he sees an ominous preview of what is to come: body bags being loaded onto planes and the exhausted bodies of seasoned soldiers taunting him as they walk by. The film clearly marks a separation between civilian life and the experience of combat. Stone visually forces the viewer to see the war experience from the position of the ground soldier. He takes us on Taylor's journey in a visual and visceral way. His film style is fast-paced, stark, and violent, which is to provide a *realistic* experience of war. Stone's status as a Vietnam Veteran also contributes to the assertions of this film being a genuine and realistic image of combat.[6] As asserted earlier, this is a common endeavor for one who has experienced trauma. Within the context of the Vietnam Veteran Narrative, the struggle for the Narrator to recount the experience of combat is, at times, more important than the larger political context of the war. *Platoon* is better understood as an exploration of the breakdown that occurs to a person under the stress of combat than as a statement of global politics. Although there is little explicit address of the war in global politics, it does not mean that the narrative is entirely ahistorical,[7] considering that it provides important insights into the struggles going on within American masculinity and culture—both at the time of the war and in its presence in American social memory. Watching Talyor move from that fresh-faced boy into a seasoned soldier and killer, I read Taylor's act of killing his superior, Barnes, at the end of the film as the final confirmation of the traumatic break in the Narrator that combat caused. The film takes us on the journey with Taylor as we watch him and his belief in America break down; we watch *order blending into chaos*.

As a young middle-class white man, Taylor (i.e., Stone) symbolizes the Narrator traversing the boundaries between *the world* and *the Nam* as well as order and chaos. Taylor did believe in America, volunteering for service and doing his part as a man.[8] As he explained to his grandma in a letter home, "I just want to be anonymous. Like everybody else. Do my share for my country. Live up to what grandpa did in the first World War. What dad did in the second." But it is not too long into the film that Taylor begins to express his confusion around what is involved in *doing his share*. As he explains to her a little later,

> Somebody once wrote hell is the impossibility of reason. That's what this place feels like, hell. I hate it already and it's only been a week. Some goddamn week, grandma.... I'm so tired. I don't think I can keep this up for a year, grandma. I think I made a big mistake by coming here.

Unable to let go of the world he left behind, while struggling in this alternate world where the rules he lived by no longer apply, nothing makes sense. As he slowly comes to terms with his disillusionment, he severs his connection and correspondence to America. "The world" is represented through his letters home to his grandmother. He reads these to us periodically throughout the film. It is in his letters to his grandmother that we understand why Taylor is in Vietnam and the mental struggles going on as he tries to integrate what is happening to him in Vietnam with the life he had in America. His letters gradually taper off and stop entirely when he severs his connection with America. As he tells his grandmother in one of his last letters to her, "Day by day I struggle not only to maintain my strength but my sanity. It's all a blur. I have no energy to write. I don't know what's right and what's wrong anymore.... I can't believe we're fighting each other when we should be fighting the enemy." The enemy, we discover over the course of the film, is within himself and America—not Vietnam.

Taylor's platoon leaders, Sergeants Elias (Willem Dafoe) and Barnes (Tom Berenger), externally embody the Narrator's internal struggle to reconcile the gap between "the world" and "the Nam." Elias and Barnes represent different aspects of masculine subjectivity experiencing combat. These representations of masculine subjectivity become fathers to Taylor, taking over the role of domestic parents that exist back in the world of America. He explains that "The war is over now, but it will always be there for the rest of my days—as I'm sure Elias will be fighting with Barnes for what Rhah called 'possession of my soul.'

There are times since I've felt like a child born of those two fathers." As a masculine subject in combat he is destroyed and remade through his negotiation of these two *fathers*. He is caught between the primal desire to survive the brutality of combat and the desire to uphold the values he had been taught, which encapsulate a noble and righteous soldier.

Elias symbolizes those noble values in the way he cares for the men he commands and the respect he holds for the Vietnamese. Barnes symbolizes the pure break with those values as he conveys the image of an indestructible fighting machine, treating the men with cruelty and holding very little respect for the Vietnamese. When the platoon comes upon a dead Vietnamese man, he tells Taylor, "That's a good gook. Good and dead." Barnes makes up his own rules in war; he is a fearsome and calculating soldier. Klein describes Barnes and Elias's representations of war masculinity in this way,

> Barnes, a brutal, effective killer and semifascist superpatriot who regards Vietnam as one big free-fire zone; Elias, an even more effective killer of the National Liberation Front (NLF), but a non-ideologue and a person who adheres to the rules and laws of the Geneva Convention. (1990, 25)

Although Klein's rhetoric exaggerates these characters' discursive positions, the point he makes is important because it emphasizes, not that the two men are on opposing sides in terms of the war effort, but that they hold a very different ethic on war conduct developed from their opposing positions within masculine subjectivity. Barnes and Elias, albeit not pure representations of the body (penis) and social power (phallus) binary that is at work in masculine subjectivity, demonstrate the tensions involved in maintaining the correlation between the penis and phallus within the experience of the trauma of combat. Barnes symbolizes social power through his investment in the inherent physical *self-will* of the masculine subject, whereas Elias symbolizes social power through his investment in the *civilized ethical* code of conduct established by the written word of law. We sense throughout the film that these two positions cannot find union in the experience of combat. Adherence to domestic rules of conduct comes into conflict and contradiction in the alternative world of war, "the Nam," where the physical form of the masculine subject (his survival) is the central concern. At the same time this representation of war masculinity becomes devoid of social restriction *and* a social conscience, separating from the ideals of America.

Over the course of the film, these men demonstrate the difficulty that the combat soldier has with maintaining the virtues of physical prowess and social morality. Taylor, the Narrator and masculine subject, is caught between these two representations of war masculinity as he tries to maintain phallic identification and belief in the dominant fiction. He endeavors to retain the honor and values he brought with him to Vietnam while surviving the brutality of combat. Ultimately, the Narrator cannot sustain belief in America *and* survive the combat experience. To complete this break with America, Taylor stops writing to his grandmother entirely little more than halfway through the film. As he explains to King (portrayed by Keith David) when he asked Taylor why he stopped writing home,

> You ever get caught in a mistake that you just can't get out of? ... It's not just me. It's the way the whole thing works. People like Elias get wasted. People like Barnes just goin' makin' all the rules up any way they want. So what do we do? Sit in the middle and suck on it. We just don't add up to dry shit.

The platoon and the war are where he experiences his break with "the world" and so he tries to recreate a cohesive sense of self within the context and perimeters of the chaotic logic of combat.

Taylor uses Elias and Barnes to try to recover his position as masculine subject. As the Narrator, Taylor experiences a deep feeling of loss upon Elias's death, especially because he was murdered by Barnes. The loss of Elias to Barnes symbolizes the incommensurability of the relationship between the masculine subject in his physical form (Barnes) and the phallic masculine subjectivity that holds social power through the upholding of the values and ideals of America (Elias). Taylor realizes that in combat he is not at the helm of the dominant fiction and that he *doesn't add up to dry shit*. He realizes that there is nothing virtuous and noble in combat. This realization does not come from witnessing his comrades fall to the Vietnamese enemy; it emerges from the internal strife of the American masculine subject breaking under the trauma of war. The rules, laws, and ideologies that comprise the dominant fiction—the story of America—are lost to the base struggle for survival. It is upon Elias's death that Taylor becomes fully cognizant that the problem is not the Vietnamese—it is America and its values (particularly in regard to masculine ideals).

When Barnes kills Elias in the jungle, he wants to erase the social conscience of America and underscore the distinction between the ideologies in *the world* and the brutality of *the Nam*. By killing Elias, Barnes violently eradicates Taylor's moral structures. As Barnes tells Taylor, "I am reality. There's the way it ought to be and there's the way it is." The reality of war cannot, in Barnes's representation of masculine subjectivity, adhere to ideals of what *ought to be*. War changes the rules of reality and must leave behind the idealism of the world, that is, America. New rules are now in order. This is confirmed through Barnes's murder of Elias, making the narrator cognizant of the reality that under the experience of trauma his social and bodily self struggle against each other for survival. As Lewis points out, "the answer is that the final repository of meaning and value become sheer physical survival.... This haven of meaning, grounded in bio-instinctual drive, kept chaos at bay.... [E]xistence and the value of its continuation is viewed as a brute fact of experience" (1985, 111). The ideals of achieving manhood, fighting communism, and being moral and noble (on the civilized world's terms), must be negated if the soldier intends to survive. This is why Barnes admonishes Elias's civilized war ethic, saying he "was full of shit" and "a crusader." As Baker notes, "the hardest thing to come to grips with is that making it through Vietnam—surviving—is probably the only worthwhile part of the experience" (1981, 315). O'Brien further supports this: "Most soldiers in Alpha Company did not think about human courage. 'Shit man, the trick of being in the Nam is gettin' *out* of the Nam. And I don't mean gettin' out in a plastic body bag. I mean gettin' out alive, so my girl can grab me so I'll know it" (1975, 141). But those ideals the soldier carried into Vietnam do not disappear entirely, which is why Taylor, the Narrator, is so stricken by Elias's death. It is also why *getting out of the Nam* requires Taylor to seek retribution for the death of his ideals and values. He has to do this because, as the narrator of the Vietnam Veteran Narrative, he needs to find a link back to the social ideals he carried into war (and which still constitute fundamental aspects of masculine subjectivity). Although Taylor has to negate aspects of his dreams of honor and valor—the John Wayne fantasy—in order to do what he needs to do to get out of Vietnam as a relatively coherent masculine subject, he cannot completely relinquish the beliefs structuring the dominant fiction.

What Taylor realizes is that he needs to kill Barnes. The primary logic of existing in the suspended world of "the Nam" is that you will eventually return to "the world" and continue with the life you left behind. In the moment of the death of the social ideals of America (that Elias represented), Taylor (temporarily) severs the link between

Vietnam from the world—America—which is what enables him to kill Barnes at the end of the film. Although Elias may not have been able to overcome Barnes's reality, Barnes cannot survive Taylor and the inevitable transition back to America. Taylor cannot hold on to the sheer brutality that Barnes represents as he makes his way back to the world of America. He must try to destroy that part of his subjective self before he can go home. The narrator has to figure out a way to reconnect the war-torn masculine subject with the social values that will (ideally) allow him to reestablish belief in American and find phallic identification. But through his murder of Barnes, Taylor commits a contradictory act that affirms the traumatic break that combat creates in the masculine subject. Taylor's act reinforces the reality that there is no way for him to return home from war the same person he was before he left. Barnes cannot be eradicated from the Vietnam Veteran. "The Nam" and "the world" are indelibly linked and coexist within the returning soldier. As Rhah (Francesco Quinn), a fellow soldier, warns Taylor, "The only thing that can kill Barnes is Barnes." Taylor's act of killing Barnes does not eradicate the traumatic break caused by combat; it confirms its presence in the Vietnam Veteran as he returns home to America.

As Taylor flies out of the jungle at the end of the film, we are unsure what will happen to the Narrator back in the world. We can believe that he made a tenuous connection with phallic identification when he proclaims, "But be that as it may, those of us who did make it have an obligation to build again, to teach to others what we know and to try, with what's left of our lives, to find a goodness and meaning to this life." Yet, we do not know how his traumatized subjectivity will manifest as he returns home. Belief in America is now mediated by the awakening of the illusion of the Narrator's relationship with phallic masculinity. He can no longer see himself so easily taking on the social position he believed would be his as a man in America. There is a visible disconnection between his existence as a man and his relationship to the structures of power in America. The feeling this evokes is that he has been able to reclaim belief in the dominant fiction and the position of phallic masculinity to be able to teach what is *good* to others. In this context, the Narrator recoups his position of power, but it is a reclamation troubled by many questions that cannot be answered until he steps foot on American soil. Flying in the air over the jungles of Vietnam still in the company of men, he can believe in the *goodness of this life*. But it is a belief that will again be tested as he returns to America and sees the world through his war experiences. If it is up to the Narrator *to build again*, how do these experiences transform the masculine subject reentering America and does it redress the dominant fiction? To answer this question we must now turn to *Born*, where the Vietnam Veteran Narrative continues.

The Third Movement: The Project of Homecoming

Born[9] tells the story of Ron Kovic's (Tom Cruise) transformation from an idealistic boy who dreams of being a hero and living the American dream with a home, a wife, and children to a broken symbol of the America he believed in.

"What can I do Ronnie? What do you want?"—Ron Kovic's father
"I want to be a man again." —Ron Kovic, *Born on the Fourth of July*

The lessons of *goodness* that Kovic teaches are ones that he, as the Narrator, first must discover for himself as he comes to terms with his position as the Vietnam Veteran. *Born* traverses the landscape of America through the Vietnam Veteran, the masculine subject who has been dislocated from phallic identification. Through an analysis of *Born*, the narrative clarity Taylor achieved at the end of *Platoon* is contingent on the Narrator's reentry into the domestic world comprising home. The suspended belief in America and the masculine subject's position in it is possible while being engaged in the war context, a central reason for their separation of *the Nam* and *the world*. For this reason, the breaks in his beliefs do not fully emerge until the Narrator reenters the world. Through Kovic we understand how "the world" and "the Nam" will remain a part of the Vietnam Veteran, making him the site of traumatic enunciation. The struggle to incorporate his experiences and losses in Vietnam into the life and values of America illuminate the disjunction. Kovic's physical paralysis confirms this break. The break is literal and symbolic. The break physically marks the Vietnam Veteran and alerts us to the deeper social break the Vietnam Veteran represents in the Vietnam Veteran Narrative.

Kovic and his father (Raymond J. Barry) poignantly bring to life the traumatic stammering that takes place as the Vietnam Veteran returns home. Helping Kovic into bed after an emotional fight with his mother, Kovic's father pleads with his son, asking what he can do to help him. But as Kovic tells his father that all he wants is to be a man again, it becomes clear to his father and the viewers that his father cannot help him. The promise of manhood falters between father and son as all the hope wrapped up in Kovic's memories of himself as a boy disintegrate in his journey through America as the Vietnam Veteran.

> This mission to manhood shows up in [men of the baby boom generation's] minds not as a promise met but as betrayal, losses, disillusionment... There had been so much anticipation, so much excitement, so many assumptions that nothing possibly could go wrong. But, somehow, it all had. (Faludi, 1999, 27)

The illusory relationship between the phallus and penis are repeatedly articulated in the film. Homecoming makes the traumatic break of the combat experience more pronounced; the illusory relationship between the penis and phallus becomes even more fragile. Betrayal of the promises America and his family made becomes the overarching theme of the traumatic enunciation. Father and son disconnect, reflecting the vulnerability of the masculine subject in the transference of social power. Kovic experiences a series of failures as he tries to enter the space of social power through the domestic realm. He cannot claim phallic identification in the realm of his family and hometown, nor can he live out the rite of passage of manhood that is marked by the transition from son to father. The film reinforces the need for the traumatized masculine subject to negate the domestic family and seek other routes into phallic identification.

As the Narrator of the Vietnam Veteran Narrative, both Taylor and Kovic leave Vietnam trying to hold on to their beliefs in America and the possibilities for the future. Even though Kovic knows his injury seriously threatens his hopes and dreams of attaining phallic identification, he maintains belief in the promises told to him before he left for Vietnam. The trauma these men experience is not only to their psyches and their bodies, but also to the discursive structures that comprise their subjectivity as American men. Like the damage to the psyche, there is a delay in our ability to recognize the effects of the initial moment of trauma. The suspended belief in America and the masculine subject's position in it is possible while being engaged in the war context within the platoon and other men, a central reason for their separation of "the Nam" and "the world." The breaks in their beliefs do not fully emerge until the narrator reenters the world. "But once removed from the battlefront," comments Silverman,

> the traumatized veteran no longer enjoys the support of his comrades-in-arms. All that stands between him and the abyss is the

paternal imago, within which he can no longer recognize himself. For the society to which he returns moreover, he represents a sorry travesty of "our fighting men and boys," a living proof of the incommensurability of the penis and the phallus. Because of the resulting crisis of faith, "reality" itself is at least temporarily jeopardized. (1992, 63)

Whatever tenuous correlation Kovic established with phallic identification in combat and in his initial return to America all but dissolves as he tries to fully reintegrate into domestic life. Removed from the reality of the brute experience of survival in combat and the support of other soldiers, the traumatic effects of war reveal themselves to the soldier and those within the domestic realm.

In *Born*, Kovic falls into the *abyss*; he is no longer able to see himself in the paternal imago. His paralyzed body—castrated as he calls it—symbolizes the fissures between masculine subjectivity and phallic identification. In *Born*, the physical, emotional, and discursive breaks resulting from trauma converge. His body is a continual reminder of the difficult transition between the worlds of America and Vietnam. As Faludi comments, "The frontier, the enemy, the institutions of brotherhood, the women in need of protection—all the elements of the old formula of attaining manhood had vanished in short order. The boy who had been told he was going to be the master of the universe and all that was in it found himself master of none" (1999, 30). *Reality* is jeopardized for Kovic *and* his family, because, like Kovic, his parents witness America breaking down as they watch their son break down. His father cannot help him become a man and is forced to face his own limitations as masculine subject. These limitations are most saliently understood in Kovic's incapacity to biologically reproduce.

As Silverman (and Stacey) points out, the family is the central organizer of the dominant fiction. Through Kovic we see how the dominant fiction relies on the imbrication of the potency of the male body (penis) with the masculine subject's social power (phallus). Kovic holds the physical body as symbolic of his social power and lack of it after his return home. The film and his memoir emphasize the Narrator's physical prowess, particularly in athletics. At the same time, success for Kovic is using his body to excel in life and this included doing well in sports, being an ideal Marine and hero, and having children and a successful family life. Reiterating Stacey's discussion of the normative American family, she explains how it signifies a heterosexual, conjugal, nuclear, domestic unit, one ideally with a male primary breadwinner, a female primary homemaker, and their dependent offspring. This unitary, normative definition of legitimate domestic arrangements is what my book [*Brave New Families*, 1990] identifies as ephemeral, and with little regret, because of race, class, gender, and sexuality diversity it has occluded and the inequities it has exacerbated. (1993, 545)

In Kovic's mind, this construction of the family was not ephemeral; it contained the one genuine route to phallic identification. It was a route that Kovic believed had no substitute. Ultimately, the Narrator has to shift this belief if he hopes to find a position within American society as a legitimate masculine subject.

Kovic's connection with phallic identification and America breaks as he rides in his homecoming parade. As part of Massapequa's Fourth of July celebration, Kovic rides in the parade and then speaks at a rally in support of the men from the town serving in the Vietnam War. As he sits in the car waving to the crowd, we sense something is not quite right. He is not the hero—the John Wayne figure—he imagined he would be. The effects of the mixtures of cheers and jeers coming from the townsfolk have a visible effect on Kovic. His presence is one of spectacle rather than hero. He tries to maintain his composure during his speech in front of the cheering and jeering faces he grew up with, who knew him before he left for Vietnam. He says to them, "I served my country. And I don't want you to feel sorry for me. Do not shed a tear. I have my hands, my eyes, my ears. I have my heart. And I have, what I feel is [pause]. I have what I feel is an un...quenchable..." He cannot continue. He stammers as he tries to enunciate phallic masculine subjectivity, as he tries to articulate his belief in himself and America. Looking out at the faces, their expressions shift as his words break down. They grow silent and uncomfortable by his inability to speak. He tries to articulate his position in America and reconnect with the world he left behind. But he is not sure what it is he believes in, and he becomes, for them, *a living proof of the incommensurability of the penis and the phallus*. The crowd's discomfort along with Kovic's fumbled words leaves all of them in a space where belief in America is untenable. The masculine subject cannot claim phallic identification and the dominant fiction breaks down, leaving all of the participants—Kovic, his family, town folks, and even veterans of previous wars—struggling to find a way to manage Kovic's broken body and stammered articulation in the context of their beliefs about the war effort and America. It is in this homecoming that America and phallic identification no longer enjoy the comfort of distance from reality, allowing the abstraction of the soldier and masculine subject to continue. No longer within the reality of Vietnam and combat, Kovic is confronted by his beliefs in America and his experiences in Vietnam.

This break draws Kovic away from his family and the domestic realm represented by his hometown. He turns to the comfort of fellow Vietnam Veterans, which is initiated by his reacquaintance with Timmy (Frank Whaley), a childhood friend who also served in Vietnam. With Timmy, Kovic feels comfortable talking about the emptiness of his goals and desires to be a hero. As he says to Timmy,

> When I was in the hospital, I thought, yeah, this makes sense. 'Cause I failed, Timmy. 'Cause I killed someone, some people—terrible mistakes. First time I got hit, I got hit in the foot. I could have layed down. I mean, who gives a fuck now if I was hero. I was paralyzed—castrated that day. Why? 'Cause I was so stupid. They have my dick and my balls now and I think—I think, Timmy, I'd give everything I believe in, everything I've got, all my values, just to have my body back again, just to be whole again. But I'm not whole and I never will be and that's the way it is, isn't it?

The reasons he went to Vietnam lose the immediacy and vitality they had before he left. In fact, the terms of being a hero appear silly in light of the larger realities and consequences of war, rendering the America he knew before Vietnam nonexistent. When he tells us that he would give up all his values to be whole again, the tension between those values and his losses are brought to the forefront. In a sense, they alert us to the beginning of his negation of the meanings of America he grew up holding so dear.

The gap between the Narrator and phallic identification becomes wider and wider as he navigates through different parts of the social world. He cannot separate his physical limitations from his more civilized values. His bodily break emphasizes his social marginality, reiterating the deeply interconnected relationship between the penis and phallus. His physical inability to conform to the physical prowess and self-will that define society's beliefs as part of the innateness of the masculine body automatically leads him to believe he cannot fulfill his role as masculine subject in the domestic sphere. This is why being *whole* is a fundamental precursor to his engagement with phallic identification. He still believes in America and the correlation between bodily masculinity and social power, which is why he initially identifies himself as a failure—*castrated*. He sees how he is subject to a larger set of ideas that incapacitate him even as they define him. That is, he believes in the story even though he knows there is no way for him to feel he has the power to script it. This, ultimately, is what it means to be in intimate relationship with lack. It does not mean that by recognizing that lack, some other reality immediately emerges. Instead, it means that one must struggle to try to reestablish belief and find a way to reconnect to the social world, while clearly seeing the impossibilities of fulfilling his prescribed role in society. He wants to feel himself filling that subject position, even if it means giving up certain beliefs. In actuality, it may be the ability to let go of those values and beliefs that will enable him to be whole once again—enacting masculine subjectivity in a different way.

Eventually, the bridge between Kovic and home breaks down entirely as he makes the final break from his family and everything that it held in place for him. In a pivotal scene, when Kovic has a terrible fight with his mother, he realizes he cannot (and will never) live up to the American ideal of the family. This fight between Kovic, the Narrator of the Vietnam Veteran Narrative and the masculine subject, and his mother, the feminine subject who represents the beliefs of home and the domestic world, signifies the greater struggle that the Narrator had with trying to reconnect *the world* of America with the experiences he had in *the Nam*. This fight underscores the important role the family plays in maintaining belief in the dominant fiction. It makes sense (even if it is misdirected) that Kovic centers his anger and frustration on his family and in crisis turns away from them. This is finalized in the last scene in which we see Kovic and his family together (about half way through the film). After an evening of drinking heavily, Timmy and Kovic's other friends drop him off at home. It is clear that this is not the first time this has happened because, when he gets in the house, his mother (Caroline Kava), a devout Catholic, reminds him that she will not tolerate drinking in her home. This sets Kovic off, lashing out at her, God, and all the ideals he feels *she* instilled in him, and which led to his decision to volunteer to go to Vietnam. He yells to her:

> I gotta live and I gotta roll around and be a reminder of Vietnam. And you don't want to know, you don't want to see us. You want to hide us, 'cause it is a can of shit and I am a fuckin' dummy! [...] I believed in everything they told us, "Go fight! Go kill!" [...] It's all a lie! The whole thing is a fuckin' lie! [violently shoves his trophies off his dresser].

All his mother can do is ask "What did they do to you in that war? What happened to you? You need help, Ronnie." Kovic yells back at her, "You need help with all your God and bullshit dreams about me! You are ashamed of me! You're embarrassed by me!" His mother watches him, helpless and angry at having to watch her son falling apart before her eyes—not to mention her beliefs in America that were embodied in her son. There is a complete severing between Kovic and his family in this scene. He feels they cannot understand what he has been through and do not want to know the pain he feels largely because he thinks they still hold those beliefs in America that are dissolving around him.

Frustrated by her son's accusations, his mother yells back at him, "I didn't force you to go!" to which he replies, "Yes you did! Yes you did! And it's all falling apart. King! Kennedy! Kent State! We all lost the fucking war!" When she tells him that is not true, he yells back at her:

> What do you know? What do you know? You tell her dad! Tell her, it's a lie! It's a fucking lie! There's no God. God's as dead as my legs. There's no God, there's no country, there's nothing. There's nothing except me and this fucking wheelchair for the rest of my life. For nothing. Me and this, this dead penis.

By pointing his anger at his mother and seeking his father's help to explain himself to her, he is clearly negating the feminine subject and all that she represents in the domestic sphere. But the paternal imago cannot rescue Kovic from the abyss. His father stands impotently witnessing the fight between Kovic and his mother. After the fight he is the one who takes Kovic to bed. He does not have the answers his son needs. In fact, it is his father who asks Kovic what he should do, because he does not know. Neither understand "that the enemy was...neither the father nor the son; that there was, in fact, no 'enemy'—only the dangerous prescriptions of manhood into which they all, fathers as well as sons, had been drafted" (Faludi, 1999, 358). The two men decide the best thing for Kovic to do is to go away to heal—in the company of other Vietnam Veterans. He, then, leaves his family—the traditional family—and seeks out another way in which he can enter society as a masculine subject reconnected with phallic masculinity. The loss of his ability to have children, his inability to communicate to this family, and his empty values leave him looking for a new kind of family in the company of others like himself. Specifically, he turns to other disabled Vietnam Veterans and then the Vietnam Veterans Against the War (VVAW) for support and understanding.

Masculinity and Its Discontents: The Vietnam Veteran as Enunciative Site of Trauma

The struggle for the masculine subject to establish phallic identification is deeply intertwined with the articulation of trauma, which takes place in the Vietnam Veteran Narrative. It is part of the *new hero* that Stone refers to below.

> "I think [Born] describes a spiritual transformation in a boy who goes to war to be a certain type of hero and he's defeated in that goal. His life on the surface is defeated at every turn. And he goes through hell and comes back from hell and he's grown into a better man than what he intended to be. He is a different kind of hero." (Stone, film commentary).

The *new hero* is the Narrator of the Vietnam Veteran Narrative who finds a social voice that looks beyond the Vietnam Veteran Narrative even as he remains caught within its structural trappings. Although the Vietnam Veteran Narrative is an alternative dominant fiction it reflects the traumatic enunciation constituting the Narrator's struggle to reclaim phallic identification. In this concluding section, I juxtapose Kovic's return home in *Born* with Steve Butler's return home in *Heaven and Earth*,[10] in order to interrogate the way the Narrator struggles with traumatized subjectivity in order to regain phallic identification. In particular, the representation of Butler and his return home reflects the Narrator's descent into the societal images of the Vietnam Veteran that dominate the Vietnam Veteran's position in society. In contrast, the narrative built around Kovic's return reflects the distinct presence of the *new hero* that initiates a story that moves beyond break that occurred in the dominant fiction.

I read Stone's comment as one where the Narrator (capital *N*) and the narrator (lowercase *n*) converge. Kovic is the Narrator/narrator struggling to claim phallic identification. For this reason, I integrate my analysis of *Born* with Kovic's written memoir. I emphasize the central source of difficulty for the Narrator after returning home to the world in navigating all those beliefs he held prior to his war service. Because the breakdown of those values in Vietnam can be neither forgotten nor fully integrated into his life at home, how do they shape the Narrator's subjectivity? Does he establish phallic identification? Or does he remain forever traumatized? These questions cannot be answered with a simple yes or no. The Narrator *does* find belief once again in the correlation between masculine subjectivity and phallic identification, but it is a tenuous connection mediated through his experiences with trauma. In the Vietnam Veteran Narrative, the imprint of trauma affects the ways in which individual narrators seek to reestablish their place as men in society.

Complementing the social layer of the Vietnam Veteran Narrative on the palimpsest is the work of Tracy Karner. Focusing on the individual narratives of Vietnam Veterans in her research on Vietnam Veterans and post-traumatic stress disorder (PTSD),[11] she develops the argument that the recognition of PTSD by Veterans Affairs (VA) and the psychological establishment (by its recognition in the DSM-III in 1980) enabled Vietnam Veterans to gain a legitimate route into recouping their losses (particularly the loss of ability to identify with phallic masculinity). As she comments,

> since many of these veterans were still seeking acceptance as men in society and had failed to gain this status through traditional male roles of breadwinner and father, the VA could become a surrogate father possessing the capacity to bestow the mantle of manhood.... As part of the government and military, the VA symbolized an authority that betrayed them in Vietnam and in a sense owed them all the things that they had lost in combat. (1995, 41)

Her discussion of individual narrators folds into the Vietnam Veteran Narrative, demonstrating that the traumatized subject is a significant component of the social monad of the Vietnam War. Providing individual Vietnam Veterans with a legitimate way of finding meaning in their war experiences, the Vietnam Veteran Narrative is a social story continually negotiated by individual Vietnam Veterans. Like the VA in Karner's work with individual narrators, in *Born* the VVAW provided answers that Kovic's father could not provide. Karner found in her interviews with Vietnam Veterans that the men relied on their fathers as symbols of their visions of manhood. Most of Karner's interviewees continually hit roadblocks in their attempts to locate themselves as masculine subjects through traditionally domestic routes (e.g., family, fatherhood). The VA, as well as groups like the VVAW (in Kovic's case), gave them another route into phallic identification that is founded on traumatic irresolution, but this irresolution does not have a singular social manifestation. For some Vietnam Veterans, like the Narrator that Steve Butler represents, it meant falling victim to this traumatic identification; for others, like the Narrator that Kovic represents, this identification was a means of finding a legitimate voice in the social world. By vocalizing his anger and disillusionment with the country in the public realm, Kovic found a way to recoup some of his losses.

Through both Butler and Kovic, we see the breadth of possibilities into how the break that occurred in Vietnam leads the narrator to create "other roles, such as their former soldier role, that further facilitated their emasculation—the ironic opposite of their desire" (Karner, 1994, 199). I emphasize this point because, although these men work to achieve different roles, they do so without transforming the structures of the dominant fiction and its reliance on the traditional routes to phallic identification. They still hold belief in the masculine subjects' position of power and in the dominant fiction of America. We see this in the intense longing they have for an essential part of themselves that was lost. The *new hero* that emerges within the traumatized subject carries on the struggle to integrate his war experience into the domestic structures of society. Depending on his status as a soldier and veteran, the Narrator/narrator's struggle for social power potentially can make him dependent upon his losses and maladies—his lack. Whether it is Butler finding the empty rewards of fatherhood, Kovic finding his empty body symbolic of the costs of war, or Vietnam Veterans articulating themselves in the context of PTSD, Narrator/narrators are bound within a set of discourses that leave them continually trying to bridge the gap between the disaffected soldier/veteran and the father and family participant.

Steve Butler demonstrates the darker side of traumatic identification. Butler, upon first arriving back in the United States, finds a tenuous identification with phallic masculinity through his position as father and husband. He tries to dominate Hayslip, who is Butler's repository of feminine and domestic virtue, and his children, but this is never enough to fortify his position of social power. His violent attempts at containing Hayslip and controlling the domestic world he inhabits cannot remedy the disempowered feelings generated by his inability to be the breadwinner of the family. While he connects with a traumatic identification by calling himself a "killer," it only makes his position in America more irreconcilable. What he was trained to do (and be) in war is not what can help him succeed as a man in America. In fact, it is a liability; he loses everything because of it.

He cannot find a civilian job, making him unable to support his family financially. When he first returns home with Hayslip and their children from Vietnam, he depends on his mother for support. After some time passes, he still is unable to find a job and Hayslip ends up supporting the family. Rather than trying to reestablish himself in a civilian context, he holds distant and futile dreams of a future when he can retire from the military and return to Southeast Asia to do the only thing he feels qualified to do. As he explains to Hayslip: "Selling arms.... It's my life, Le. It's the only thing I know how to do. At least I'll be makin' more money for doin' it." But his dream disappears when his actions in Vietnam come back to haunt him. He is left to bear the burden of his self-proclaimed status as a killer. The military dishonorably discharges him because of his actions in Vietnam, destroying any chance for him to have a military career. The Narrator's traumatic identification puts him in a precarious position whereby the Narrator can easily be identified as the social harbinger for the moral and ethical quandaries that war produces. Not only do we see how difficult it is for the Narrator to reintegrate into *the world*, we also are shown how the Vietnam Veteran Narrative leads the Narrator (who can easily be confused with the individual narrator) into symbolizing aspects of the Vietnam War that America has difficulty addressing structurally (within the military institution, for example). Ultimately, Butler's, the Narrator's, traumatic identification destroys the fragile connection he made with phallic masculinity through family and situates the social trauma of the war within the Narrator.

There was a brief moment after his return when Butler could hold on to phallic identification. Defending Hayslip from attacks by his family and other Americans, Hayslip calls him her hero. Their bond soon breaks apart, though, as Hayslip acclimates to American society, finding a job and achieving success in business. Butler becomes remote and distant, continually asserting his beliefs and values upon Hayslip. As a feminine subject and symbol of domestic values, her independence from Butler further dislocates him from claiming phallic identification. This leads Butler to violently react to her growing independence. Telling her that her "Buddha don't know shit!" and when she complains that he is spending money they do not have on guns, he says to her, "I don't need you to tell me what I should or should not have. They're my sons too. And I'm gonna take 'em up into the mountains and learn how to hunt and shoot. Thank you! They're gonna learn what it takes to survive in this world." It is a violent scene. Butler towers over Hayslip as he screams these words at her, physically dominating over her. But Hayslip does not back down and yells at him, "I've seen too many guns in my lifetime. Killing people won't protect anything. I don't want guns in my house no more." She proceeds to tell him to get out of the house. At her threat he becomes more physically violent, loading and then pointing his shotgun at her head. This marks the beginning of Butler's downward spiral from which he never recovers. Unable to improve his position, the tensions between Hayslip and Butler continue. Eventually she leaves him. Butler cannot take it, though, and he ends up kidnapping his sons, threatening Hayslip:

> You want to see 'em again, you do exactly what I tell you. You write a letter to that bitch lawyer of yours. Tell her you're dropping all the charges against me. Tell her that you want the house all our stuff put into my name. Tell her you're dropping the divorce.

Hayslip agrees to this, fearing that she will never see her sons. When she talks to Butler again later that night, she tells him

> I know you hate me, but I don't hate you. Let me help you. Let me try. I feel your pain. You come back home. No police. Just you, me, the children. We make this right. I'll go to your church. I'll try harder. I'll put the shrine away. I love you Steve. I love the man I saw in Vietnam. I'll find you again. He's still there, Steve.

But he is no longer in Vietnam and no longer that man. He breaks upon hearing her willingness to sacrifice all of herself—her work, her religion, and her autonomy. He shatters completely. He knows he has lost his family—the only thing holding him to the social world. The next time we see him, he is dead; he committed suicide. Unable to resolve the break between *the world* and *the Nam*, Butler's death symbolizes the way traumatic identification can destroy the Narrator's social existence, reflecting the incommensurability between *the world* and *the Nam.*

Kovic finds a more productive way into phallic identification than Butler.

Kovic turns away from the domestic world entirely in the film; we never again see him with his family or establishing a family in the normative sense. Instead, he creates a new family with other Vietnam Veterans, becoming a part of the VVAW and establishing a career as a political advocate. The film ends with him on the threshold of speaking at the 1976 Democratic National Convention. We want to feel great promise and hope as he moves out to the center stage. But we experience an odd discomfort as he makes his way from the backstage to the podium. We are forced to take on the perspective of Kovic from his wheelchair, having people physically impose themselves on him as they ask him questions about what he will say in his speech or to sign his recently published memoir. In this social environment he finds the words to express his frustration and disquiet. This is very different from his speech at the Fourth of July parade when he fumbled for words. He feels more in control of his social existence. Although we do not hear his speech in the film, we sense a great deal of promise, which we hear in his response to a reporter who asks him what it is like to address the entire country. Blurring *I* and *we*, he finds a connection with phallic identification when he says, "Overwhelming. Honor. It's been a long way for *us*. Just lately *I* felt, like, *I'm* home. You know? Like, uhm, maybe *we're* home" (my emphases). Home is structured, not around the normative family but around his reclamation of a social voice; a social voice that is valued. Articulating the trauma he experienced in war and claiming traumatic identification provides the Narrator with that legitimate social voice, even though his body symbolizes and situates the trauma of the Vietnam War within the Narrator. In different ways (and with distinct ramifications), both Butler and Kovic take on the enunciative site of the trauma of the Vietnam War in their images as the Narrator of the Vietnam Veteran Narrative.

In the filmic version of the narrative, Kovic, the Narrator and masculine subject, completely bypasses the domestic realm of society. He is unable to speak to his family and hometown, but finds his voice both in his memoir and in his public addresses. When he speaks of his decision to use his disability to force America to see him as a wounded soldier, he asserts the *goodness* he found in his war experiences and his damaged body. He explains,

> I went totally into speaking against the war [...]. I went into it the same way I'd gone into everything else I've wanted to do in my life—the way I'd gone into pole vaulting or baseball or the marines. But this was something that meant much more than being an athlete or a marine. I could see that this thing—this body I had trained so hard to be strong and quick, this body I now dragged around with me like an empty corpse—was to mean much more than I had ever realized. (Kovic, 1976, 149)

The *more* he describes is identifying himself as a physical symbol of the damage of war and the contradictions of America and masculine ideals. Although he finds solace and hope in speaking to the public, it is tempered by the intense longing for an earlier time when Kovic's body, beliefs, and dreams were still intact. The book's ending conveys more ambiguity in his loss of his hopes and dreams in the domestic sphere than the film. Yet, read together, we can see how the film and the book enforce the construction of this *new hero*. By making the connection between *I* and *we*, Kovic, a narrator of a Vietnam Veteran narrative is also the Narrator of the Vietnam Veteran Narrative, reclaiming a legitimate social voice and position—however tenuous it may be.

At the end of his book, we read how Kovic longs for the time when he still believed in America and the man he thought he would be. "I remember it was a beautiful spring day and we were young back then and really alive and the air smelled fresh. This song was playing and I really got into it and was hitting baseballs and feeling like I could live forever. It was all sort of easy. It had all come and gone" (1976, 224). In both versions (the film and his memoir) of Kovic's narrative endings, we are left to wonder how he navigates between the representation of the Vietnam Veteran and the masculine subject functioning in the present social world. The Vietnam Veteran Narrative leaves the Narrator trying to be a new kind of hero who, rather than questioning the gender constructions that led to his feelings of failure, tries to reestablish his position of power through his lack. Yet, both Butler and Kovic carry the trauma of the Vietnam War within them, locating them as the site of trauma within which America articulates and contains the difficult aspects of this historical event.

The story of the Vietnam War contains these layered narratives of the Vietnam Veteran. It is with these tangled stories that the men and women I interview tell as they begin to develop their own narratives, constituting a third narrative layer on this palimpsest. They, as we will see in chapter three, expand the story of the traumatic event of the Vietnam War out and beyond the original event, ultimately expressing the complex dimensions of the social monad.

CHAPTER THREE

Exploring the Social Monad through the Crisis of Articulation

The Vietnam Veteran and Father as Narrative Foundation

If the Vietnam War is the epicenter of the social monad, narratives of children of Vietnam Veterans (COVV) constitute one of the ripple effects radiating out of the initial shock of this historically traumatic event. As Bissell writes,

> For the growing-up children of many [Vietnam] vets the war's remoteness was all but impossible to gauge because it had happened pre-you, before you had come to grasp the sheer accident of your own placement in time, before you recognized your reality—your bedroom, your toys and comic books—had nothing to do with the reality of your father. (Bissell, 2004, 567)

The real problem of trauma [is] that of the second generation (Felman, 2002, 47), because the monad emerges as part of the social reality that the second generation has always known. Why is this a problem? Well, it is not so much a problem in the sense that it undermines the lives of the second generation. Rather, it is a problem because the trauma with which the second generation must contend opens the door to a set of historical tensions that comprise the social world that, at least initially, had nothing to do with their subject position. It is unsettling for the second generation to see how they are at once intimately connected the social monad of the Vietnam War and yet remote and distanced from its original shock. To live in moments when networks of social interactions come to life before your eyes poses a productive problem, a problem that, painful or not, initiates alternative questions about the role of trauma and memory on subjectivity.

In this regard, COVV interact with the social monad, not through direct memories of the experiences during the Vietnam War, but through their fathers and the Vietnam Veteran Narrative. This is a fundamental distinction from the expression of trauma for the first generation. Rather than discussing the event and experience itself, COVV focus on their fathers and the subject position of the Vietnam Veterans. As Sandy, one of my interviewees, explains, "If someone brings up the Vietnam War I immediately think of my dad." In their narratives, COVV clearly express that the Vietnam War is something that their fathers embody and carry with them. Most of my interviewees could not disentangle the event of trauma from their fathers' status as a Vietnam Veteran. COVV negotiate meanings of the event of the Vietnam War through their father and their relationship with him. This is very different from the Vietnam Veteran Narrative, which focuses on describing the original event of trauma and the break it caused in their masculine subjectivity.

An in-depth analysis of several men and women's narratives, supplemented with some of the other interviews I conducted, demonstrates how COVV articulate trauma *through* their fathers. Engaging the concepts *crisis of articulation* and *intersubjectivity*, my analysis reveals the way these men and women recognize their fathers as the embodiment of the Vietnam War. Building on Caruth's *crisis of truth* and *crisis of survival*, I demonstrate how the crisis of articulation can be utilized as a tool with which to understand the expansiveness and limitations of language. By centering their narratives on their fathers, rather than the event, these men and women develop their own stories, resituating the Vietnam War in the language of affective intersubjective relations that go beyond trauma and memory as it folds into a particular social presence. COVV's correlation of the war with their fathers uncovers a distinctive connection between the past and the present that reworks the Vietnam Veteran Narrative break between *the world* and *the Nam* in such a way that it produces questions about society's relationship to war, masculinity, and fatherhood. The crisis of articulation takes place not in the struggle to retell the original moment but in the struggle to define the meanings and effects of the war on their fathers' and their own lives. The significance of COVV's intersubjective relationship to the father cannot be overestimated. Because their process of remembering and articulating the trauma of the Vietnam War hinges on their father, COVV demonstrate the way the past becomes a shared experience.

When I asked Danny what came to mind when the topic of Vietnam was brought up, he said to me, "My father. It's a very individual thing." With few exceptions, this was the response given by my interviewees. While some of them simply stated "My father" (Mark), others started to make more complex connections between the war and their father. Regardless of the depth of their initial response, the war was never just about the event; their articulation of the trauma of the war always relied on linking the war with their father. As Tammy told me, "I think of my dad. The tragedy he's seen and the friends he's seen get killed." It is on this deeply tangled relationship between their father and the event of the Vietnam War that my interviewees build their narratives. The level of their awareness of their fathers' service, along with their formal knowledge of the war, demonstrate how they navigate the articulation of trauma through a complex weaving of personal and social knowledge. As Stan explained to me, "Just knowing what I know about my dad and, you know, his service. Just—I mean it was an unpopular war and just, you know, the way things shook out for him." He cannot disentangle the war's social memory from his memories (and awareness) of his father's struggle with the trauma of war. Greg makes similar connections, going further to include his own discomfort with the topic. "It's kinda an uncomfortable feeling. Because I was born in the '70s, it's, uhm, well, it's this thing that happened before I was born and I know my father went through this and I know it is something that tore the country apart." The interviewees are sensitive to the negative images of the war as they draw the line of connection between their fathers and the war. They are keenly aware of the pain and suffering experienced by their fathers and have a heightened awareness of the war's negative impact on the country.

Greg's response to my question draws out another important point. He makes it very clear that the war was not something that he personally experienced. Being born in the 1970s, when the war was almost at an end, he continuously doubted his understanding of the war, in part because he could never experience that moment the way his father did. *For the growing-up children of many [Vietnam] vets the war's remoteness was all but impossible to gauge because it had happened pre-you, before you had come to grasp the sheer accident of your own placement in time.* It is always a distant and ambiguous part of the past, even though he believes it deeply impacted his father and the country—and is still a part of his father's present. This was a common source of struggle. COVV are deeply aware of the presence of the war and personal struggles it caused, which does not allow them to categorize it as a distant and remote part of history. At the same time, they did not have as intimate of a relationship to that moment as their fathers did and, therefore, never feel they can fully understand the event. Stacey exemplified this as she described a time in middle school when she had to write a war journal for history class. She asked her father for help, rather than seeking out the information on her own, because she knew he had experienced the war firsthand. She remembered this incident because "my history teacher accused me of plagiarizing it. Like taking it out of a book. But then I told her that my dad helped me and she said I had to put his name on there." Knowledge of the Vietnam War always felt out of reach for Stacey precisely because she was aware that formal knowledge of the war would never enable her to understand it as intimately as her father. She does try (and want) to learn, though; the mock journal demonstrates a moment of shared knowledge between her and her father. The journal's coauthorship is a literal testament that the memories are not purely hers, nor any longer purely her father's. It also initiates us into the crisis of articulation, which many of the interviewees experience as they try to discuss their understanding of the war. In this sense, they struggle, not with articulating the Vietnam War, but with articulating its presence in their fathers. History, trauma, and subjectivity are tangled up with one another.

Anna Vidali's research on the transmission of trauma of the Greek Civil War reinforces this point. In her analysis of interviews she conducted with a woman who lived through the war and her daughter who was born after the war, Vidali found the daughter, not trusting her own knowledge and opinion of the war and politics in Greece, relies on her mother's assessments instead (1996, 38). This, I argue, has to do with the narrative transition from a focus on the traumatic event (in the narrative of the person who experienced the traumatic event firsthand) to the traumatic subject. Stacey's knowledge of the war and her attempts to articulate its trauma rely on her intersubjective relationship with her father. As she told me, "I know more about the war from [my father] than from, like, school or from any history book." She trusts her father's knowledge of war and feels it provides her with greater depth of understanding than formal knowledge because of his firsthand experiences in Vietnam. She deferred her own knowledge and opinions of the war to what she perceived as a more *realistic* account of the event.

Contrasting COVV's narratives to the layers of the Vietnam Veteran Narrative deepens our insight into the process of engaging with the social monad. Trauma moves into the next generation through a series of intersubjective shifts that depart from the original moment of trauma. Instead of reading the traumatic event, the gaze shifts to the traumatic subject. This complicates the way society relates to historical events, requiring social discourse to look at history not as a linear series of events, but as a series of dynamic interrelationships moving the event through time with varying degrees of momentum and with shifting intensities of meaning. Part of the *real problem of trauma* is transcending the crises of truth and survival, which shape traumatic narratives. The ensuing result is the crisis of articulation that the second generation experience as they attempt to transcend the gap between formal knowledge of the Vietnam War and its social maladies and their intimate awareness of the pain and suffering resulting from the firsthand experience of trauma.

Uncovering What Was Always There: Comprehending the Truth of Trauma

[The Vietnam War] wasn't something that was discussed, people didn't just sit around and share war stories—but it was always there and you knew it was there. (Montana)

What I explore in this section is how the Vietnam War was *always there* and how my interviewees *knew it*. Although my interviewees correlate the war with their father, they had a difficult time telling me how they learned that their fathers were Vietnam Veterans. In their minds, they always knew. Part of the struggle to explain how they always knew about their fathers' status as a Vietnam Veteran comes from their fathers' inability to find the truth of their traumatic experience. Therefore, uncovering how COVV learned about their father's service in Vietnam becomes part of their struggle with the crisis of articulation. These adult children start connecting the fragments of disjointed stories that they have heard over the course of their lives to develop their own stories about the Vietnam War and their fathers' experiences there. The interviewees go through a process of *piecing together* their memories of and experiences with their fathers, along with different combinations of history books, films, memoirs, print media, and other societal sources. This process also consists of their interpretations of the stories, which are tinged by their interactions with (and feelings for) their fathers. Making this process more difficult is that the stories were rarely conveyed in a clear and direct manner.

Because *people didn't just sit around and share war stories*, the interviewees struggle to explain to me how they learned that their father served in Vietnam. As Ted explains, "It was always just this thing where it was always something that was never regularly discussed and it was just something that was in a box in the basement, you know." This is part of what makes it so difficult for my interviewees to identify a clear moment when they became aware of their father's service. As Holly told me when I asked her how she learned her father was in Vietnam, "I mean, I always knew he had been in the Army; it was just one of those things. And I don't remember [...] when I put it together that it was Vietnam." It was up to her to make the connection between her father's service in the Army and his presence in the Vietnam War. Mark told me something very similar. He said, "It wasn't a 'sit down son, I have something to tell you: I was in the Vietnam War.' I don't think it was like that. And it's a rough memory. A rough memory. A learned type of thing." Outside of one exceptional case (discussed in chapter five) there is little certainty about how they found out that their fathers are Vietnam Veterans. In fact, the interview process provided a space for many of the interviewees to explore and develop their articulations of how they learned about it, piecing together the ambiguities their fathers articulated along with the social images they were well aware of. Ted did this as he tried to explain to me why his father did not like to talk about the war.

> I think that, that a lot of it was a situation where my father just kind of pushed it aside. I think a lot of guys just push it all aside. [...] It's like a part of their lives when it's over they couldn't wait for it to be over. When it was over it was done with and then it was time to move on.

Their fathers' attempts to *move on* did not keep my interviewees from being aware of the importance of the war to their fathers, nor did it keep them from providing me with numerous insights into their fathers' service. Ted, for example, knew that his father threw the uniform he was wearing into the trash when he returned home "and put on civilian clothing because he didn't want anybody to see him with a uniform." This story intimately reinforces his knowledge that the war was not well received by the American public.

Ashley brought out another aspect of why the war is such a difficult topic for her to broach to her father. She repeatedly asserted the incomplete knowledge she had of her father's experiences. She told me how she knew her father had a Purple Heart but it was not until a year ago that she learned what earned him the medal. He had been shot in the foot and she explained that her father never spoke of it and "he always wore socks," rendering his wound invisible to her. This draws out the importance of how the invisibility of the memories often makes it a difficult topic to bring up or discuss for COVV. Ashley's knowledge of the medal is not the same as understanding the circumstances for which her father earned that medal. The crisis of truth explains how difficult it is for the survivor of trauma to discuss traumatic experiences. This can be doubly difficult for the survivor when trying to find the words to explain he did and saw to his daughter (much in the way O'Brien expressed difficulty in answering his daughter's questions). Ashley's father was able to curtail discussions about the war by rendering his wound invisible to his daughter. This covering of memories of the war by Ashley's father contributes to her inability to see and better understand his experience of trauma, creating a host of ambiguities around her father's experiences in Vietnam.

This by no means renders the social monad empty and irrelevant in Ashley's and the other interviewees' lives. On the contrary, its presence is a significant aspect of their relationships with their fathers. This reinvokes Bissell's comment: "Despite its remoteness, however, the war's aftereffects were inescapably intimate. At every meal Vietnam sat down, invisibly, with our families." That remoteness and invisibility is the catalyst behind the interviewees' numerous strategies to try to understand what those effects look like and feel like, working within the crisis of articulation. Whether they seek out knowledge in other places (e.g., history books), focus on an intimate moment of connection with their fathers, or create an imagined understanding of the war, it is up to the COVV to fill in the gaps and missing pieces in order to generate their own story about the war and their fathers' experiences in it; that is, they must manage the gift of a traumatic history handed to them.

From the Crisis of Truth to the Crisis of Articulation

This silence and its ensuing ambiguity open up social discourse to the implications of the *crisis of articulation*. I turn my attention to the interviews with Samantha and Renee, two women who are sisters. Like the other interviewees, they asserted that their father did not talk about the war, or, when he did, it was usually in the form of terse and finite comments. For that reason, these two women felt they had very little to tell me about their father's war experiences. Yet, despite their belief in their lack of knowledge, each woman had important stories to tell me about her father's war experiences. Their lack of *understanding* of the trauma their father experienced effectually contributes to their assumptions about their lack of *knowledge* of his experiences.

The *crisis of articulation* reflects a gap between *knowing* and *understanding* a traumatic event. Samantha and Renee rely on the wound their father sustained to his leg in the war. For them (unlike for Ashley), his wound was something visible and tangible to them. Both women *know* their father was in the Vietnam War and they *know* about the physical injury he sustained in the war. They never feel, though, that they *understand* the impact of those experiences. Because the effects of trauma manifest belatedly, creating problems for the survivor to ever fully retrieve that moment, articulating it to others results in a host of struggles for COVV to manage. The struggle to refine their articulation of the connection between the war and their fathers produces an interesting contradiction. COVV rely on their father being a Vietnam Veteran to shape their understanding of this difficult historical moment, yet they never feel that they clearly comprehend their fathers' personal experiences in the war. It is one thing to *know* that your father is a Vietnam Veteran, it is quite another to *comprehend* the effects that has on their knowledge of the war and of their father.

The interviewees' struggle to understand their fathers' relationship to the Vietnam War is one effect of the crisis of truth that their fathers grapple with as a result of their experiences with war trauma. The truth of what happened is impossible to reach. Caruth emphasizes the temporal delay that exists between the experience of trauma and the survivor's ability to gain a definitive meaning of the event in his present life. Gaining insight into a traumatic experience, then, is as much about understanding the effects as it is about understanding the event. In a sense, it is through the effects of trauma that we (and not just the survivor) recognize the event itself. "The problem [of truth] arises not only in regard to those who listen to the traumatized, not knowing how to establish the reality of their hallucinations and dreams; it occurs rather and most disturbingly often within the very knowledge and experience of the traumatized themselves" (Caruth, 1995, 5). The survivor consciously and unconsciously works through his own understanding of what happened to him as those who listen to his struggles try to establish some sense of *reality* to what they are hearing and witnessing.

COVV provide us with a possibility of linking the gap between knowing and understanding the effects of trauma, because they no longer focus solely on the event to articulate trauma. They must rely on their father and the Vietnam Veteran to initiate their discussion of trauma. They know (have always known) that their father is a Vietnam Veteran and must navigate what that experience means to the man who is their father. As they reflect on their personal and emotional relationships with their fathers, they work to build a linkage between the past and the present. Samantha and Renee provide greater depth of understanding into both the crisis of articulation and the way memories of the war are embodied and enacted through the relationships in our present lives.

Layers and Gaps of Knowing: From the Wounded Leg to Familial Crisis

It was all just there. (Renee)

Caruth writes,

> But we can also read the address of the voice here, not as the story of the individual in relation to the events of his own past, but as the story of the way in which one's own trauma is tied up with the trauma of another, the way in which trauma may lead, therefore, to the encounter with another, through the very possibility and surprise of listening to another's wound. (1996, 8)

Both Samantha and Renee work through the crisis of articulation at the site of their father's wounded leg. His leg is the physically locatable site of trauma for both women and so they use it to begin telling me about what they know of his experiences in Vietnam. When I asked Samantha if she remembered when she first learned that her father had served in Vietnam, she said to me, "I don't remember a specific time, but my father was injured in the war. So, uhm, I knew, I knew of his situation early on because my father [pause]." Like my other interviewees, she cannot pinpoint the exact time and way she learned that her father is a Vietnam Veteran. She makes the link between the war and her father as she explains the way she must have found out he was a Vietnam Veteran: through his wounded leg.

Samantha hesitated, though, as she tried to connect the knowledge of her father's physical war wounds to a definitive understanding of what her father experienced in the war. She went on to say, "So, I know the story...like the story of how he got into Vietnam and everything but..." She trailed off and then added, "And I know most—I think he was one of the few survivors of his platoon." She fumbled as she tried to make the connection between her knowledge and understanding of the trauma she feels her father experienced in Vietnam. The story of their father's wounded leg, and what it can tell us about the trauma he experienced in Vietnam, eventually breaks down. The story of the wounded leg cannot provide for Samantha a sense of what it must have been like for her father to lose his platoon and a part of himself in the jungles of Vietnam. The story of the wounded leg enables Samantha to tell me how stoic and strong-willed her father was as he found the internal and external strength to walk again, but the complexities of the psychic trauma are not so easily correlated to the physical trauma sustained to his leg.

The crisis of truth surrounding her father's war experiences affects Samantha's ability to talk about and understand its impact on her father. As Caruth comments, "For the survivor of trauma, then, the truth of the event may reside not in its brutal facts, but also in the way that their occurrence defies simple comprehension" (1995, 153). The gap between knowing and understanding the truth of the event is essential to the struggle within the crisis of articulation. Her assertion that she does not know very much about her father's experiences, then, is the result of the gaps of understanding between the injured leg and the psychic and emotional injuries he suffered in Vietnam. It is here that we see the crisis of articulation taking place in her narrative.

Repeatedly, both women insist that they do not know much about their father's war experiences and that their father never tells them very much about his service. Yet, each of them has extensive knowledge of the *brutal facts* surrounding their father's service. Samantha explained all about her father's entry into the Marines, as well as the events that led to his injury and his stay in a Veterans Affairs (VA) hospital. Both women knew a landmine went off as their father and his platoon were hiking in the jungle, nearly causing him to lose his leg. Samantha and Renee also knew that their father spent months in a VA hospital in traction, surprising his doctors by walking when they believed he never would. But the brutal facts surrounding their father's wounded leg never seem to explicate enough. The crisis of articulation provides a unique space to delve into the limitations of our knowledge and the language we use to describe past events. It provokes questions about what it means to know in a factual sense and what it means to understand in an experiential and a visceral sense. As my interviews with these women unfolded, I could hear them struggling in this space, each in her own way, building a narrative around that gap through their own experiences and relationships.

The women try to better articulate their understanding of the trauma their father went through by telling me about a traumatic event the whole family experienced. Through this story, Samantha and Renee begin to find words for their understanding of the emotional pain their father experienced in Vietnam. They begin to advance the stammered connections they made between their father's wounded leg and the psychic trauma he experienced. We see how, to bring back Felman's notion of the gift, *the real problem of trauma [is] that of the second generation.* Their father's own uncertainty about the truth of the event affects their own narratives. These women (and all my interviewees) have to work through layers of disjointed stories surrounding their father's service, as well as their own stories and experiences, to make sense of the event of the Vietnam War. In this gap, they begin to recognize that there is a breakdown of articulation, and within those ruptures they are compelled to question their uncertainties and frustrations within the context of their own narratives.

The fragmentation of remembrance, the *gift* as Felman describes it, that is given to them comes in the form of their father's reactions to the death of their sister at a young age (their sister died at age 7; Samantha and Renee were 15 and 12, respectively, at the time of this incident). This fragment provides each woman with a space to address a particularly painful moment in her own life, as she finds a way of speaking within the ruptures of her understanding of her father's war experiences. In their individual interviews with me, both responded to my question about whether or not they witnessed their father having a flashback by drawing on their sister's death. This moment resonated for both of them as a time when their father's war experiences had returned, ultimately contributing to their father's difficult grieving process for his daughter. When I asked Renee if she ever witnessed her father having a flashback, she said to me, "I would say, that when my little sister died, [my father] went through a very strange series of emotions and I think that there were probably a lot of flashbacks in there." She goes on to tell me,

> I cannot say that for certain, but he was in such a, uhm, he was in such a state at that point that it was really frightening. I mean, my father had always been this very strong Marine, you know. I had never seen this side of him that could not function.

Up until that time, his war experiences held a more distant and ambiguous position in their family life, a position that was more of a curiosity than anything else. Therefore, witnessing her father's breakdown after knowing the strength it took for him to heal from his injuries in the war was significant for Renee. She identified herself as "daddy's little girl," "the apple of his eye," when she was a girl. She saw him as a hero who went to war and would sacrifice anything for his family. She remembers a very strong emotional bond between them from a very young age, which lasted through high school. So, when he *could not function* after the death of her sister, Renee was scared and uncertain about what was really going on with her father. Yet that uncertainty gives her an entry into thinking through the traumatic effects of her father's war experiences. It also provides a space for her to talk about a difficult time in her own life. She recounts for me a rather disquieting scene of her father trying to resuscitate her sister. The depth to which this moment affected Renee is never directly discussed with me, but her confusion about her father is deeply tangled in her own attempt to understand what she saw the morning her sister died. She explains to me,

> And the day that my sister died, uhm. [My dad] found her and I went down the hall, my mom was screaming and he was lying above her and turned to look at me and he had you know. [pause] Her lungs had filled with fluid, so there was blood coming out of her mouth and he turned and had a little, like, dribble of blood there and he just looked back and he was breathing into her. He was trying to give her mouth-to-mouth and there was just this kind of funny stopper sound, like there was a stopper there blocking the breath.

Her reflections describe a disturbing image she witnessed as a young girl. The colors and sounds of the memory are most vivid as she tries to explain to me what had happened. Renee tells me this story as a way to find the words to articulate what she understands of her father's war experiences. Her own painful past is deeply interwoven with her father's traumas. She then went on to describe the struggles her father went through as a result of the loss of her sister.

> He never got out of his flannels. He had a flannel bathrobe and flannel pants—for about a year. Never even did anything...He was just foggy. So, I'm sure that at some point in that period, there was a lot of *review of loss*. And a lot of review to have him be the one to find her and to go through that. And to be, you know, 'cause he—obviously—I'm, like, sure a lot of the guys, you know,

had to see that and they saw a lot of stuff over there [in Vietnam] that they didn't want to see and a lot of friends go. And I think it just, like, *it was just all there*, so I would say that was definitely a huge part. *But besides that I can't really say.* (my emphasis)

It Was Just All There

The reexperiencing of trauma is not isolated to its own space and time. It intermingles with a complex of events of everyday life. Speaking of this loss in the context of her father's experiences allows Renee to reflect on a difficult moment in her own life. Here we hear the voice, *not as the story of the individual in relation to the events of his own past, but as the story of the way in which one's own trauma is tied up with the trauma of another.* Renee identifies her father's struggle with the loss of her sister as part of a way of coping with the numerous other losses he incurred in his life. In this narrative, she fumbles for a way of speaking about the death her father had to see in Vietnam. Recognizing her father's war trauma through her sister's death, she begins to piece together the fragments of memory that help her gain insight into the profound emotional pain her father has/had to contend with.

Reflecting on watching her father deal with the death of her sister, it becomes clear to Renee that his grief during that time reflected the profound wound that penetrated into those layers of trauma that haunt his present experiences—and her own. "History, like trauma, is never simply one's own,...history is precisely the way we are implicated in each other's traumas" (Caruth, 1996, 24). Renee tells me about the trauma she witnessed, as she finds words to bridge the gap between her father's physical and emotional injuries. His history is inextricably a part of her history. Yet, she is hesitant to make a direct link. *But besides that I can't really say. Besides* recognizing the pain of her father's war experiences during the time of her sister's death, she cannot tell me very much about her father's experience with trauma and flashbacks. Yet *it is all there* in complex layers. The gaps left in the story of her father's wounded leg are punctuated by this story of familial loss. What I mean by this is that it at once illuminates and addresses the breach between knowing and understanding a traumatic event. There is not a sense of resolution for Renee, but it sheds light on the emotional complexity of trauma, making her sensitive to what her father went through. While Renee believed I was looking for stories that explained the factual experiences of her father, in this story she tells me, it became clear to both of us that the story of her father's trauma could not be told without her telling me her stories and experiences. The ghosts of the Vietnam War haunt Renee's memories of the loss of her sister. The embodiment of the war in her father means that his story is not a static and an isolated expression of trauma. The original *event* of trauma may be the story that he tells, but the *effects* and the trauma of war (and his way of articulating it) become part of Renee and her family's narratives. She remembers the image of her father trying to resuscitate her sister as well as him wearing his flannels for a year; and those memories overlap with her father's own traumatic past.

Renee makes the connection between her father's reactions to her sister's death and the trauma of his war experiences in her description of an intimate exchange between her and her father on the evening of her sister's death. This moment conveys the powerful emotional link between father and daughter. She said to me, "Later that day he came into my room when I was lying in my bed and held me and he was just mumbling and, you know, and talking and saying really strange things." When I asked Renee if she remembered what her father had mumbled to her when he was holding her, she explained to me the very confused state her father was in, while simultaneously tying together the layers of loss. She replied:

> He was, he was. You know, he was kinda talkin' to his dad; he was kinda talkin' to [my little sister]; he was, you know, "Why? I've seen so much, why would you do this to us?" You know? And I look back on it and I think, he's a pretty strong guy to have been able to pull himself out. You know, on his own at the age of 15 and been through deaths right in a row there and then going to Vietnam. And witnessing all the death in everything there and then coming home and then, you know, when you finally get on your feet and you have life in this family—to be hit again and still be able to come out of it.

The past takes on an insistent presence in Renee's awareness. Her articulation takes place as a simultaneous telling of her own experiences at the intersection of their shared grief. Her story of their interaction carries a profound emotional intensity, as well as an insight into her father's suffering. The link between the emotional bond Renee had/has with her father and him coming to her in a moment of personal pain cannot be overemphasized. The father-child relationship has much to tell us about trauma through its effects, demonstrating the intersubjective nature of our processes of remembering. Her father as a Vietnam

Veteran and traumatic subject is what drives her understanding of the event of trauma (the Vietnam War). It is not a reenactment of the past that Renee witnesses; it is a recognition of the presence of the traumatic event(s) in their lives; it is *a review of loss*, as she so succinctly comments.

For the person who experiences trauma firsthand, there is no return to that initial moment of trauma; new experiences continually enter into our lives, mediating our interpretations of the past. The temporal delay between the event and its coming to the surface is striated with the events of the present and the relationships bound in that present. The Vietnam War is not simply an event that lay in history books. For Renee, Samantha, and my other interviewees, it is a significant moment for their fathers, producing an ethereal existence in their lives. They know it is part of their father, yet they are unsure what it really has to do with them. Not until I can delve deeper into the personal nuances of their relationships with their fathers do I (and the person I am interviewing) start to develop a means of articulating the war's presence. Even in those moments, we see the ambiguity that is woven into the emotional and experiential dynamics of the present.

Through my interview with Renee, we both learn that this is a pivotal experience in her life, both because of its traumatic impact on her and her family and because it helps her develop a more complex understanding of her father. The story of his lapse during the time of his daughter's death complicates and strengthens the imagery of her father as the strong Marine, which both women steadfastly adhere to throughout our interview. The traumatic subject interjects itself into her imagery of her descriptions of her father, ultimately complicating her view of him. Near the end of our interview, Renee provided an insightful description of the traumatic aspects of her father's subjectivity. When I asked her to give me several words to describe her father, one of them was "multifaceted." She goes on to explain what she means be this. "He appears to be a very strong, stalwart, you know, determined, set-in-his-way person. And yet if you turn him just a little bit, I think there's definitely this sense of sadness and [pause] wondering and questioning. It's all underneath, so I think sometimes he appears what he's not really. It's like it's a—it's a façade."

The façade initiates questions regarding the way people navigate societal expectations and images with the complexities of lived experience. The hero and stoic Marine have other sides to consider that do not fit easily into our societal understandings of the Vietnam soldier and Vietnam Veteran. It is not easy to draw together a soldier's strength and heroism with the pain and darkness that such service carries. This is a point emphasized by Gail Hosking Gilberg in her memoirs of her life with her father, a career Army man, who died during his service in Vietnam. Here we see how Renee struggles with the meaning of masculine subjectivity and the break the trauma of the Vietnam War produced in men such as her father. After his death, Hosking Gilberg's father was awarded the Congressional Medal of Honor. For Hosking Gilberg, this medal is a painful memory of her father; it symbolizes the costs of war that she feels she is still paying. For years, Hosking Gilberg could not integrate the medal into her memories of her father. "[T]o discuss the medal was to discuss blood—that real blood that comes with any medal, no matter what war, in what time, in what country. It was to remember why [my father] was awarded the medal..." (1997, 191). Remembering her father, and who he was as a soldier, is to provide an image of the men who fought in Vietnam that neither fits within the idyllic images of warrior or father. Hosking Gilberg could not maintain a view of her father that was purely good, or purely bad. As with many of my interviewees, she is trying to find a place in which to speak of her father as a good father and man in light of what the combat experience and trauma may have done to him. My interviewees often do this by relying on societal images seen in films, books, and television. This is something that is quite salient in Samantha's discussion of her father.

Complicated Images, or Seeing the Crazy

Samantha (like Renee) tries to link her knowledge of her father's service with an understanding of its traumatic effects through the moment of her sister's death. It is her closest approximation of witnessing her father having a flashback.

> I think that was directly related to Vietnam. Because, uh, he had seen a lot of people die around him in Vietnam. And, but to then see it, you know, his own child die and to think about all that. [pause] I've never seen him have a flashback. No. That's not to say he hasn't had them.

Again, her ability to connect the death of her sister with the death he witnessed in Vietnam is shaky and uncertain; yet they clearly are connected in her mind. She recognizes the time of her father's grieving of his daughter as something that incorporated his losses in war. Renee and Samantha each have their own way of expressing that time but they are no less aware of the way layers of trauma permeate their father's (and their own) life. There is a tangled series of events that cannot be separated: their father's early losses, his Vietnam experience and now the loss of his daughter.

In Samantha's story of that time, she expands on the impact that these traumatic moments had on her father *and* herself. I quote her at length, because the way she connects the war with the loss of her sister and her own feelings is quite complex.

> I mean. He said. [pause] I walked into her room once; he wouldn't leave her room for weeks at a time. And, uhm, he stopped shaving. He. [pause] My mom could barely get him to bathe. He would just sleep on her bed. We barely. [pause] And I went in one time to talk to him and he said to me he saw, in me, himself. He said when he was 15—this is a horrible thing to say to a child—he said when he was 15 that's when his hell on earth started. You know, that's when his father died. When, uhm, he died they were scuba diving. So he was there. He witnessed it. And, uh, he said that he thought. [pause] He saw so much of himself in me and he felt like I would be living his life and he then told me—I said something about she's in heaven or something—and he said, well she's gotta be better off than here because. [pause] He said because, uhm, we are living in hell. This is hell on earth. What kind of world would have war and have people dying around you—have people struggling and suffering just to make ends meet? And what kind of world do we live in? He said this is hell. So anything has to be better than this.[...] I remember thinking, you know; I remember just being a mess after he told me that. I thought oh my god, you know my dad's really screwed up. For him to say that to me.

Samantha, like her sister, has a conversation with her father that provides her with a very particular understanding between her father's experiences in Vietnam and the loss of her sister. In part, the distinctions between their conversations with their father reflect the differences between the personality and ages of the two women. Samantha is a very straightforward and confident woman; Renee is a far more intuitive and receptive woman. Both women are very articulate and observant, but their receptions of their father's experiences at this time drastically differ. Renee's memories revolve around the more sensitive unspoken bond she had with her father. Samantha's memories are marked by her father's explicit fears and uncertainties about the world he and his daughters live in. Samantha told me about the heated arguments she would have with her father when she was growing up. She identified herself as a very similar person to her father—strong-willed, stubborn, driven. She integrates her descriptions of her father's comments and concern for her into her own self-identification. His comments filtered into her own grieving process and made them all the more salient in her memory, which, by her own admission, deeply impacted her outlook on the world and her father.

At the same time, it informed her awareness of some of what her father may have experienced in Vietnam. As she comments,

> The way he dealt with [my sister's death], I think brought a lot back for him, because he hadn't.... He had things pretty good since he got out of traction. He met my mother; they got married. He got a college degree. Got a good job. And all of a sudden—[pause] he thought. I think he started to think that he was invincible or something. And he had sort of seen the worst and then passed it. Because what could be worse than war? But then your child dies in her bed and doesn't wake in the next morning [...]. That was—that was at a time I really saw a different side of my father. And I saw the, *the crazy*, you know? (my emphasis)

Here, the crisis of articulation generates incomplete understandings of the original experience of trauma. At the same time, it is clear that Samantha is navigating within the social monad of the Vietnam War. She uses the expression *the crazy* to describe the vulnerable and affected state of her father after her sister's death. Her use of this word, though, is a reference to an earlier part of our interview when she was discussing the negative societal images of Vietnam Veterans. Samantha feels that her father was facing the numerous losses of his past during his grieving of her youngest sister. It was not just a review of loss; it was forcing him to confront the parts of his past that she did not feel he had faced. She identifies this moment as a time when he could no longer forget that past, forcing everything to penetrate to the forefront of his mind. At the same time, it drew out an aspect of her father that she had not really seen before. Like Renee, Samantha was faced with seeing her father in a very vulnerable state, where he could no longer function. Samantha identifies this as *the crazy*, but this expression means much more to Samantha than the narrow content implies.

At the beginning of our interview, I asked Samantha to tell me what first came to her mind when the topic of Vietnam was brought up. She immediately said the film, *Born on the Fourth of July*. But it was not just the content of the film that was important; it was the memory of her father making her and her family see the film together, along with his subsequent response to the film, that stuck in her mind. She told me,

> We all went to the theater to see [*Born on the Fourth of July*]. My father thought it would be good for us to go see it. And he hated it. He was furious afterward. He thought it made all Vietnam Veterans look like total, you know, [in a whispered tone] fuckups. He was—he was upset. He thought it made them all look like they had problems.

She continued to talk about this experience, taking it into a larger discussion about her understanding of the way Vietnam Veterans have been represented in the media.

> And, and, you know what? I think that the ones that don't seem like they have problems are just sort of uhm—just made the best of a bad situation. In some ways just sort of buried everything or swept it under the carpet and just don't think about it. Don't talk about it—as in my father's case—and then think everything's okay, you know? I guess, the other thing that I would think about is, when I think about Vietnam, I think about a lot of sad veterans.[...] Not sad, emotional sad, but sad circumstances. And I do think maybe part of that is a reflection of the movie or what the media has done to the Vietnam Veterans since they finally acknowledged them. Once they were acknowledged, they were acknowledged as people who were kinda screwed up.

We went on to talk about media images of the Vietnam Veteran as crazy and screwedup and the problems her father had with those images. Yet, when she needed a word to describe her father's emotional breakdown after the death of her sister, she relies on that very imagery to try to capture the vulnerable side of her father that she saw. She has no other way of articulating the traumatic expressions her father displays than by connecting them to the societal images with which she is familiar. The pain of her father's suffering is connected to the crazy images of the Vietnam Veteran. *The crazy*, then, should not be read as a derogatory comment about Vietnam Veterans and her father. Instead, it is a term she uses to speak within the crisis of articulation. It is a means for her to express the emotional impact of the war on her father and other soldiers—an emotional impact much of the cultural imaginary has trouble articulating to the American public other than through *the crazy*. Yet, we begin to see how it is an incomplete and easily misunderstood description. Language not so much fails here as it expresses the contradictions at work in the struggle to reconcile the gap between knowing the facts of war trauma and comprehending their latent manifestations on individual and social life. Samantha's father's behaviors during the time her little sister died demonstrate to her that her father does struggle with the past of the Vietnam War. But she is uncertain how that fits into her own ideas and the expectations she has for her father.

To some degree, *the crazy* represents survivors' struggles with war trauma. Yet, her father's inability to function, which she witnessed as he grieved for his daughter, left her without a way to articulate how this strong and determined man could be affected and vulnerable. This reflects the gap between knowing that there is a significant amount of pain and suffering as a result of a traumatic experience and witnessing its effects. This leads to a host of dilemmas that cannot necessarily be resolved. Samantha illuminates the gap, which places her within the crisis of articulation. She sheds light on a common struggle for the interviewees. Many were concerned about saying anything too negative about their fathers out of fear that it would taint the image I (and others) had of him. Ultimately, they did not want the struggles their fathers have with the trauma of war to overshadow the men, who are their fathers. This concern underscores the problem of trauma for the next generation. They have to navigate between social history and personal history in order to tell the story of their lives with their fathers that does not deny his war experiences, yet does not allow it wholly to determine who their fathers are as men. Samantha goes back and forth between holding up her father as a symbol of strength and moments of frustration, when that image cannot hold as he falls into what she perceives as negative images of the Vietnam Veteran. These are tensions surrounding the process of establishing the connection between their fathers with phallic masculinity (which I discuss in chapter five).

Negotiating the Interstice between Knowing and Comprehending

The gap between knowing and comprehending trauma makes the articulation of trauma full of irresolution. Part of the crisis of articulation and the struggle to bridge this gap resides in the difficulty that my interviewees have in connecting their father with his war experiences and status of soldier and Vietnam Veteran. My interviewees rely on their relationships with their fathers to develop their understanding but it continually leaves them wanting more. Samantha's peek into her father's painful experiences, struggling to make a connection between the man she knows—the stoic father and Marine—and the man she saw profoundly affected by the war, left her with more questions and hesitation than answers. It is easier to think of the men who are their fathers and the men who were soldiers as two different men because it is seemingly impossible to integrate the broken, affected, and traumatized man into the strong invulnerable father. It is the gray area between the Vietnam Veteran and the father that is difficult to navigate, making the connection between their father and phallic masculinity vulnerable to dislocation.

My interviewees may rely on things such as medals, wounds, and photographs to generate their story and understanding of the trauma of war but their tangibility belies the deeper realities of the lives and memories within those objects. Hosking Gilberg explores this gap in her book about her father, which she centers around the photograph books he made over the course of his life as a soldier *and* father. The process of looking through *his* photographs and telling *her* stories (trying to make connections between the man she knew as her father and the man who fought in Vietnam) answers some of her questions but provokes many new ones. She writes,

> Many in this country, peers and soldiers included, [...] believed that the strong were absolutely strong and the weak absolutely weak. What was and remains is the gray area in between—the most difficult to look at. Just as with my father's photograph collection, no part can stand for the whole, no whole can stand for its parts. (Gilberg, 1997, 10–1)

She recognizes the difficulty she and the country have with looking at the complexities of *the gray area in between*. Coming to terms with the ambiguities that lived experiences produce disrupts the tidy black and white categorizations, which shape the order and meaning of the social world, particularly around masculine subjectivity. But she also sees the value of recognizing how the whole is a complex reality that can never be *wholly* understood. This is reminiscent of Renee's description of her father. The gray area where her father's identity as a father and soldier intersect and where his strengths and weaknesses overlap is difficult to look at; yet, this is where Renee finds strength in her father. The event and experience of the trauma of the Vietnam War, which produced a break in masculine subjectivity, is a provocative site in which we can see how the social subject never fully captures the complexity of an individual's lived experiences. In fact, it can limit and pose problems for individuals who may not be able to fit into the prescriptions of the gendered expectations at work in society. To try to define their fathers in the context of his presence as a father in COVV's lives never captures the full scope of their fathers' lives. It is as limiting as isolating the Vietnam Veteran from any other part of his life experiences. He is not one or the other. The problem of the second generation of trauma is about bearing witness to how that moment generates fissures in our understanding of the social world. To speak of the man they know is nearly impossible in light of the limited social references to the Vietnam Veteran as an integral and productive member of society. Some of my interviewees, like Hosking Gilberg, are compelled to understand the ways these parts of their father connect and inform one another. But it never provides definitive answers.

The nuances that emerge out of the crisis of articulation make it difficult to find the words to explain the gray areas within which some of my interviewees recognize their fathers. Samantha navigates the line between her father's stoicism and strength *and* his vulnerability and weakness by using the term "the crazy." This word opens the door to a deeper understanding of her father *and* the Vietnam Veteran, even as it seems to rely on black-and-white language that isolates and reifies the Vietnam Veteran as someone wholly separate from their familial ties. She explained to me how seeing the film *Born on the Fourth of July* with her family provided her with the opportunity to gain more insight into her father's war experiences and how they affected him. Samantha told me that she did not understand what the soldiers had to deal with upon their return from Vietnam. "I hate to say it [...]. I didn't realize that when these guys came back from the war they were treated so poorly. And that they didn't receive a hero's welcome." She uses the film to inform her knowledge of the war, inquiring about the accuracy of those images from her father. She even asked her father if his experiences in the VA hospital were like those of the men portrayed in the film. She explained to me,

> After seeing the movie *Born on the Fourth of July*, I asked him questions. Like [were] there rats crawling on these guys, and he said, 'Yeah. That's what happened [Samantha]. [...] It was horrible conditions. I mean I remember him telling me about it and after

that fact I don't remember him mentioning it since. But he had bedsores—unbelievable—because they just weren't getting the attention and medical care they deserved.

In this sense, she starts engaging in a deeper understanding of the struggle her father went through after his return home from Vietnam.

Images in the film reflect the sadness she saw in that moment of her father's grief over his daughter. Nevertheless *the crazy* is a contentious term with many negative connotations. Although Samantha does not want to insult or deny the struggles her father and other Vietnam Veterans face, she cannot provide an alternative word to describe what she saw in his struggles. She identifies her father as strong and passionate but it bothers her that he tries to push away the more difficult aspects of his past. At the same time, when she did catch a glimpse of her father expressing his emotional pain, he did it in a way that scared her, making her uncomfortable and confused, because she did not know what to do with it.

Recognizing the gray area that defines the complications of lived experiences can be fruitful in engaging with the effects of trauma and gaining comprehension of the experience of trauma, but it can be overwhelming and scary to see different parts of their fathers emerging from those insights. As my interviewees move between their father and his war experiences, they develop a greater desire to make coherent connections between the war and his present life, a frustrating task. At the same time, they try to narratively construct an understanding of their fathers that enables them to mend the breaks in masculine subjectivity that are part of the imagery of the Vietnam Veteran.

Active Social Subjects: Moving Beyond Survival

COVV engage with the social monad of the Vietnam War in such a way that these subjects exchange and transform meanings within the social monad. This is not done in a way that generates a unified meaning of the social monad. Rather, it radically shifts the subject's relationship to history, disrupting the possibility of a singular narrative. COVV are not passively subjected to the social monad of the Vietnam War so much as it is subjected to them. What a way to conceptualize this process! The social monad—a traumatic event—is the problem of the second generation. It is a problem, because it is the work of COVV to shape other meanings within the social monad. They are not tragically fated to live out the trauma again in an eternal repetition. This is not what it means to be of the second generation. COVV's work is not simply a process of rewriting history, although revisions could result from the work of articulating a different relationship to the Vietnam War. Throughout, the men and women I interviewed demonstrated an active relationship to the social monad of the Vietnam War. Whether it was actively forgetting aspects of the Vietnam War or actively invoking it into their narratives, the gift of history is not simply passed on but becomes infused into their personal narratives and experiences with their father.

From Crisis of Survival to Crisis of Articulation

The interviewees not only work to bridge the gap between knowing and understanding trauma, they also must develop a way of making sense of the trauma that Vietnam Veterans experience within the context of their present lives as fathers. The way that a person survives trauma has a variety of implications on how other people make sense of the person and the traumatic event. The crisis of survival grounds the traumatic event within the individuals who experience it. As the survivor passes out of the moment of trauma, his struggle with the crisis of survival shapes the way trauma moves from one generation to the next: it becomes part of the way COVV know their fathers. How a person survives, the way he lives life and comes to terms with the past, profoundly affects (and is affected by) his relationships with others and the social world. In particular, the ways my interviewees' spoke about their fathers and the war depended on how successful they felt their father was/is at rebuilding his social position. It is his survival from the trauma of war and his ability to take on the role of the father and engage with the dominant fiction that marked their discussions. The crisis of survival denotes the intersection between the memories of the traumatic event and the survivor's present-day life experiences. The struggle to integrate the pain of the past within the context of the present helps us understand what Caruth means when she calls trauma not only a "repeated suffering" but "a continual leaving of the site" (Caruth, 1995, 10). Surviving trauma means that the event/experience will always be a part of the survivor's present life, affecting who he is as a father.

Interrogating historical trauma as a social monad widens the focus. The traumatic event is not the only focal point; the subject of trauma— the survivor—takes on a significant role in understanding the terrain of historical trauma. In the shift to the second generation, the narrative does not develop around how the combat experience and the Vietnam War broke down the survivor's belief in the dominant fiction; it develops around the desire for COVV to align the survivor—their father—with phallic masculine subjectivity and establish belief in the dominant fiction. The crisis of survival that their fathers experience shapes the way my interviewees see their fathers, not only as a father but as a man and a Vietnam Veteran. Ultimately, it affects my interviewees' descriptions of their fathers as masculine subjects. Working within the perimeters of the social monad's carapace, COVV utilize preexisting social discourses governing the social monad. Yet, they generate a new discursive layer through their active presence. Remember, they are happening to the social monad. They are enlivening it through engagement with these preexisting discourses. But silence and affective intersubjective relationships shape their responses and reactions to those social discourses. COVV's presence strengthens the social monad even as they search for a way to articulate themselves out of its dynamic social interactions.

Because of the negative portrayals of the Vietnam Veteran and the Vietnam War in American society (through media and education), discussing their fathers in the context of masculine subjectivity is not an easy task. As such, the relationship that COVV have with their fathers intersects with the social history and the social memory of the traumatic event, creating obstacles for my interviewees as they shape their narratives. This harkens back to Greg's expression of a feeling of *awkward anxiety* as he negotiated the space between his understanding of the man who is his father and the man who served in Vietnam. These men and women work through issues of trauma and masculine subjectivity through two routes. Some see their fathers and his service in black and white, drawing a nearly impenetrable line between *the Nam*—the world of Vietnam and combat—and *the world*—their present with their family life and father. Others cannot make such clear lines of distinction and see these two worlds seeping into each, developing meanings of their fathers and relationships in the murky gray spaces where *the world* and *the Nam* are intimately interconnected. Here, right and wrong and good and bad are not static or mutually exclusive realms. In the following sections, I explore how these two narrative structures take shape in two of my interviewees' discussions of their fathers: Mark and Montana.

In particular, both Mark and Montana must navigate between the ideals and expectations they hold about fatherhood and the images of the Vietnam Veteran (both societal and personal). Although they articulate this process through different routes, their discussions of the subject of trauma and the hero rely on their ability to reconnect their father with phallic masculinity, even if the connection is contradictory or incomplete. While the survivor works to script himself back into the story of the dominant fiction by finding social legitimacy in his service, COVV do this by concentrating on the story of the survivor's success as a father. Ironically, the association of the Vietnam War with their fathers provides them with a means to do that. While Mark utilizes his father's service in Vietnam to fortify his father's strength and dedication to his family, Montana utilizes her father's service to explain and justify why he was not a strong ideal father figure. My interviewees' navigation of their father in this manner alerts us to ways that the Vietnam War continues to be a space where the tensions in masculine subjectivity are disputed. In this sense, COVV return to the break in masculine subjectivity that is such a central part of the Vietnam Veteran Narrative as they look at the connections between their fathers and his service in Vietnam. COVV have a different point of focus from their fathers as they work through the traumatic break that took place during the Vietnam War.

Active Forgetting: Seeing in Black and White

Mark's respect and admiration for his father shapes the way he navigates the relationship between his father and the Vietnam War. As he told me, "My father is very strong, strong-willed—he's a strong man. Stubborn. I, I betcha indirectly that having the Vietnam experience helped him become a person who sees above and beyond the material things in life, which he passed on to me." Over the course of the interview, it became clear that he held an idyllic image of the Vietnam War within his father and relied on this image to support his contention that his father was/is a strong father figure and role model. He did this by maintaining a clear line between the world of combat that his father experienced in Vietnam (*the Nam*) and the world of his family (*the world*). Mark resists integrating specificities of his father's service that could potentially taint the image of his father and so makes the conscious decision to *not* seek out information on the particularities of his father's experiences. He consciously refuses aspects of the discourses going on within the social monad. By doing this, he demonstrates how some of the interviewees see their father's survival from trauma in black and white, fortifying the view that *the strong are absolutely strong and the weak absolutely weak* in order to keep the images of their father contained to a manageable present. Although the interviewees with this narrative focus constitute a minority in my sample—and their views are not as uncomplicated as they would like them to be—they demonstrate how the second generation of trauma still rely on idyllic images of heroism and masculine subjectivity even if their fathers experienced a break with those ideals and values. The dominant fiction of America is still a story deeply ingrained in the lives of all my interviewees but they manage its presence differently. This set of interviewees ground how COVV look to the dominant fiction for social meaning in their individual narratives.

Mark's narrative exemplifies a structure that relies on the containment of the Father as the symbol of sacrifice and masculine virtue, which is why I initiate my discussion with him here (I discuss this set of interviewees in more depth in chapter five). Such interviewees focus on drawing their fathers out of the traumatic abyss and back into the paternal imago (to use Silverman's language). The Vietnam War becomes a sign of nobility and virtue rather than a symbol of failure. In a sense, these interviewees try to formulate an official rescripting of the Vietnam Veteran by upholding their fathers as exemplars of (traditional) masculine virtue.

Mark described his father's service in a way that reinforced the strength of his belief in his father's moral values and willingness to sacrifice for his family and country. He made this link by asserting that his father's appreciation for life and family came from his experiences in Vietnam:

> You're in a foxhole and you may not come home. And you got people in the states who know that you may not go home. It gives you a different perspective on life, I think. [...] Life is important. Waking up every morning is important. And it instills in you more than just the monetary world.

Calling his father a "true American," Mark looks up to his father, admiring him for his service and sacrifice. Because it is vital for Mark to connect his father with idyllic images of the Father, he concentrates on the heroic images of the warrior, resisting the presence of any negative connotations the Vietnam Veteran may hold. This enables him to bridge the gap between his father and the Vietnam War in a way that resists the historical precedence of the war being a difficult social memory.

It also enables him to connect his father with phallic identification, reinforcing his belief in the dominant fiction of America.

As he does this, he actively resists his knowledge of the Vietnam Veteran's precarious social position. He repeatedly told me that he does not like having discussions with his father about his service for fear that it might incite too emotional a response, revealing a vulnerable side to his father that does not fit into the image he has projected on to him. He explained to me that he sees his "father in a certain light" and has no desire to know what his father did in Vietnam. Although he values his father's emotionally demonstrative personality, he shies away from expressions that convey any sign of powerlessness. He did not want to ask his father any questions about the war out of fear of provoking a reaction he could not handle. "I wouldn't even ask questions. I didn't wanna—I didn't want to bring up something that maybe wasn't there. I didn't want to be the person who brings a situation out that dad had to remember." Whatever *might* be beneath the surface of his father's life with his family was not something Mark was capable of integrating into his image of his father. These fears are partially the result of him witnessing his father have "a negative reaction to watching fireworks" when Mark was a boy. He noticed his father jumping every time the fireworks exploded, so he asked his mother why he acted so strange. She explained that it was because of the Vietnam War. "And from that point forward, I never really wanted to really ask questions to my father about the war. I let him volunteer the information." The anxiety he holds toward seeing his father struggle with difficult emotions causes tensions in Mark's narrative about the war's presence in his father. He explained that his father frequently watched war films, often crying while viewing them. This led Mark to conclude: "I always associated his crying with Vietnam." He further elaborated on his fears of seeing the emotional vulnerability of the war provoked by saying, "Yeah, it's a selfish thing, it's like I don't want to deal with [my father crying], I can't deal with this. Never tried to probe and figure out what's wrong. I just kinda stepped away, you know. I never wanted to get involved." He did not want to "figure out what's wrong" because he sensed it would affect the view he had of his father and he could not handle the irresolution between the darker side of combat and the idyllic images he holds of service and sacrifice.

But Mark goes beyond not bringing up the topic of Vietnam to his father; he actively avoids it. He made this clear in his refusal to watch *When We Were Soldiers* with him. His father came to visit Mark and brought the film, hoping to watch it with his son. Mark refused to watch it, though, telling me,

I don't really want to watch it. And the reason I don't—I've never seen *Platoon*. I've never seen—I don't watch any Vietnam War movies, because I'm afraid. I see my father in a certain light and, like, I hear the things that soldiers do and [pause] smoke pot through their guns or whatever. If he did, that's fine. I don't want to know about it. So I'm afraid if I watch these movies not only will it show me what he, he went through from a combat standpoint, but then I don't want to know about the other stuff. For some reason I just don't.

Although it is *fine* if his father did engage in what he viewed as negative behaviors in Vietnam, Mark did not want to know about it. To know would threaten Mark's ability to see his father *in a certain light*. From his comments, he is actively foreclosing (i.e., forgetting) the connection between particular discourses surrounding the Vietnam Veteran and his father. It is not that Mark is naïve or ignorant of those discourses. In actuality, he has a heightened awareness of those images that might threaten his images of his father. It is significant that even though he claims to have never watched *Platoon*, he is fully aware of a scene within the film that he considers unflattering and troubling. This action resembles some of Nietzsche's notions of *active forgetting* (1997). To actively forget something one must first be aware of its presence. In the case of a social monad like the Vietnam War that has dense social discourses moving through it, it draws out interesting questions about what it means to actively forget something that has a strong social presence. So strong in fact that one does not actually have to watch a film or read particular books to be cognizant of the myriad discourses and images—negative or positive.

Mark's coherency and ability to connect his father to phallic masculinity—and I would venture to add himself—hinges less on forgetting than on managing the variety of discourses within the social monad. He does this in a way that quells the anxiety and tension necessarily a part of the social monad (we visit this theme in chapter five). As Ramadanovic (2001) explains, "active forgetting is hence a process in which a past measure is abandoned and a new measure is continually reconstituted on the basis of new experiences. This way of doing history does not reduce the new to the old... but perpetually recreates the new/old such that the outcome of historical processes is reflected in the degree of happiness achieved." Happiness in this sense reflects cohesion between the dominant fictions of society and one's individual subject position.

Yet Mark's resistance to the negative images is countered by a "reserved fascination" (as he called it) about the Vietnam War and his father's status as a Vietnam Veteran, and it is important to emphasize his father's *status* of Vietnam Veteran is what he highlights in his narrative. This generates a degree of certitude that alleviates some of the tensions and anxieties regarding the negative discourses surrounding the Vietnam Veteran. His *reserved fascination* enabled him to be aware of the negative images of the war circulating in society. He explained to me that "even pre-college you heard of stories of people having negative reactions to the Vietnam War." Yet, he did not want those images to intervene with his view of his father as a Vietnam Veteran. But because it is important to know the history of the war, Mark sought out knowledge of the Vietnam War through college courses. He did not want to provoke difficult emotions in his father (nor emotions in his father that he felt incapable of handling), so he did not seek information from his father. Mark prefers to know the facts of war—the chronological history, the causes, and the political issues of the war; he did not want to complicate that knowledge with particularities that he felt distorted and tainted that knowledge. Yet, he took the classes to get a better handle on the war's social history, which he felt made him more informed about his views. Unlike Samantha and Renee, Mark has no desire to bridge the gap between knowing and understanding. For him, managing the crisis of articulation means not disrupting the break between knowing and understanding the complications of trauma that war produces.

Yet the gap between knowing and understanding—the crisis of articulation—does seep into his narrative. The ambiguous emotions that the trauma his father experienced are there, informing his hesitations and qualms about what it really means to be in combat and fear for your life. The distance Mark keeps from such emotional reactions instructs Mark's vision of his father's survival from the trauma of war. He felt the war was there for his father but it never impeded on his ability to be a father. For Mark, the memories of the war were at a safe distance for him and he was unaware of the specificities of the war's emotional impact on his father. Aside from the incident with the fireworks when Mark was a boy and his father's reaction to war movies, he could only remember one other time when his father visibly (to Mark) reacted to the war. It was a moment initiated by Mark through a Christmas gift he gave his father a few years before our interview. He gave his father a framed photograph of a man standing in front of the Vietnam Veterans' Memorial. He described the photograph to me, saying

> It was the Vietnam wall. A businessman with his hands against the wall, leaning in and weeping. And a shadow of the people on the other side of the wall—are the people he served with—and they are touching hands together on the wall. [...] and, it...pretty emotional, moving type of thing.

The separation and distance he tries to maintain between knowing and understanding the war experience is not as clear as Mark tries to make it in our interview. He does try to extend himself to his father, revealing his sensitivity to the pain involved in losing friends in war. It is a gesture that demonstrates his desire to understand what his father might have experienced as well as an attempt to connect with him on an emotional level. He went on to tell me how his father "lost it" that morning when he opened the present. So even though he works to maintain a conscious ignorance of the brutality he assumes is part of the combat experience, he cannot completely disengage from his awareness of the war experience or the emotional tie he has with his father. This gift to his father allows Mark to connect with his father in a way *Mark* can manage. By giving his father a photograph that reinforces the honor and sacrifice involved in war service, Mark can access an emotional tie with his father that supports a division between the absolute strength of the war hero, disallowing a view more vulnerable view of the warrior.

His gift of this photograph supports Mark's narrative containment of the image of his father as a *true American* through his willingness to volunteer for service. To engage in the deeper pain and reality of the war experience was something he could not readily integrate into the ordered distinctions between the trauma of war and honor of service and sacrifice, something he held in high esteem and that he connected to his father's service. "If I had to think of a word to describe what I learned as a child from my father would be the word sacrifice. My father volunteered. So that shows me he was willing to sacrifice for his country." Upon these images, he builds his narrative of his father and the Vietnam War. He keeps a mindful distance from the trauma of war, building a wall between knowing and understanding. He finds resolution to the crisis of articulation by relying on his father's strength and virtue rather than allowing the tensions of trauma to disrupt his knowledge of the Vietnam War. The active subject of the second generation takes the gift of a traumatic history and integrates it into his narrative.

As such, Mark is successful in making clear connections between his father and the Vietnam War, so long as it supports the view of his father as a strong and a good man. Throughout the interview, I could see his curiosity was always carefully mediated by his fear that the negative images of the war could damage his view of his father. In turn, this mediation helps him maintain the connection between his father and phallic masculinity, solidifying his belief in American ideals. He builds his views of manhood on the values that his father instilled in him. That is why he *can't deal* with the possibility that his father might hold some of the negative images of the Vietnam Veteran he has seen in other places. He works hard to build a narrative that keeps the grayer areas of lived experience at bay. But what emerges when aspects of the social monad are not—cannot—be forgotten and are instead remembered?

Seeing Gray: Understanding the Failed Father

Montana cannot navigate the relationship between her father and his service in Vietnam in terms of black and white. She was not able to see her father as strong and heroic; nor was she willing to conclude he was a failure. Although she discussed how her father was an alcoholic and died because of complications from his damaged liver, she could not pass judgment on him as a failure. Instead, she identified him as a traumatized subject who had been deeply affected by his experiences in Vietnam, and so made the connection between Vietnam and her father in order to explain why her father was not the father (or man) he could have been. In contrast to Mark, Montana actively remembers the more difficult discourses surrounding the Vietnam Veteran. Mark was able to actively remove those discourses from his own narrative because he could easily identify his father as a successful masculine subject by the standards of the dominant fiction. Montana could not do that. Instead, she relies on the more difficult components of the Vietnam Veteran Narrative in order to draw out connections between her father's struggles and failures with his experiences as a Vietnam Veteran.

Montana could not simply categorize her father as an alcoholic and move on from there. Caruth reminds us that "the attempt to gain access to a traumatic history, then, is also the project of listening beyond pathology of individual suffering, to the reality of a history that its crisis can only be perceived in its unassimilable forms" (1995, 156). Those unassimilable forms encompass a host of individual suffering that intersects with sociohistorical events. By identifying her father's alcoholism and depression as something beyond his individual affliction, she connects the traumatic event to the Vietnam Veteran. The Vietnam War shapes and becomes part of her father's life; Montana cannot disentangle the event from her father's subjectivity. The imbrication of the event of trauma with the subject position of the father and Vietnam Veteran opens up the perimeters of war trauma to include the lives of those who survive trauma and the relationships they develop. Such narratives demonstrate how trauma moves between people and events, perforating the line between the personal and social. As Montana explained to me, "When I think of war, I connect that with him and his experiences and I can only assume that that's been many people's experiences. I don't think he was alone."

Montana continually connected the war with her father. In response to my question about what comes to mind when the topic of Vietnam is brought up, she replied, "A feeling comes to mind more than a thought does. I immediately feel sadness. I'm trying to think. [pause] I think tragedy. That's probably the closest approximation to what I think about." When I asked her what she felt caused this feeling of sadness, she said, "My father's experiences there. My father, uhm. My father lived a very sad life. And most of that was the result of his experiences in Vietnam." With this response, Montana not only connects the war to her father, she also initiates an explanation for her father's life since the war, that is, his survival. His inability to move on or cover up the pain he feels from his experience of trauma is deeply imbricated in his inability to be the father Montana so desperately wanted. It also makes it impossible for her to ignore the impact of the war on her father. She repeatedly discussed how her father's experiences in Vietnam contributed to his difficult life. She continually negotiated her father's struggle with alcoholism and depression, which led to his death two years before our interview, in the context of his status as a Vietnam Veteran. Montana works through the various fragments of her memories of her relationship with her father in order to piece together a cohesive narrative of her father and their life together.

For Montana, the war is about the suffering that has occurred since her father returned home. That sadness is not isolated to her father; she recognizes it as part of the traumatic event of the Vietnam War, which includes the survivors and their families. As she goes on to say,

> So, I'm sad for him. I'm sad for my family's experience. [...] I'm sad for all the people that suffered there. And their families. It just [pause] spreads. People think Vietnam and they think the veterans; they think the troops and there's no understanding of this ripple effect that gets sent out into everyone's families and friends and hearts. And it's very wide and I don't know why people don't get that.

Montana cannot isolate the war to an event in the past. It is part of her father and her family. Understanding the war means recognizing the way that the event became part of her father's life. She articulates this through her father's psychological maladies, connecting them to her explanations for the limitations the experience of trauma placed on his ability to be a father. She did this with the hope of finding a resolution between his failures at home and his experiences in Vietnam.

COVV begin their narratives at the point of the survivor's departure from trauma. This means they develop an understanding of their fathers and the Vietnam War through their relationships with him, as well as through their own experiences and interpretations of their fathers' behaviors. Montana's understanding of the Vietnam War comes from years of watching her father struggle with his war memories. Her negotiation of her father's survival is what drives narratives of the trauma of the Vietnam War. She tells me stories, not of the Vietnam War, but of the way he suffered in his life after Vietnam. She tells me that the war was always there, even when it was not directly spoken or referenced. She explained to me,

[A]s I remember my father from 12 years old onward, he was always *in it*. He was always reading about [Vietnam], watching movies about it with his veteran friends. It just consumed his life. So it was all of these little subtleties that sort of built up into this growing awareness that that is what his life was centered around.

The subtleties that Montana speaks of involve the intersubjective components of their relationship, which lead to her assessment of the war consuming her father's life.

It was not just his drinking, nor his continual reading of books and watching of movies on Vietnam that made her sensitive to his struggle with his memories; it was also her recognition of the memories of his emotional attachment to that time in his life, which came from interactions that defied words. "I never understood why my father seemed to kind of just *get right in it*. I mean he surrounded himself with it. And it so obviously caused him pain and I never understood why he did that." The gap between knowing and understanding may be illuminated by our own experiences of loss and trauma but it is through the piecing together of fragmented narratives and memories that the attempt to articulate trauma takes place, albeit with great difficulty. This has become an important process for Montana, because within it she struggles to make sense of her father as a masculine subject, searching for a way to connect him to phallic masculinity. There is a great deal of ambiguity and irresolution in her narrative, but she uses her father's status as a Vietnam Veteran and the trauma she feels he experienced there to reflect on his failings and incapacity to be a strong and supportive father to her.

Her parents divorced when Montana was very young. When her mother remarried, Montana and her new family moved from Alabama to Western New York—and away from her father. Her memories of her father are filtered through her yearly visits with him in the summer, which continued into adulthood, until his death. Their relationship was never built on deep conversations. As she explained,

> We did see each other so seldom. And I had this separate life that he had no awareness of. And every time he saw me, I was a year older and a year different. But we were both bookworms, so we would be in the same room and we would both read. Or we would both watch TV. We didn't do a lot of talking.

Montana felt disconnected from her father physically and was never able to establish a strong father-daughter relationship. Her once-a-year visits never enabled them to know each other as well as she would have liked. "It was always sorta strange," she told me. "There was my, like, life here. And then there was my dad in [Alabama]. And that was like two separate worlds." This inhibited their interactions and created a distance in their relationship. It is that distance that Montana has been trying to reconcile since her father's death and is instrumental in her desire to find an explanation for his failings as a father.

She expressed nostalgia for that time with her father even as she explained their disconnection and her growing awareness of her father's mental and physical deterioration. His depression and alcoholism became clearer to her, making visits difficult as she grew older. The last time she visited her father before his death became a pivotal time for her, because she knew that her father would be in a deeper state of disrepair. She comments, "The last time I saw him before he died I remember being really upset before I went and talking to my partner, saying, *why am I going? Why am I doing this?* I'm just gonna go and see him after another year's worth of deterioration." She emphasized to me that

> Dad was just less there over the years. He was—he was always drunk. He always had alcohol in his system but. He somehow seemed more drunk those last few years [she laughs uncomfortably].

> He seemed. [Pause] He just kind of fell into it, like. When I was younger he was always drinking but he was always functional. He got less and less functional over the years. No work. He got very antisocial. He used to always have friends. [...] There were no friends in the end. He was constantly alone. And it was self-inflicted. He was just very reclusive and I hated seeing, seeing him like that. So that's the mental deterioration I'm talking about. Just this isolation and this increasing dysfunctional attitude and behavior.

In this explanation we see both the awareness of her father's painful emotional state as well as her discomfort and difficulty reflecting upon and explaining what she witnessed over the years.

In that last visit she makes the connection between the deterioration that frustrated her so deeply and the trauma of the war, providing greater insight into the complexities involved in surviving and articulating trauma. She explained to me,

> But the last summer that I visited before he died, he, uhm, he handed me a binder that he kept his mental health records in. He was an immaculate record keeper and he had every, like, psych report that had ever been done. He was in and out of the VA hospital in [Alabama]. This—he spent quite a bit of time in the psychiatric ward there. So, you know, he handed me this binder full of psych reports and just wanted me to read. He wouldn't talk about it. He wanted me to read it. And he also handed me a government report of some type. He had to go to Washington and go through some sort of files, uhm, to obtain, like a report [sighing] of a bombing that had happened where he was and it was part of his claim that he submitted to the VA—for compensation. And he had me read that. And I tried to ask him a question about it, uhm, and I guess I asked too deep or something. He wouldn't answer. He said I, I'm, I can't answer that—or something like that. But he, he, he wanted. He said something like you need to know. [Begins crying] He says you need to know what happened to your father or you need to know me. That's what he said, you need to know this about your father. [Words broken up by crying] That I can really remember. That was the only time that he was very direct.

I quote at length to provide the intimacy she felt between the two of them, even though her father could not speak to her directly about the reports. Her own memories of that time are filled with tremendous pain and emotion. The importance of the act of him sharing that binder, sharing that part of himself, however limited his words and their relationship were, shaped her way of speaking of her last visit. She never communicates to me directly what those reports articulated to her about the war, but the brutal facts that are often found in bureaucratic documentation are tempered by the visceral, emotional impact of him trusting her ability to understand what was within them. Even more so, her memory of him telling her that she needed to know this about her father stuck in her mind. In a sense, the brutal facts become less important than the exchange itself and the emotional impact it had on her memory. The crisis of articulation, which pursues the gray areas of our understanding of the experience of trauma, reflects the importance of the emotional exchanges shaping the father-child relationship. Montana, just as Renee and Samantha, engages in this task but finds it difficult to develop a clear causal relationship between the experiences of war and her father's subsequent maladies. This is a tenuous relationship. She seeks an explanation to her father's absence in her life, but she can never completely solidify it through her father's experiences in Vietnam.

Articulating the Vietnam Veteran within the Father

Analyzing narratives of COVV through the crisis of articulation compels us to consider the way trauma is a shared experience that moves beyond the individual and into the complexity of relationships that constitute the social realm. Individuals act in concert to find ways to reestablish belief in the ideals and values that were broken down because of the traumatic experience. The event of the Vietnam War becomes part of Vietnam Veterans' subjectivity, infecting Vietnam Veterans' relationships with their children. As a result, the event of trauma becomes part of the way COVV negotiate their understanding of masculine subjectivity and fatherhood. COVV traverse the boundary between their relationships with their fathers and their understanding of the Vietnam War as a social event. Here we see the importance of looking at the traumatic subject and their relationships to gain greater insight into a historically traumatic event such as the Vietnam War.

As I go into deeper analyses of my interviewees' narrative of their relationships with their fathers, the embodiment of trauma and affective personal relationships emerge as a central component of the discursive layers at work within the social monad. Resolution is not found in any static answer to what the war means to the individuals I interviewed; instead, it is seen as part of their process of living and acting in the social world. How COVV's fathers survive shapes the way they work through the crisis of articulation, generating not only their own narratives of the Vietnam War, but also greater dimension to the social monad.

The work involved in articulating the presence of the Vietnam War is necessary, yet full of hesitation. Like Montana, Hosking Gilberg implicates herself in finding resolution for her father as she simultaneously seeks a resolution in her own life.

> How do I resolve a soldier father's life in a villainous war? What is the resolution after this long journey? [...] I am the resolution. I conquer your death through my own personal acts. I am more than a daughter of a dead soldier, just like you were more than a soldier in a hideous war. (1997, 200)

While Hosking Gilberg identifies writing as her personal act to conquer and make peace with the death of her father, Montana identifies her studies and desire to be a social worker as her way of giving meaning to both her and her father's lives. The daughter knows the event of trauma through her father. And it is this knowledge that expands our understanding of the traumatic event of the Vietnam War. We come to understand the war within the dynamics of lived experiences that are often submerged between political debates and media images of the Vietnam War and Vietnam Veteran.

CHAPTER FOUR

The Vietnam Veteran Father: Reconfiguring Hegemonic Discourses of Masculine Subjectivity

The Vietnam Veteran Father

At the 2004 Democratic National Convention, Alexandra Kerry made the following statement: "To every little girl her father is a hero. It's taken some getting used to, that my father actually is one. And not just in the obvious ways." To children of Vietnam Veterans (COVV) such as Alexandra Kerry, their fathers embody not only the traumas of war but also its heroism, teaching them about freedom, peace, and the meaning of sacrifice. Alexandra considers her father a hero *not just in the obvious ways* that a woman might idolize her father, but in ways that reach into the myths America holds about war. Yet, she does not do this by talking about her father's heroics in Vietnam. Instead, she tells about his heroics as a father. In her speech at the 2004 Democratic National Convention, where she introduced her father, Democratic Presidential Candidate John Kerry, she described the hero who is her father by invoking a story about his willingness to jump into a lake to save her sister's hamster. She explained that "when he loves you as he loves me and my sister and his family, as he loves the men who fought beside him—there is no sacrifice too great." By elaborating on their fathers' strengths and sacrifices as a father, the men and women in this chapter, like Alexandra Kerry in her speech, work at the discursive intersection of the ideal Father and socially marginalized Vietnam Veteran. That is, they do not just rely on the myths America holds about the Vietnam Veteran, but also notions of ideal fatherhood. Like Mark's narrative in chapter four, these men and women's narratives reconfigure forms of hegemonic masculine subjectivity. Highlighting how individuals develop their own narratives within the overly articulated spaces of the social monad, they find a voice that addresses the silences and clichés that permeate the traumatic event of the Vietnam War.

As these men and women contend with both the ideal forms of the Father and the broken and maligned image of the Vietnam Veteran, they develop a form of phallic masculinity with which to identify their fathers. By emphasizing aspects of social discourse that support this identification, they manage to build a narrative bridge between the Father and the Vietnam Veteran that generates a story of the Vietnam Veteran Father. Over the course of the interview, many of these men and women felt it was their responsibility to correct the image of the Vietnam Veteran as the symbol of the broken masculine subject by expressing what a wonderful father *their* father was and is. They negotiate popular images of the Vietnam Veteran within their experiences with their fathers. As Moser remarks in his article on popular memory and oral histories of Vietnam Veterans, "deep structures of popular memory are important not because they explain all the facts, but because they indicate the nature of cultural processes which assign meaning to and reconstruct the past" (1990, 118). At the same time, popular memory of the Vietnam Veteran deeply impacts the way my interviewees think and talk about their fathers, leading them to develop responses that critique the image of the Vietnam Veteran through their intersubjective relationships with their fathers (and their subsequent narratives). Their memories of their fathers are mediated by those images, which, consequently, further illuminate the social monad of the Vietnam War. Rather than leaving behind this traumatic event, it goes through another iteration as the second generation use their fathers' status as a Vietnam Veteran to demonstrate why their fathers fit the model of the ideal Father.

These shows are a reminder of the way the war tested the values and beliefs of our nation, even if they do keep us at a safe distance from the more troubling moral questions that exist about war and its ongoing effects. Individual Vietnam Veterans, though, cannot distance themselves from the moral questions that the Vietnam War provoked. As Christian Appy comments,

> For veterans torn by confusion about the war they had fought, and struggling to feel some pride in what they had done, the protestors' passion, self-assurance, and sense of purpose could generate a nagging—if unspoken—envy. Faced with people so sure the war was wrong, vets were convinced their own morality was under siege. (1993, 302)

Vietnam Veterans often felt that they were the only ones experiencing the moral ambiguity of war, believing that those at home "seemed to have such a wonderful, safe time" (302) without having to face the dissolution of American values in the dangers of the jungle. In this sense, the Vietnam Veteran easily manifests as the symbol of the unresolved issues the war provoked. The Vietnam Veteran as an imagined source of social maladjustment becomes an easy way to dislocate the larger break in American idealism that occurred in the event of the Vietnam War, but it leaves the COVV in a precarious position. The COVV have to navigate between social images of the Vietnam Veteran and their fathers in order to maintain belief in the dominant fiction. They cannot easily displace the trauma of the Vietnam War into the Vietnam Veteran because their father *is* a Vietnam Veteran. Moral ambiguities filter into COVV's narratives, and these interviewees try to dispel those uncertainties; they are plagued with moral ambiguity in a fashion similar to their fathers. To combat this, some interviewees try to describe their fathers as noble and heroic men with moral certitude. The social imaginary's articulation of the trauma of the Vietnam War through troubled and traumatized representations of the Vietnam Veteran requires my interviewees to work within those images to negotiate their understanding of their fathers.

In her speech, Alexandra Kerry does not tell the story of her father saving her sister's hamster simply to be frivolous or humorous, but to dislodge her father from the symbol of a traumatic past. By generating a tangible and humane image of her father as kind and benevolent, she draws on images of the noble hero in order to move away from the cultural stereotype of the Vietnam Veteran. By doing this she conjures the symbol of masculine virtue: the Father. Similar to Alexandra Kerry, the interviewees work through masculine subjectivity and American mythology through the lens of the Vietnam War, their fathers embodying these cultural dynamics. These actions are an effort to configure an alternative memory of the Vietnam War by rehabilitating the image of the Vietnam Veteran into a Vietnam Veteran Father. Here again we see how the social monad of the Vietnam War is *a personal thing* that is deeply enmeshed with societal discourses surrounding the war.

The Ideal Father and Phallic Masculine Subjectivity

Leonard Benson, in his 1968 book titled *Fatherhood: A Sociological Perspective*, draws out the significance of the father as a symbol of the social order and stabilizer of the dominant fiction. Reinforcing the relationship between the father and masculine subjectivity, he provides one of the earliest sociological examinations of fatherhood. Overall, though, fatherhood has had a rather benign existence in social research, not unlike the research done on masculinity. With the exception of Benson's work, the father has held an elusive position in social research, often existing as an uninterrogated role within the family.[1] Research on fatherhood can be found in a variety of fields, ranging from popular psychology to sociology to history. Until recently, the area of masculinity studies has given little attention to fatherhood and when researchers in masculinity have focused on fatherhood they rarely explicitly examine the relationship between fatherhood and the construction of masculine subjectivity.[2] As Deborah Lupton and Lesley Barclay assess in their book *Constructing Fatherhood: Discourses and Experiences*, "many influential book-length academic works that feature extended discussions of masculinity...either ignore fatherhood altogether or mention it only briefly" (Lupton and Barclay, 1997, 3). At the same time, "little attention has been focused on the social, cultural and symbolic dimensions of fatherhood. Nor have contemporary writings on subjectivity and gender been adequately employed to theorize the ontology of fatherhood" (4). Lupton and Barclay's critique centers less around the lack of research done on fatherhood than on how the Father has remained unexamined in the context of masculine subjectivity; this is a reflection of the depth to which the father permeates the structures of the social order. The literature utilized in this section, then, was selected because it focuses on the relationship between fatherhood and masculine subjectivity. This relationship is of utmost concern because it addresses the ways we generate links between the masculine subject and phallic identification, thereby enabling the structures of society to continue through time. Because my interviewees rely on idealizations of the Father to structure their narratives, we can see how individuals work to regenerate a belief in the dominant fiction of society through the Father. Trauma is managed, not simply through trying to retell the event, but in trying to attach belief structures to the social subjects we interact with in our daily lives. It is a seemingly benign process of maintaining the social order; a social order that necessitates societal belief in the power of the masculine subject.

The Traditional Father

Kind. Caring. Family-oriented. I wanted to try to give you an amalgamation because I think [my father] would do anything for his family. (Tara)

My interviewees discuss their fathers' success as a father through the way he upholds traditional beliefs and values in what defines a father in society. What are these traditional values, though? Benson defines a set of aspects of the father's (traditional) role in society and the family. He identifies the significant components: reproduction, material support, survival skills, handling crises, and providing security (see Benson, 1968, 39–65). In his book, *Fatherhood in America: A History*, Robert Griswold points to the way breadwinning has defined men's position as father and social subject and how that started to change, coincidentally (or not so), near the time my interviewees' fathers were coming of age and serving in Vietnam. Benson and Griswold's books, together, generate a broad history of American fatherhood through the lens of the masculine subject in America. Essential to this image is the role of the father as breadwinner and the way his success and failure in this realm defines his success and failure as a man.

Griswold writes,

For over a hundred years, male breadwinning undergirded patriarchal authority, helped define male identity, and even provided some commonalities across chasms of race and class. But its hold was always tenuous. Fathers who could not support their families—breadlosers—suffered terribly. (1993, 268)

The breadwinner role is arguably the central component of traditional (and modern) fatherhood. Combined with the other aspects outlined by Benson, the picture of the traditional father is one who is strong, stable, and (above all) economically successful. This means that traditional masculinity finds phallic identification through the masculine subject's capacity to embody and display these qualities. Benson writes,

The breadwinner task is unquestionably father's key responsibility in the United States. It lies at the core of our ideology of fatherhood, fuzzy as that may be. It constitutes the effort that most thoroughly satisfies the man's family obligation: he is the instrumental leader of the household primarily because his is accountable for its economic well-being. The father's activity as breadwinner has long been established as the chief embodiment of his masculinity.... (1968, 271)

Much like motherhood for women, fatherhood is a defining marker of manhood; it shapes men's capacity to claim phallic masculinity in society. The traditional model of fatherhood shapes the power of the masculine subject in society. Kovic's intense experience of loss and emasculation when he found out he could not biologically have children reflects the significant role fatherhood plays in the masculine subject's route to phallic identification. As the progenitor of social life, the masculine subject's power comes through both the biological capacity to father children and the social power to pass on established values and social beliefs. Ultimately, we measure the masculine subject's failures and successes at taking on the role of social progenitor through his capacity to procreate *and* economically provide for his family.

It is not surprising that, when they describe their fathers and try to identify him with phallic masculinity, my interviewees depend on his ability to provide economically for them. When Stacey was describing her relationship with her father, she explained how he has been a good provider and would do anything for her and her sister. When I asked her what types of interactions she has with her father, she said, "We'll talk about school—what the money situation is. What needs to be done. If I have a problem then I tell him and he fixes it [giggles]. That's about it." After telling me this, she added, "I mean, he's a dad. He's a good dad." For Stacey, he is a *good* dad, because

> He's always been there. No matter what—like not just money— but no matter what my sister and I need, he always makes sure that even if he's gone without that we have, you know, whatever it takes to make us happy. So we don't get picked on—you know— can't wear holes in our shoes. We don't have a lot of money but my dad—he's always made it so we do have the best. And he'll, like, go without—like he'll have holes in his shirt and three-year-old shoes so we can have stuff.

While it is *not just money* that he sacrifices for her and her sister, Stacey contextualized those sacrifices in material terms. He is a *good* father precisely because he placed his children's needs above his own. They may not have had a lot of money, but he did ensure their comfort and security. This was a continual theme she returned to throughout the interview. She was also very careful not to say things that might convey her father as vulnerable. I felt the weight of the image of the maligned Vietnam Veteran continually present in our interview even though she never directly spoke of it. Her only mention of her awareness of the negative images was through her repeated refutation of knowledge about the Vietnam War. "But like again, I don't know what the war was about. I don't even know who was president at the time." This assertion is made more as a *refusal* to know about the particulars of the war, than simply a testament of *not* knowing. It reveals (in less explicit ways than we saw with Mark) her apprehension of the way the Vietnam War and Vietnam Veteran are articulated in society.

Unlike Mark, Stacey expresses many more situations where she has seen firsthand her father's struggles with post-traumatic stress disorder (PTSD) and was visibly uncomfortable telling me these stories. One example was the first time she watched her father have a flashback. The moment deeply affected her but she wanted me to know that "It doesn't make me think that he's wacky or anything." Instead "It kinda made me feel, like, worse for him. Like, like, to understand that he *does* remember and it *does* affect him still" (my emphasis). In this expression she works through the crisis of articulation, demonstrating how understanding that her father still deals with his memories of the war extend far beyond any factual knowledge she may or may not have of the war. Yet, it is apparent that she not only has a working knowledge of the negative images of Vietnam Veterans but she actively negotiates her father's image in terms of this awareness by asserting that she does not think her father is *wacky*. She wants me to know that even though her father has a hard time with his memories of the war it does not mean he is crazy, nor does it incapacitate his ability to be a *good dad*.

Stacey is highly sensitive to the ongoing presence of the war in her father. The discussion of her father's struggles with PTSD is contextualized within the assertions that Stacey's father is a good father who would sacrifice anything for both her and her sister. Stacey's resistance to know about the war, coupled with her understanding of the intimate ways in which her father has been affected by the war, enabled her to build a narrative of her father as a model of the traditional father. That she articulates her father as a successful breadwinner, even though her family did not have a lot of money, reflects her ability to connect her father with phallic identification in ways he may or may not be able to do himself. At the same time, by refuting her formal knowledge of the war, Stacey generates an alternative history of the Vietnam War that relies on the personal and human legacy of the event. By doing this she reveals how powerful the need to create a coherent and consistent narrative around the dominant fiction of America can be (even for the second generation) as we work through memories of a traumatic event that disrupted our systems of belief. Creating clear demarcation lines between her father's experience of combat and his present life structures facilitate the development of a narrative that is in line with the dominant fiction of masculinity, precisely by negotiating against and through the (dominant fiction) of the debilitated Vietnam Veteran.

Similarly, Tammy described how her father upheld traditional ideals of fatherhood by telling me, "[My mother] never worked a day in her life.... As children, we were never allowed to be without mom in the house." She then went on to tell me how her father not only provided for her family but also her maternal grandfather. "And he took in, actually he bought the house my mom was raised in—to take care of my grandfather who had Alzheimer's. And paid for medical care for my grandfather to stay there." She also told me that "He gives me—if I ask him for a $100 tomorrow—or yesterday or today—he would hand it over." Through these descriptions of her father, Tammy exemplifies the way her father is both an economic foundation and the purveyor of social values and morals. Not only did she describe him as a great provider, but she also praised his moral strength and willingness to take responsibility for her mother's father. She emphasized how her father embodied the values of service and sacrifice—making connections between both his service in Vietnam and his status as a father and husband. Tammy invoked images of the ideal hero and father rather than the Vietnam Veteran in order to try to separate her father from that image and history. Structuring her articulation of her father and his service around the ideal image of the Father that is without moral ambiguity, Tammy was able to express a great deal of pride and admiration for her father's status as a Vietnam Veteran. Like Stacey, Tammy develops a clear separation between her father's service in Vietnam and the work he does at home in the community. Her emphasis on his community service and commitment to his family provides a means of removing moral ambiguity from the descriptions of her father. By describing her father as "loyal" and "honest," Tammy creates a picture of him that is the epitome of the masculine subject and American citizen. She explained that

> He works long hours during the day and then comes home and he wants—he does family things, you know. He always wants to be with the family. He's always helpin' out family members or things like that. And then the amount of volunteer work that he does. He drives food to homeless people. [...] He'll drive out 500 miles to deliver food to somebody [laughs].

For Tammy, her father is a good father, an exemplar of the ideal. Tammy asserts that his work and service ethic provided her with a strong work ethic and commitment to service. "My father has definitely instilled the volunteer work in me." Through this narrative she counters the social image of the Vietnam Veteran as socially dislocated.

Tammy also believed that her father's military service provided her with a greater sensitivity to the military and the people who serve in war. She told me that being a child of a Vietnam Veteran enabled her to "appreciate those who fight in the war—more than I think anybody else" and that she values "knowing more about the war than anybody else would—normal person would." As a child of a Vietnam Veteran, Tammy believed that she held a unique perspective and awareness that extended beyond general knowledge of the war. Although she could not precisely express what that understanding consisted of, it connoted a sense of greater awareness of the sacrifices involved in service. She also believed that it was her responsibility to uphold the values of service and loyalty that her father embodies. Although Tammy knows very little about the specifics of her father's war experiences she held his service in high regard. This point was expressed in the story of how she made a display case for her father's medals. Honoring him in this fashion underscored her belief that duty and honor are what is most vital to the memory of her father's service in the Vietnam War. Unlike Hosking Gilberg, who could *not* think of her father's medals without thinking of the blood and pain of combat, Tammy dissociates the brutality of war from the ideal images of the noble war hero. Like Alexandra Kerry, who told us that when her father *loves you as he loves me and my sister and his family, as he loves the men who fought beside him—there is no sacrifice too great*, Tammy (and other interviewees) rehabilitate the Vietnam Veteran as a humane and heroic figure by emphasizing their successes as a father (to them), enabling my interviewees to connect their fathers to phallic masculine subjectivity. By focusing on these traditional ideals of the Father, my interviewees *combat the ambiguities created by paternal weakness and general social upheaval.*

Negotiating the New and Traditional Father as Ideal Father

The significance of the traditional Father never leaves the narratives of COVV. Regardless of whether or not these men and women feel that their fathers were successful at being a father, it was discussed in relation to notions of the traditional father. "Even films that critique the traditional father and the patriarchal position signal the importance of it as a determining model" (Bruzzi, 2005, xvii). Much in the way Stella

Bruzzi's research on images of the Father in Hollywood conveys the significance of this model, societal discourse of the Father filters into COVV. Whether or not a father fits into the social discourses of ideal fatherhood, this ideal structures and determines the way these men and women narrate their experiences and the expectations they hold about their fathers. But this does not happen in a unified way.

As Griswold alludes to the above, social changes took place that shifted the image of the traditional father in American society. Some of my interviewees incorporate what Griswold calls the "new father" into their image of the ideal father. This *new* father does not contain *new* ideas of fatherhood so much as it identifies the growing dominance of an image of the father that addresses the masculine subject's changing position in American society. As Griswold argues, social changes in the last 25 years have provoked a reorganization of the father's role in society and the family.

> The tremendous increase in the number of married women and mothers in the work force fundamentally challenged ideas about manhood, masculinity, and attendant breadwinning and fatherly responsibilities.... The effects of this change were augmented by the reemergence of feminism in the mid-1960s, which made all the gender assumptions, including those about fatherhood, problematic. (1993, 244)

The new father that materializes from this shift asks fathers to be more involved in their children's lives—to know them and contribute more energetically to their development. No longer was the expectation for fathers to be distant and passive role models who did not actively participate in the daily life of their children and home. They could not just go to work and be dismissed from familial responsibilities. The ideal of the breadwinner did not disappear, though, and what emerged is an ambiguous expectation of fathers being both a provider and an active participant and caregiver in their children's lives.

This active role is heavily invested with middle-class ideals and capacities.

Much of this dual-role is understood as an *augmentation* to the mother's role of caregiving, rather than relieving her of the more onerous duties of childcare. As Griswold comments,

> The new fatherhood, then, can become a badge of class, a sign that one has the knowledge, time, and inclination to embrace

progressive visions of parenting.... For these men, pushing a pram becomes less a sign of a wimp than a public symbol of their commitment to a more refined, progressive set of values than those held by working-class men still imprisoned by outdated ideas of masculinity. (1993, 254)

Griswold does not make this comment to support that the middle-class ideals *are* more advanced than working-class ideals. He makes this comment to reinforce the way the values of the new father *present* themselves as a more advanced system of values that *all* men should embrace. Here we see again how images of fatherhood and masculine subjectivity are deeply connected, each shaping the other in their position within the dominant fiction. The way one takes on the role of father is a measurement of his position as masculine subject. This shift in fatherhood is part of the transitions that were taking place in masculine subjectivity, part of which contained progressive values and greater acceptance of gender equality.[3] What is interesting in the interviewees' comments about their fathers, though, is that, regardless of the more progressive images of masculinity and fatherhood that may exist, they still privilege the act of breadwinning.[4]

Ted exemplifies this process as he reflects on the way he has come to terms with his father's limited physical presence in his life. He told me,

> I always thought, I guess when I was younger, I always thought that I wished my father had been there probably more than he was. At least my perspective was that he wasn't [around enough]. But I have a different perspective now, because I realize now my father was the only one working. My mother was at home with four small kids; she couldn't work. And it was really tough on them financially. [...] I have a different perspective on it now because I realize that what my dad was trying to do was provide, you know, as good a life as he could.

He resolved his father's lack of presence growing up by emphasizing how his father worked hard for his family and his ability to be the sole provider for Ted's family. Like Stacey, he reveres his father's hard work and sacrifices for his family, focusing on how that demonstrates his virtues as a strong masculine subject.

Tara moves back and forth between these images in different ways, in part a result of the fact that Tara's family has had a nontraditional living arrangement. Her father has not lived in their family home since she was in the sixth grade. She is now 23, but she considers her family home as the one she grew up in with her mother and her sister. Tara's father maintains a separate home over four hours away. Her parents are not divorced and she explained they have a strong relationship but he moved in order to take a better-paying job without displacing his family. She is adamant about projecting an image of her father as an ideal provider, even though he was not involved in her day-to-day life while growing up. Tara said, "He has done whatever he could to keep our family afloat." She went on to explain,

> I think just in his struggles to support his family, to make sure that, you know, we had what he thought were necessary means. I mean he could have lived in the same town as us and grown up with us and we could have been scraping by but he wanted us to go to the best schools, have cars, have clothes; he wanted the type of lifestyle that, uhm—or my parents wanted the lifestyle that they didn't have when they were growing up.

Tara resolved that her father's decision to live apart from her family was the ultimate sacrifice to provide for her and her sister. Similar to Stacey and Ted, Tara emphasized his sacrifices, muting her feelings about his absence. She developed an understanding of her father's actions that support his success in the role of father. He wanted to improve the station of his family's lives so they could have a better life than he did. The ability to provide economically mitigated her father's physical absence in the home.

Yet Tara is profoundly affected by her father's absence and tells me how devastated she was when he stopped living with them, only returning home on the weekends. She recently tried to initiate a closer relationship with her father, explaining that "I sent him an e-mail once that said, 'I want to get to know you and be able to, you know, have stories to tell my children.' [...] And so I think he realized that and he's gotten better at it." Although she primarily identifies her father's success as a father through his economic strength and stability, Tara feels he has made an effort to communicate with her more, and it is that effort that she references when she explained to me how she knows her father loves her. Since her e-mail to him, she feels their relationship has improved. As Tara explained, "I mean, it's not like the level I would like to be with my dad, but nor is he the type of person to be that type of father anyway, so it's at the level we are both able to come to an agreement." While she may not be entirely satisfied with her father's ability to be more aware and involved in her life, she resolved that he is not the type of man who can give a lot emotionally. She values the effort he has made and used it as a means of reinforcing his success as a father.

At the same time, discussions about her father's experiences in Vietnam are greatly minimized. She resisted any attempt to correlate her father's experiences in Vietnam to her frustrations with her father's emotional dislocation. While I do not want to make false connections between her family life and her war experiences, there are several hints of tension that her father's experiences in Vietnam may be a greater factor than she was willing to admit. As we were finishing our discussion of the ways in which the Vietnam War is brought up, she said,

> I wanted to add on to that and say, uhm, when I was growing up, my father was a kind of borderline alcoholic for a number of years. My mother says that it was because he was trying to forget some of his experiences. And he, since, you know, has—hasn't been as violent as he was in the past.

She said this rather tersely and would not go into too specific a detail about her father's behaviors at that time. Yet, when I questioned if she thought any of her father's actions were the result of his experiences in Vietnam, Tara did not mention her father's drinking problem, making the point later that "nobody knows [the causes of his drinking problem] for sure and that's something that's kind of like—nobody ever talks about it in my family [nervous laugh]." Tara resists making a causal link between her father's drinking problem and difficulties he may or may not have experienced in war, preferring to concentrate her discussion on the more honorable qualities of his war service.

> In fact, she told me that
> I think [being a child of a Vietnam Veteran is] a privilege, to be quite honest with you, because, while I don't know how honestly I would have felt at the time [of the war], I think it's such a privilege and honor to be related to someone who's been in the military. [...] I gave a fleeting thought to being in the Air Force because my father didn't have any sons. [...] I tried to make it appeal to me in my head, you know, "maybe [I] should consider this to honor my father" but I just couldn't do it. But I definitely feel it's a privilege and an honor.

When I asked her why it was an honor, she said, "I think that the traditions that the military has, you know, go back for years. There's so much honor involved there, because they're serving their country and they are willing to, you know, die for freedom. And I think that that's amazing." By focusing her attention on the honor of service with very little insight into the war and her father's experiences, she actively shifts her attention from the negative images of the Vietnam Veteran and potentially negative aspects of the war's effects on her father to maintain a view of her father that enables her to preserve alignment with the dominant fiction and masculine subject's position in it.

The expectation of having a father as both traditional provider and emotionally invested, builds an image of the ideal father against which my interviewees describe their fathers. The interviewees' successful constructions of their fathers' ability to uphold these ideals and be *good* fathers allows them to draw the connection between their fathers (as masculine subjects) and phallic identification. In this narration they counter the negative images of the Vietnam Veteran. Let us turn now to some of the types of images my interviewees engage with in their conversations with me.

The Vietnam Veteran in the Social Imaginary: Traumatic Repetition in Prime Time

> Even though we didn't talk about the Vietnam War in a negative way, it always just seemed to convey negative thoughts and reactions because it was a war that nobody wanted a part of. (Tara)

My interviewees engage with the social monad of the Vietnam War through their continual negotiation of the negative images of the Vietnam Veteran. Specifically, they focus on how poorly Vietnam Veterans were treated when they came home and how they were dealt with in American media. Some of my interviewees, like Samantha, rely on films to support their assessments, recalling (given in chapter three) how she did not really understand how badly Vietnam Veterans were treated until she watched the film *Born on the Fourth of July*. Others, like Ted, mention that the media's focus on the crimes and violent acts that Vietnam Veterans commit, only bring back the stigma that Vietnam Veterans and their families have faced since before the war ended. These images cast shadows over the COVV's ability to understand their fathers and the Vietnam War. D. Michael Shafer, in his book *The Legacy:*

The Vietnam War in the American Imagination, emphasizes how "since the war, we have ignored Vietnam Veterans or treated them with a hostility reflecting the common view that they are a 'bunch of whining vets,' or losers, druggies, and, possibly, psychopaths" (Shafer, 1990, 80). In this section, I explore public representations of the Vietnam Veteran in two popular television shows. These episodes exemplify the stories we as a society tell about the Vietnam War. They do this by relying on the *comforting* social narrative of the troubled Vietnam Veteran, which keeps the trauma of the Vietnam War isolated to the *bleary eyed veteran* (to invoke O'Brien's earlier point). This social narrative, though, is not a comforting story to my interviewees; in fact, it is the social narrative of the troubled Vietnam Veteran that produces a great deal of anxiety in their personal narratives, creating an intense urgency to repudiate the negative images of the Vietnam Veteran.

Regardless of whether or not the news media tries to be sensitive to the struggles Vietnam Veterans faced in their transition back into civilian life, the public representation of the Vietnam Veteran as a traumatized subject dominates his public image. Coupled with the violent and deviant images of the Vietnam Veteran in Hollywood films, the crystallization of the image of the Vietnam Veteran as a socially troubled masculine subject (e.g., see O'Brien, 1979; Shafer, 1990; and Appy, 1993) has continued to plague the American memory of the Vietnam War. Shafer, like O'Brien, speaks of the way that this problematic image is a reflection of American society's inability to face the "human legacy" of the Vietnam War (see Shafer, 1990, 80–1). Even now, America has trouble facing this human legacy. The troubled image of the Vietnam Veteran continues to persist in current representations of him, demonstrating the way America still struggles to make sense of Vietnam War's impact on society. My interviewees must manage these public images as they discuss their relationship with their fathers, reflecting how the Vietnam War continues to affect the COVV in intimate ways (whether or not they are explicitly aware of it). The way the interviewees generate their narratives around their fathers and the war reveals the depth of this image's impact, regardless of how accurate or wrong they may find it to be. The social construction of the Vietnam Veteran leaves my interviewees working to integrate deep-rooted social narratives—pieces of the dominant fiction of America—into their personal narrations of their fathers and the Vietnam War, which often stand in contradiction to (or with far greater complexity than) these public representations.

A study done in the early 1980s by Josefina Card is an example of the contrast between public representations and personal life experiences.

In her research, she found that the men who served in Vietnam had not been as severely socially handicapped as media representations might have us believe. In her study, published under the title *Lives After Vietnam: The Personal Impact of Military Service*, Card found that although the men who served in Vietnam had higher rates of anxiety and depression, the rates of substance abuse and criminality were no higher than their peers (Card, 1983, 91–2, 100). At the same time, although Vietnam Veterans' educational attainment and home ownership were comparable to their peers, they suffered from higher rates of job instability and unemployment, having "more problems than their peers in getting on track in their work and in abiding by rules to stay on track" (1983, 70–1). Although there have been few other studies to support, refine, or refute her findings (or more recent studies looking at Vietnam Veterans' present social status), her work demonstrates the differences that exist between media representations and the reality of these men's lives. It also reinforces the association of the Vietnam Veteran with a traumatic subjectivity, substantiating society's use of the Vietnam Veteran as the symbol of the trauma of the war. The impact this has on the real lives of Vietnam Veterans and their families, though, is a reminder of how symbolic imagery intimately affects the way individuals orient themselves to the social world in which they live.

Episodes of *Without a Trace*[5] and *Cold Case*[6] provide images of the Vietnam Veteran in the present, contributing to the social monad of the Vietnam War through these representations. In particular, each show (with variable degrees of complexity) explores the way that the Vietnam Veteran as a masculine subject still struggles to connect with phallic masculinity. *Cold Case* provides an atypically nuanced portrayal of the masculine subject struggling with the trauma of the Vietnam War; *Without a Trace* presents a more typical image of the Vietnam Veteran and damaged masculine subject. Despite these differences the Vietnam Veteran in both episodes still symbolizes our unfinished business with the Vietnam War through his inability to connect with phallic masculinity. In both shows, the Vietnam Veteran—Brian McCormick in *Cold Case* and John Carver in *Without a Trace*—is visited by a dark past that he has spent the last 30 years putting behind him. The dead return as a haunting reminder to America that the past is far from resolved and that the social monad of the Vietnam War is still a dense presence in the American imaginary. When the dead speak, it is not only to tell us about the irresolution of their own deaths, but how their deaths are part of the American memory of the Vietnam War. *To be haunted is to be tied to historical and social effects*; the dead's presence reflects how the Vietnam Veteran still carries the social effects of the Vietnam War. In particular, the struggles of war are expressed, not through the conflict with the enemy, but through and within the American Vietnam Veteran. The Vietnam Veteran provides us with a comfortable distance from the trauma of the Vietnam War, but he must be read as a stark reminder that the war still weighs on our social consciousness.

The discrepancies between the image of the Vietnam Veteran and their fathers daily lives leave many COVV, like Tammy, Mark, and others, engaging in discussions that remediate these images, often moving to the other extreme in their idealization of their fathers as noble men and heroes. I turn now to my analysis of two popular television series' episodes to better understand the social narrative with which COVV work. Ultimately, these popular images (versus the interviewees' negotiation of those images) "obscure our understanding of both the Vietnam War and its human legacy. No less important, [we understand the way] they blind us to how badly we as a nation have dealt with the war..." (Shafer, 1990, 81).

(A)Historical Trauma: Another Iteration of
the Bleary-Eyed Veteran

The image of the Vietnam Veteran in the *Without a Trace* episode titled "Kam Li," which first aired on March 13, 2003, provides a facile representation of the Vietnam Veteran in popular memory. Twenty-five years after O'Brien's statement that the bleary-eyed veteran carries the emotional baggage of the Vietnam War for the nation, we see yet another iteration of him on prime-time television. Through the different variations of the image of the Vietnam Veteran in the show, it provides viewers with an image of the Vietnam Veteran that is an estranged and socially dislocated subject who cannot make a meaningful connection with the social world. Providing several variations of the image of the Vietnam Veteran, the show creates an amalgam of the broken masculine subject. The tainted image of the Vietnam Veteran emerges out of the circumstances of the death of a comrade (Lewis) in Vietnam. Ultimately, it is this absent soldier (who never made it home as a *living* representation of the Vietnam Veteran) who is the only figure in this group of men *not* imagined as a tarnished subject. The cause of his death in Vietnam is a tension I center my analysis on because it is the grounding upon which the image of the Vietnam Veteran develops, demonstrating the ways in which the Vietnam Veteran still carries the weight of the irresolution of the war in present popular memory.

This irresolution is found in the isolation of the Vietnam Veteran to his experiences in Vietnam and disconnecting him from other socially viable domestic images. In particular, none of the Vietnam Veterans in this show are represented as successful fathers. Rather than conveying the image of the *good* father, the Vietnam Veteran is seen as an object "through which the nation could express its unwillingness or inability to face the Vietnam War" (Moser, 1990, 108). The Vietnam Veteran's isolation to the sphere of war, regardless of whether he is lionized or criticized, locks him in as a symbol of the traumatic effects of the event without any other accessible social existence.

While it may seem a matter of commonsense that the Vietnam Veteran, as a subject of a television show, would not necessitate a connection to the domestic world, it is precisely that *commonsense* understanding that intrigues me. The normalcy of the notion that the Vietnam Veteran has little domestic social presence 30 years after the Vietnam War ended conveys him as an iconographic figure of the Vietnam War that enables social discourse (at least in prime-time media, which is a decidedly significant venue) to sidestep a meaningful engagement with the original event. As Moser continues to point out, "the 'crazy vet' and the 'baby-killer' became cultural objects, emblematic of the evils of war.... [A] 'crazy vet' can be more easily ignored than a war hero or fellow citizen" (1990, 109).

This is precisely why Alexandra Kerry explicitly emphasized her father's successes as a father in her speech. By actively managing this public representation of the Vietnam Veteran as she describes her father as a hero and citizen, Alexandra integrates a domesticated image of a social subject that is traditionally isolated from domestic social life. Such an integration redirects the symbolic meaning of the Vietnam Veteran into the Vietnam Veteran Father into a less easily ignored and more human social subject. To portray the Vietnam Veteran as a successful and *good* father shifts his presence in a way that turns the social monad of the Vietnam War into a domestic conversation that is accessible to issues such as the family and fatherhood. Because the social imaginary is unable to engage in such a conversation in media (such as television shows and films), COVV's narratives are a vital contribution to the social monad of the Vietnam War. The second generation only knows the Vietnam War as an intersection between war and family—something their fathers embody.

Trapped in a form of traumatic repetition, the social imaginary cannot find a space to articulate the Vietnam Veteran Father. None of the images of the Vietnam Veteran in the show symbolize a present and active father. The show opens at a reunion of a group of Vietnam Veterans celebrating the retirement of their platoon leader in Vietnam, John Carver. At the end of the night Carver turns up missing and the show proceeds to investigate his disappearance. In their search for Carver, the detectives question his daughter, who has a distant and remote relationship with her father. She had not spoken with him in over a year, and when she did, she was disinclined to interact with him. She explains her estranged relationship with her father to Detective Malone, "I'd never seen him so...vulnerable. And, uh, I didn't reach out to him at all. And when he called from Atlantic City and said he'd like to come to church with the girls, I...I doubt I sounded very enthusiastic." Malone consoles her by revealing that he, too, was raised in a military family, telling her "My father was in the Army. I know how hard that life can be." His reassurance implies an inarticulable bond that children of veterans and military men have, which includes the assumption that their fathers were never truly capable of being fathers to them. None of the other representations of the Vietnam Veterans gives the viewer any indication that the Vietnam Veteran has a successful home life. He is portrayed with varied *public* success (which produces variation within the image of the Vietnam Veteran), but none rely on his status as father to secure his present social life. Considering how vital the position of father is/has been to the construction of masculine subjectivity, the absence of the Vietnam Veteran's role as father enables social narratives to contain him within the boundaries of war and a one-dimensional traumatized subject. By foreclosing the symbol of the Vietnam Veteran from fatherhood, the measurement of his position as masculine subject is tenuous and suspect, regardless of how successful he may appear to be in the public sphere. Because fatherhood is such a defining factor in a man's life, his incapacity or failure at it renders him a fragile masculine subject. As the investigation uncovers that Carver's disappearance is linked to Lewis's death in Vietnam, the image of the Vietnam Veteran takes on the trauma of the Vietnam War.

Although Carver is the central figure constituting the image of the Vietnam Veteran in the show, the other characters support this image. As the plot unfolds, we discover that Carver killed Lewis in Vietnam and that the other men had confronted Carver about his actions at the reunion. It is this confrontation that leads to Carver's disappearance.

Actually, he did not simply disappear; he committed suicide. All of the characters are entangled in Carver's death and carry aspects of the Vietnam Veteran. Wallace Sykes, the depressed and morally weak Vietnam Veteran, exists on the fringes of society. He lives alone in a remote cabin addicted to a variety of drugs. At the other end of the spectrum, Congressman Whitehurst, the politically successful Vietnam Veteran, conveys a cold distance and an emotional detachment. The detectives continually look at him as a primary suspect who had the most to lose by his involvement in Carver's disappearance. As a Vietnam Veteran in a position of social power, he is portrayed as a threatening presence who impedes the investigation. The detectives continue to believe that "he's hiding something" even after Whitehurst is cleared of involvement in Carver's disappearance. The other Vietnam Veterans symbolize the brotherhood of the platoon, holding their allegiance to their fellow comrades even after many years of not seeing one another.

Even in present conceptions of the Vietnam Veteran, America cannot imagine him as anything other than a problematic and traumatized subject. By showing him as an absent, a nonexistent, or a failed father, it is easier to isolate him as the harbinger of America's unresolved memories of the Vietnam War than to address the structural implication of the war on American society (for example, how war may or may not affect family life). Carver represents the morally debilitated Vietnam Veteran and it is his actions in Vietnam that contain the corrupt actions attributed to the Vietnam Veteran. The image of the Vietnam Veteran in the show enforces the immorality not of the *war* so much as of the *men*, leaving the actual context of the Vietnam War as little more than incidental background to the social subject. But history is never incidental; "history... is that ghostly... totality that articulates and disarticulates itself and the subjects who inhabit it.... It is always a site of struggle and contradiction between the living and the ghostly" (Gordon, 1997, 184). The show's focus on Carver's immoral acts of killing a fellow soldier and attempting to rape a Vietnamese woman compels the viewer to focus on the (im)morality of the Vietnam Veteran rather than contemplate the ethical issues of the Vietnam War. In that fateful moment in Vietnam, Carver took a Vietnamese woman into the jungle to rape her. Lewis knew Carver's intentions were not good, and went into the jungle to stop him. Carver ended up killing Lewis after he confronted Carver. Sykes knew this and had been carrying this secret all those years. Like *Platoon* and *Born on the Fourth of July*, the struggles of war are expressed, not through the conflict with the enemy, but through and within the American Vietnam Veteran. America's ongoing nightmare of Vietnam may be rooted in structural meanings and causes of war, but it is imagined through the lacks of the individual men who fought there. In this episode, the image of the Vietnam Veteran still carries the traumatic baggage of the Vietnam War for us. Individual corruption and limitations of the Vietnam Veteran pervade public discourses of the Vietnam War. This show follows this public narration and leads the viewer to place the anxieties within the social monad onto Carver, the Vietnam Veteran.

The circumstances of Lewis's death touch all the Vietnam Veterans, the taint of Carver's actions permeating all of the representations of the Vietnam Veteran. They are not portrayed as heroes and citizens. Instead, they form an amalgamated image of the Vietnam Veteran, which is a damaged and fallible hero. Carver takes on the image of the morally corrupt Vietnam Veteran, whereas Sykes takes on the image of the morally weak Vietnam Veteran. Both of these men commit suicide in the show because of their involvement in the death of Lewis. Are their deaths an attempt as closure, a way to shatter the social monad's hardened carapace? I think not. Instead, this imagery succeeds in conjuring up the tensions at the heart of the social monad. But it does it in a way that diminishes the presence of the original event (the Vietnam War) for a new generation. The tension between the images of the Vietnam Veteran and the not-so-incidental context of the Vietnam War structures the way we watch the detectives solve the mystery of Carver's disappearance. The viewers, like the detectives, can stand apart from history as they watch the darkness of the Vietnam Veteran surface to the forefront of the plot. The other Vietnam Veterans easily take on the role of complicit actors in this dark moment of their service in Vietnam, augmenting the image of the Vietnam Veteran as the traumatized subject. It induces the viewer to focus on the corrupt actions and moral ambiguity of the Vietnam Veteran rather than recognizing the problematic aspects of the Vietnam War (and pursue questions about the reasons why the image of the Vietnam Veteran is a returning figure in popular culture).

Even after 30 years, the social imaginary does not know how to reimagine the Vietnam Veteran in order to face the trauma of the Vietnam War. As David Anderson comments in the introduction to the book, *Facing My Lai: Moving Beyond the Massacre*,[7]

> One of the most contentious questions has been whether My Lai was an aberration or an operation.... Does the moral burden fall on a few individuals, on the military and civilian chain of command,

or on the entire American way of war? How one answers these questions about the past determines how one lives with the traumatic memories of the present and guards against such disasters in the future. (1998, 6)

Considering the image of the Vietnam Veteran in popular culture, public discourse heavily relies on the individual subject—the Vietnam Veteran—to carry the moral burden of traumatic memories in the present. Rather than our popular memory engaging with the ghostly presence of Lewis in order to ask new questions about the Vietnam War and *guard against such disasters in the future*, public representations of the trauma of the Vietnam War erupt through the Vietnam Veteran. Social discourse returns to the Vietnam Veteran in moments of residual uncertainty about the presence of war in society (the show originally aired as the United States embarked on the war in Iraq), and even then we use it as a means of generating a tenuous resolution to irresolute aspects of war.[8] "The pressing problem of the present is the disjunction between historical rupture...and the remaking of subjects" (Gordon, 1997, 171). Ultimately, the image of the Vietnam Veteran in popular memory is made and remade through its relationship with America's struggle over the trauma of the Vietnam War. That is, the image of the Vietnam Veteran is made and remade as a traumatized subject who contains the historical rupture that the Vietnam War caused in the dominant fiction. All of this occurs within the perimeters of the social monad, enabling us to see it at work in social discourse. Unfortunately, social discourse struggles with the existence of the Vietnam War in modern society and has yet to find a way to resolve its presence in a way that moves beyond the image of the Vietnam Veteran as an object of derision and instability.

The Traumatic Return of the Prodigal Son

In the *Cold Case* episode titled "Revolution," which aired February 20, 2005, the rupture that the Vietnam War caused in the dominant fiction is more complexly represented in the image of the Vietnam Veteran and masculine subject in this show. Specifically, an analysis of the male characters reveal the variable ways in which the Vietnam War caused a break between the masculine subject and phallic identification. Centering on the renewed investigation into Eleanor McCormick's murder in 1969, the show engages with the social monad. Revisiting her death is a reentry into the wounds of the Vietnam War. The return of the primary suspect, Warren Cousins, to Philadelphia is the impetus behind the renewed investigation and emergence of the historical rupture that is at the heart of the social monad. Because Cousins represents the prodigal son/hippie-flouter (to use Faludi's terms), the show initiates an exploration of the social monad through the shifts taking place in the dominant fiction of phallic masculine subjectivity. Throughout the show, Cousins's presence disrupts and problematizes the Vietnam Veteran, uncovering his fallibility. Brian McCormick, Eleanor's brother, represents the Vietnam Veteran and her killer. It is through the images of the prodigal and good sons that the tensions in masculine subjectivity erupt.

As previously discussed in the work of Faludi, the good and prodigal sons are a significant component of the representations of the Vietnam Veteran and his antiwar counterpart in the social imaginary. Brian symbolizes the virtues of the good, working-class son who went to Vietnam and fought for his country. He returns damaged, though, and that physical damage is what plagues the image of the good son, giving us a visually tangible stigma that signifies far more than just the loss of his ability to walk. Warren is the prodigal son who and is part of the counterculture movement in that era. He sings in a rock-and-roll band, does drugs, and goes to Canada to avoid the draft. Refusing to go to Vietnam, he outwardly expresses his disagreement with American actions there. On the surface, these images emulate traditional stereotypes of the service men and antiwar activists of the Vietnam War. Warren's return, though, goes beyond a rearticulation of these traditional social markers. Not only is he a disruptive reminder of the unsolved murder of Eleanor (the feminine subject and symbol of home and domestic life), but his presence opens up unresolved issues of the Vietnam War also. His return reveals the permeation of the war's trauma through space and time. Over the course of the episode, though, the image of the Vietnam Veteran shifts, revealing cracks and fractures in the representations of all these masculine subjects and their struggle to claim phallic identification.

Initially, Brian (the Vietnam Veteran) appears as a pitiable subject, even as he symbolizes aspects of sacrifice and virtue. When coupled with the additional loss of his sister at that time, viewers cannot help but sympathize with him and his losses. As he tells the detectives when they first question him, "It's been most of my life now, but it never settles with ya—not being somebody's older brother anymore." But that is not the only thing that never settled with Brian. He returned from Vietnam a paraplegic and, at the outset, this constructs a tragic image. As the show unfolds, greater losses emerge that are key to his break with phallic masculinity, ultimately resulting in the murder of his sister. As the Vietnam Veteran, Brian represents the broken masculine subject, containing the fears and anxieties surrounding the war. The reactions to Brian's broken body are shown in a variety of ways over the course of the episode. Terry, another representation of the good, working-class son (and the husband of Eleanor's best friend), is mortified at the possibility of going to Vietnam. He says to Eleanor, "I'm flipped out. You know I'm going to 'Nam, right? El, I saw your brother during the wedding. Katy [Brian's girlfriend] lookin' around during the dance songs. Embarrassed to be with him. *That can't be me*" (my emphasis).

In another scene we watch the way Brian and Eleanor's parents refuse to talk about the damage to their good son. When Eleanor tries to ask her brother what the war was like, he tells her, "Muggy. Mosquitoes there like freakin' crows." When Eleanor persists, asking "How about the war part?" she is scolded by her mother and father and informed by Bud, her fiancé (at that time), "Ellie, if your brother wants to *brag*, he'll do it with me over beers" (my emphasis). The assumption that Brian's stories of the war would be heroic tales of bravery closes off the topic of the war as something traumatic and painful. This renders the topic of the Vietnam Veteran's experiences as taboo, especially for Eleanor, the feminine subject, and limited to stories full of bravado. This leaves the Vietnam Veteran isolated from domestic social life and unable to talk about the trauma of the war with most of the people around him—a common theme of the Vietnam Veteran's return home. Key to the traumatic presence of the Vietnam War in the show is the way in which the image of the Vietnam Veteran is unavoidably visible, yet the war itself is a taboo topic of discussion. Instead of focusing on the meanings and circumstances of the war, the viewer is shown images of the way the other characters negotiate the Vietnam Veteran's physical impairment. In addition to the interactions described above, the viewer sees how the Vietnam Veteran is dependent on others, requiring help with basic activities. For example, the viewer is shown his need for the assistance of his father to navigate his wheelchair in their home. These images, coupled with the visible discomfort his girlfriend displays when she is with him, separate the Vietnam Veteran from the other characters and distance him from the viewer. Like in the Vietnam Veteran Narrative, society imagines the Vietnam Veteran as a traumatized subject who cannot claim phallic identification.

Terry and Bud—both of whom represent variations of the good, working-class son—provide greater insight into the image of the Vietnam Veteran and the prodigal son, shifting the way we think about these forms of masculine subjectivity. Because Terry and Bud represent the good son who is *not* the Vietnam Veteran,[9] they provide a more nuanced image of the good son as it diverges from the Vietnam Veteran's distinct position in social monad of the Vietnam War. At the same time, Warren, the prodigal son, is considered suspect by the detectives. The hippie-flouter image is what incited the detectives' derision but it is the qualities of his seemingly progressive views on social issues (especially gender equality) that shift the image of the prodigal son into a more progressive "new" masculine subject. Juxtaposed next to the stereotypical images of provincial working-class masculinity that underlies the good son, Warren represents a more socially advanced masculine subject. In fact, he carries many of the qualities of the "new" father and masculine subject, reinforcing Hondagneu-Sotelo and Messner's assertion of the "New Man" being portrayed as sensitive and egalitarian (see endnote 3). Terry and Bud, as more typical working-class men, represent an outdated good son, who is antagonistic toward women. We learn that the feminine subject, Eleanor, had broken up with Bud before her death, leaving him for Warren who she identified as a freethinking man who let her see "she was better than this place [Philadelphia]." Viewers are presented with this appraisal of the "New Man" as they are shown Eleanor's best friend's bruised face—the victim of the working-class good son's (Terry's) abuse.

This intersection of images reinforces the transitions occurring in masculine subjectivity over the last 25 years. The good son appears backward and provincial—unable to acclimate to the shift in the feminine subject's social position. At the same time, the prodigal son is represented as a sophisticated masculine subject who more readily embraces changing gender relations. As the prodigal son-turned-new (father and) phallic masculine subject, Warren is portrayed as the more informed and conscientious man of the four male characters. Keep in mind, though, that these images do not necessarily convey the facts or realities of men's experiences. But these *deep structures of popular memory* express how social discourses *assign meaning to and reconstruct the past.* This means that although these images project a symbolic reality, that reality is always working with and against experiential reality shape meaning.

At the same time that the prodigal son displaces the good son's position within phallic masculinity, he dramatically fractures the Vietnam

Veteran's social presence. Through the prodigal son, the viewer becomes aware of ways in which the Vietnam Veteran falls into the social abyss. The prodigal son expresses a greater level of sensitivity to the Vietnam Veteran's situation; he is more willing to speak of the trauma the Vietnam Veteran carries than the two good sons who exhibit intense fear of the Vietnam Veteran's broken body. Warren suggested that Eleanor, when she expressed helplessness about her brother, "just talk to him," which she did. The prodigal son is also the one who recognized that Brian was addicted to heroin. In fact, he is the one who helps the Vietnam Veteran see his position in society more clearly by helping him detoxify from the drug. Coming off of heroin, Brian, the Vietnam Veteran becomes painfully aware of his fractured connection to phallic masculinity.

The final climax of this break occurs when the act of Eleanor's murder is revealed through a flashback. Watching Eleanor prepare to leave for Canada with Warren (she had decided to move to Canada with him), Brian's vulnerable connection to American society surfaces. For the Vietnam Veteran, the prospect of losing his sister (feminine subject and symbol of home and domestic life) to the prodigal son is a damaging blow to his shaky belief in the dominant fiction. The Vietnam Veteran's homecoming breaks down the suspended belief in the dominant fiction and the masculine subject's position within it. As he tells the detectives when he confesses to her murder, "Aw, God. For the first time in so long, I was clear. I could see right to tomorrow. And all the way down the line," and it is obvious that he does not like what he sees. The physical damage to his body is symbolic of the deeper breaks he sees in his position as a masculine subject. While he tells Eleanor that "I don't work how men do," he means this at a level that goes deeper than his physical potency. When Eleanor tells him, "Brian that's not what a man is. It's how you treat [women]. How you love them," he tells her, "Ohh, but that's where it's all rotten." In that moment, the viewer understands that his physical damage is a portal into the darkness plaguing him on the inside. He explains,

> That little girl who [wounded me]. She recognized me. That's why. Because we went into her hut and we dragged out her parents and her grandparents and we threw them in a bunker and tossed in a grenade. She finds me later. So starving, she's probably 40 pounds wet. And all I was thinking was I should've killed her too. El, you are the only one I can tell these things to.

Terrified by his confession, Eleanor tries to console him, but he lashes out at her, saying "But you don't know, okay. Because you get to leave and *forget* and I am stuck here. What about me?" (my emphasis).

Brian *is* stuck. The Vietnam Veteran is an isolated social subject trapped by the memories of the war. The moral quandaries of war and of America's actions in Vietnam (and the idealism we took there) are all contained in the Vietnam Veteran's painful confession of not only his actions in Vietnam but also in his violence against his sister. As the Vietnam Veteran lunges at Eleanor (again, the feminine subject and symbol of home and the domestic world) from his wheelchair, strangling her, the (impossible) resolution between the trauma of war and civilian life is finalized. In that moment of killing his sister all he can say is "I'm stuck! I'm stuck! I'm stuck!" The meaning behind Brian's comment that *it never settles with ya—not being somebody's older brother anymore* takes on a dark irony that captures the way his actions reach beyond his position as Eleanor's brother, extending into his position as a Vietnam Veteran—and expressions of *the image of the bleary-eyed veteran carrying all that emotional baggage for us*. In that moment, it is vital to understand that the other good sons recovered from the Vietnam War in ways the Vietnam Veteran could not.

But Brian is not the only one stuck in the trauma of the Vietnam War; American social discourse is trapped as well. We as a culture impart these meanings into the Vietnam Veteran through public discourse. The Vietnam Veteran may be carrying the baggage of the Vietnam War in popular memory but we are all a part of the war's irresolution in society. "The ghost cannot be simply tracked back to an individual [subject's] loss or trauma" (Gordon, 1997, 183); it is a part of the social world in which we live. The effects of trauma are not the Vietnam Veteran's alone, even though America articulates its unresolved memories of the Vietnam War onto him. Brian, the Vietnam Veteran, has been *stuck* in trauma and his body since he returned from Vietnam. Although he managed to create a life for himself after he killed his sister, he stayed trapped in that moment, not unlike he was trapped in his body. We are flashed back to his act in 1969 and returned to the present to see this man, now in his 50s, living out that bleak future he forecasted. He continues to be *stuck*. From the little bit that we see of his current life, the Vietnam Veteran is visibly unhappy and alone. He works the night shift, because he cannot sleep at night. He still lives in his parents' house, although they are no longer there (we do not know if they died or moved). There is no sign of him having a family of any sort. Eleanor, the ghostly feminine subject, has been living on as an unresolved break between his life and the domestic world, her death the result of the traumatic event of the Vietnam War. The act of murdering that part of his life that provided a glimmer of connection to the domestic world of America secured his break with the dominant fiction. He destroyed her, turning her into a victim of his damaged self.

The feminine subject and all that she represents is the victim of the masculine subject's impossible recovery. Eleanor is intimately tangled in the struggle of the masculine subject's reclamation of phallic identification. But that effort failed for the Vietnam Veteran and as much as she was muted by his trauma, he was consumed by it. Neither of their lives were the same—nor was America. Brian—the Vietnam Veteran—was/is not the only one paying the price for the trauma of the Vietnam War. Eleanor—the feminine subject and symbol of home and civilian life—was caught between shifting images of masculine subjectivity and had to make a choice about how to envision her own relationship to the dominant fiction. While we might try to believe that by uncovering Eleanor's killer we recovered in some way from the trauma of the war, this could not be further from the truth. The show provides insight into how all the people suffered from the trauma of the Vietnam War. The other men also are stricken by the impact of the war on masculine subjectivity but, in the end, it is the Vietnam Veteran who still carries the greatest weight of those memories in the American imaginary. The other men *seem* to have recovered. They found a way to reconnect with phallic masculinity and establish their belief in the dominant fiction but they were not unaffected by the traumatic effects of the Vietnam War on our narrative of phallic masculine subjectivity. What makes their recovery possible is (in part) the discursive containment of this traumatic event in the Vietnam Veteran. The fact that America still looks to the Vietnam Veteran as the symbol and carrier of that trauma reveals how difficult it is for the dominant fiction to recognize the complexity of the Vietnam War's presence in current society.

Although the focus on the Vietnam Veteran may provide momentary comfort from the trauma of the Vietnam War, trauma and memory are not that simple. In this journey through the traumatic break that occurred in the event of the Vietnam War, viewers discover that old wounds did not heal; they only lay waiting to be revisited. As the returns to the event of trauma, our understanding of the event becomes more complicated. The deeper we explore the more difficult and painful questions we uncover about ourselves and what we value and believe in under the dominant fiction of America. Although masculine subjectivity is radically destabilized, social discourse cannot go too much further without running the risk of surfacing more difficult questions about the shifting meanings of hegemonic masculine subjectivity and the expectations and demands it carries for men trying to recover phallic identification. Ultimately, social discourse resettles into the image of the traumatized Vietnam Veteran in order to contain the irreconcilable demands (e.g., the tensions between traditional and new father/masculine subject) placed upon the masculine subject. And we can only wonder how many more women and family members are silenced by the need to maintain and contain belief in the dominant fiction.

Encountering the Human Legacy

Images such as these leave the men and women I interviewed struggling to defend their fathers as individuals. Caught between the image of the Vietnam Veteran in popular memory and the men who are part of their lives, the interviewees must navigate between the crystallized public representation of the Vietnam Veteran and the dense reality of their intersubjective relationships with their fathers. The troubled public images of the Vietnam Veteran leave the interviewees with the unenviable task of narrating the disjuncture between those images and the experiences with their fathers that contradict and problematize those images. This compels some of my interviewees to narrate an ideal image of their father, asserting their fathers' sacrifices and willingness to do anything for them as they confound the public representation of the Vietnam Veteran as a social subject incapable of living a normal life. They rely on images of the Vietnam Veteran as their point of departure. By re-narrating and renegotiating the Vietnam Veteran and the Father, they attempt to dispel crystallized public representations of the Vietnam Veteran by focusing on their fathers' strengths and what they know of him as a father, defining him as an honorable man and honorable soldier. The effect is to generate a new narrative that can tenuously be called the Vietnam Veteran Father.

Looking at the ideals surrounding the Father and masculine subjectivity in the context of problematic images of the Vietnam Veteran still present in American media provokes a number of questions about the way the trauma of the event is displaced and crystallized within the Vietnam Veteran. The anxieties surrounding masculine subjectivity that took hold in the event of the Vietnam War are projected onto the Vietnam Veteran in popular media. He carries the problems of the war, not just in the context of our political motives for the Vietnam War, but also in the way we do not know how to manage the shifting context of masculine subjectivity that broke down during that era. Although Sturken asserts that the survival narrative of the Vietnam Veteran "retrieves and refigures traditional notions of masculinity and warriorhood" (1997, 255), it is not the Vietnam Veteran alone who engages in this process. It is as much a personal process as it is a cultural process; this is similarly the case with COVV.

For example, Ted's narrative clearly counters these images. Describing his father as "intelligent, positive, and not a complainer," Ted emphasized repeatedly how his father always has a positive outlook, even in regard to his war experiences. He explained that the

> war gave my dad a kind of general philosophy about things. And I think for the most part, maybe a lot of veterans—and this may just be my perception—kind of have a negative view of the situation they were put in and everything like that. And if my father looks at it from a negative standpoint, he's turned it into a positive thing. Where he's kind of always taught us to only worry about those things that you can control. You know, don't be a complainer— that kind of thing.

He stresses how his father turned the negativity of the war and stigma it held into something positive, unlike *other* veterans. Ted not only idealizes his father, he separates him from the *other* Vietnam Veterans, who had more difficulty recovering from the moral ambiguities of the war. He not only tries to separate his father from the symbol of the Vietnam Veteran but also from other veterans who have not been able to find positive meanings in their experiences in Vietnam. According to Ted, his father valued his life after returning from Vietnam, appreciating the things he had. "I think that experience has taught him, you know, don't be a complainer no matter how bad the situation is. Nothing could be as bad as somebody wanting to kill you for a year."

The contest over meanings of the Vietnam War creates a complex set of interrelations the least of which is COVV's struggle to navigate between the cultural articulations of the Vietnam Veteran and their intersubjective relationship with their fathers. COVV find themselves relying on an ideal image of their fathers to rehabilitate the Vietnam Veteran, revealing that traditional images of masculinity and warriorhood may be a response to the deeply ambivalent treatment of the

Vietnam Veteran in cultural discourse. Whether or not they actually adhere to these images in their own conceptualizations and performance of gender is less clear and alerts us to the complexity involved in the second generation's understanding of gendered subjectivity. Family is a significant force in these interviewees' lives and their fathers are deeply twined into their conceptions of family, gender, and nation. We can look at Mark's claim that his father is a *true American* and Ted's focus on how his father taught him to *not be a complainer* as ways of retrieving their fathers from the moral abyss within which the Vietnam Veteran exists in the cultural imaginary. We can also assess the idealization that Stacey, Tammy, and Tara hold about their fathers' ability to provide and sacrifice for them as a way to humanize their fathers. In both cases, the interviewees try to recapture traditional notions of the Father and masculine subjectivity in order to convey the love and honor they have experienced with their father. Even if this belies larger historical truths surrounding the war in general or their father's personal actions in Vietnam in particular, the power and strength of the intersubjective relationship these interviewees have with their fathers cannot be underestimated. As we turn to more ambiguous narrations of the father and Vietnam Veteran, the bond between my interviewees and their fathers never falters. What happens, though, is that it becomes harder and harder to maintain an ideal image of the Father, which leads us to further questions about the Vietnam Veteran and Vietnam War.

CHAPTER FIVE

Narrative Disruptions of the Dominant Fiction

Engaging with the Ghost of Traumatic History

Gordon reminds us that "we are part of the story, for better or worse: the ghost must speak to me in some way sometimes similar to, sometimes distinct from how it may be speaking to others" (1997, 24). As we discovered in chapter four, intergenerational narratives of trauma rely on the fixed form of the Father to reimagine the negative public representations of the Vietnam Veteran and Vietnam War that permeates the social imaginary. As will become clear in this chapter, some of the interviewees refuse to reimagine the Vietnam Veteran and Vietnam War, instead questioning the fixed form of the Father. The variability of the ways in which children of Vietnam Veterans (COVV) work through their relationship with their fathers as they address public representations of the Vietnam Veteran and Vietnam War in society demonstrates the dynamism at work within the social monad. That COVV rely on these societal images as they navigate their relationships with their fathers alerts us to the way historically traumatic events are inscribed into the intersubjective dynamics of individuals' daily life. Being part of the story of the Vietnam War, these interviewees raise questions about images of the Father and the Vietnam Veteran in American society. Focusing on their narrative negotiations of these categories enables me to analyze issues surrounding masculine subjectivity and its reified position of power in the dominant fiction. What emerges from this analysis is that the deeper belief structures of American society—in this case, hegemonic gendered identity structures that constitute the dominant fiction—are not as solid and impenetrable as represented in the dominant fiction. The interviewees in this section negotiate crystallized aspects of the Vietnam Veteran and the Father, enabling an analysis of the way these fixed social forms intersect with the more fluid and in-formation aspects of lived experience. The interviewees recognize the presence of these social forms but life experiences alter their meanings and effects on their lives. The presence of the ghost of the Vietnam War enters their narratives in variable ways that lead to shifting questions about what it means to be part of a shared public memory where stories overlap and change as they are read against one another. Reading these narratives through the lens of the traumatic event of the Vietnam War upbraids the stories that the dominant fiction tells us about the Father and the Vietnam Veteran.

Although Bissell commented that "at every meal Vietnam sat down, invisibly, with our families" (2004, 57), this does not mean that the war sat down in the same way for all my interviewees. Speaking to them through their fathers and through public discourses, the ghost of the Vietnam War is not received and engaged with in the same way by interviewees. This can make the analysis a bit unsettling but it reminds us how, although trauma and history are part of all of the lives of my interviewees (and other COVV), it does not look or feel the same. The social monad may have a static shape but the complex relationships working within it are fluid and shifting, undermining any single formula for tracing the motions of social life. My interviewees tell me stories of the Vietnam War, Vietnam Veteran, and Father that change and shift under the weight of their intersubjective relationship with their fathers. *As these stories overlap they change.* Here I tell their stories, drawing them together in order to build a greater understanding of how deeply interconnected and intensely particular the relationship between the individual and the social is. Through these narratives, we can rethink the presence of such overwrought social categories as the Father and the Vietnam Veteran that produce the gaps that exist between social belief structures and intersubjective relationships. In this chapter, I dig deeper into COVV's narratives to understand the contradictory and conflicting ways the Vietnam War moves through individuals, breaking down our conceptions of the chronological ordering of time and history.

The ossified images of the Father and Vietnam Veteran, which grounded the narratives in chapter four, continue to move through these interviewees' narratives. The images shift, though, demonstrating the work involved in developing narratives in and around structured forms of social life. Many of the interviewees had a variety of experiences with their fathers that prevented them from holding on to an untainted belief in the black and white imagery embedded in societal ideas and structures. Reading their narratives, then, requires an attention to the haunting nature of the structure of feeling as a tool for understanding how COVV navigate the rocky terrain existing between the Father and the Vietnam Veteran in the context of their experiences with *their* fathers. Their intersubjective relationships with their fathers—the deeply emotional affective impulses that generate intimate relationships—capture the struggles in working between definitive categorizations of lived experience and the dynamics of the unstable motions continually at work throughout our seemingly mundane life experiences, all of which define and shape the social monad of the Vietnam War. As Raymond Williams explains,

> We are talking about characteristic elements of impulse, restraint, and tone; specifically affective elements of consciousness and relationships: not feeling against thought, but thought as felt and feeling as thought: practical consciousness of a present kind, in a living and interrelating continuity. We are then defining these elements as a "structure": as a set, with specific internal relations, at once interlocking and in tension. (1977, 132)

The structure of feeling as discussed by Williams, and which I developed in chapter two, opens up a recognition of the *living and interrelating continuity* at work between the persistent presence of the historically traumatic event of the Vietnam War and the *practical consciousness* of a present life being lived in all its layered complexity. While all my interviewees live a complex life in which they must navigate between ideological structures and contradicting life experiences, the interviewees' narratives in this section more explicitly rely on contingent modes of understanding the way the Vietnam Veteran pokes through their conceptions of the Father, capturing the way social experience is actively lived and felt through, against, and within our conceptions of fixed social forms.

From going through family tragedies such as the death of a sibling and mother, to watching their father deteriorate before their eyes from alcoholism, these interviewees must restructure the systems of belief that permeate society to develop a coherent narrative of their fathers; that is, they must negotiate between the unformed present and the unassailable past that holds the trauma of the Vietnam War. The disillusionment, disappointment, and irresolution they experience in their lives with their fathers are mediated by his status as a Vietnam Veteran.

In particular, having this historically traumatic event as a focal point from which they can engage with their father's weaknesses and vulnerabilities allows these interviewees to retrieve a sense of meaning in the structures dominating social life. The dominant fiction is a far-reaching story of belief that permeates the way these men and women understand masculine subjectivity. As we saw in chapter four, the father's presence in the family—in its traditional form—is a strong guiding structure in my interviewees' narratives. The patterns of belief in the ways in which the masculine subject—the Father—is the purveyor of social life continually returned in these men and women's narratives even as they struggled against the constraints imposed by those ideals. Structuring my analysis around the point where my interviewees' discussions of their fathers touch on the aspects of the Father, the Vietnam Veteran, and the hero allows me to interrogate how these crystallized structures work as interlocking identity categories defining the masculine subject's position in the dominant fiction of America. In this chapter, I reinforce the way these structures animate individual social presence, even though most people can never live up to the ideological structures that so deeply ground us into the social world. It is at once frustrating and yet quite understandable that the Father and family have maintained a relatively static existence in the social imaginary even as so many variations of patterns emerge from the lived experiences of those unable or unwilling to fit into the ideals. Whether or not one wants to see oneself in the ideals constituting social forms, they seep into the individuals' narratives as they struggle to either affirm or negate their presence in their lives. As Gordon assesses,

> A structure of feeling is not the subjective or the personal as we have conventionally understood them as a self-contained other of the sociological object. A structure of feeling is precisely that conception, or sensuous knowledge, of a historical materialism characterized by the tangle of the subjective and the objective, experience and belief, feeling and thought, the immediate and the general, the personal and the social. (1997, 200)

Objective and subjective experience are not mutually exclusive; they are tangled into a sensuous knowledge that cannot be easily categorized or inserted into binaristic structures of social analysis. Through this analysis of my interviewees' narratives, we can read the way the Vietnam War marks my interviewees' relationships with their fathers (and life experiences), making it impossible to disentangle their subjective experiences from historical objectivism. Because the Vietnam War has such a peculiar and extensive presence, it is more easily discernible in the subjective experiences of my interviewees. The articulation of the trauma for the second generation is laden with the layers of a previously inscribed history that is itself constituted in and through a dominant fiction that relies heavily upon patriarchal structures of masculinity and family. This, in turn, is inflected onto these men and women's narratives as they seek explanations for the significance of this historical event in their lives. The traumatic implications and realities of this event are a vital component of their narratives and create a point of reference for my interviewees' discussions. The traumatic consequences of the ghost of Vietnam sitting down with these interviewees include the dislocation of aspects of the ideals surrounding the Father and Vietnam Veteran as they simultaneously disturb the masculine subject's *manifest destiny, supplementing and suspending the lack-in-being* that constitutes the fragility of his social position in the dominant fiction. This is a critical point and one that requires our attention if we are to understand historically traumatic events beyond the perimeters of traumatic repetition.

(Re)Structuring Feeling:Incomplete Erasures and Narrative Inscriptions of the Heroic Father

[My father] was in the hospital when they gave [the Purple Heart] to him. And just this sense of huge loss. And it was much more than his leg. So much more than his leg. Just like a loss of a dream—kind of. [...] And I think his hopefulness, in a sense, [that] he could go over and make a difference and come back and be wounded and knowing that he didn't feel like he made much of a difference at all. (Renee)

The narratives of Samantha, Renee, and Danny emerge from their inability to maintain strict lines between their lives and the meanings of heroism and the Father that the dominant fiction inscribes on phallic masculinity. Yet, they rely on them in ways that enable a reworking of the meanings of those categorical structures that deeply affect social conceptions of the traumatic event of the Vietnam War. In this section, I explore the confrontation that develops between structured patterns of belief constituting the hero and the Father within the dominant fiction of America and the residue of the traumatic break that occurred in these structures due to the Vietnam War. What emerges from these interviewees' discussions of their father is a reconceptualization of what it means to be a hero and father with physical and emotional strength. The structure of feeling provides a guidepost by which to analyze the way lived experience intersects and cuts through fixed social forms of understanding. The result is a tension between the easily discerned structures of society and their more in-formation counterparts in my interviewees' narratives. This creates a struggle that invites our recognition of, re-invoking Williams's words, *thought as felt and feeling as thought*. The palimpsest provides a metaphorical frame of sight through which we can discern the layers of inscripted past(s) that never entirely disappear from our sense of self in the world. We see (in a variety of experiential ways) the shadowy remnants of a past that insists on its presence in the lives of individuals such as my interviewees. Converging with a not-quite-present reality, the historically traumatic event becomes part of that yet-to-be-understood present that the interviewees struggle to articulate in their narratives.

The Vietnam Veteran has never been conceived as a hero within the perimeters of socially prescribed views of war and heroism. Public discourse's frequent default to the troubled hero and marginalized masculine subject leaves present conceptions of the Vietnam Veteran marred by the image of a socially castrated and defective masculine subject. True to the Vietnam Veteran Narrative, O'Brien poignantly tells us how he felt the Vietnam War had stripped him of his values and dreams.

> This little field [in Vietnam], I thought, had swallowed so much. My best friend. My pride. My belief in myself as a man of some small dignity and courage.... I'd seemed to grow cold inside, all the illusions gone, all the old ambitions and hopes for myself sucked away into the mud. Over the years, that coldness had never entirely disappeared.... For twenty years this field had embodied all the waste that was Vietnam, all the vulgarity and horror. (1990, 184–5)

Revisiting Vietnam with his daughter, they went to the place—a small field in Vietnam—where he watched his friend die. As he explained, he lost much more than his friend: he lost his beliefs about what it meant to be a man. This break experienced by the narrator of the Vietnam Veteran Narrative is managed in the different ways my interviewees recognize and integrate that break into their own narratives. While the interviewees in chapter four wanted to connect their fathers to the traditional imagery of a heroic Father (within which the Vietnam Veteran had to be socially reimagined), Renee and the other interviewees in this section made no such attempt in their narratives. Renee (discussed above in chapter three and in more detail below) understands that her father's losses, like O'Brien's, were immense and that heroism is not just a symbol of guts and glory. Vietnam was where her father lost *much more than [the use of] his leg*. She discusses how her father had gone into the Marines to fight in Vietnam because he wanted to do something important and meaningful but his wounded leg crushed his hopes for having a career in the Marines. He could not go to candidate school because of his disabled leg and she reflects on how sad it made her feel that her father's dreams were lost in Vietnam. Her sensitivity to that loss reminds her of the costs of war on individual people, complicating traditional understandings of heroism. As is discussed below, this sensitivity left her with a desire to prevent her father from being associated with negative public representations of the Vietnam Veteran even though she was unwilling to do this by idealizing who he is or what that service did to him as a person. She "gives notice, not, for example, to the cold influence of a given and discernible ideology or class structure upon individual thinking, but rather to the proceeding looming present" (Gordon, 1997, 198). That *looming present* evokes the recognition of how strong a person Renee's father became (to her) in light of the losses he experienced in Vietnam. Renee reflects on and questions the costs of war through her recognition of her father's losses, rather than through a *denial* of their presence. As such, her narrative can be read as an articulation of presence that negotiates the noble hero within her father's individual life trajectory. Her articulation of the intersubjective relationship she has with her father dislodges the cold ideology of crystallized belief structures, revealing how a hero is far more complicated than the impervious John Wayne image that was such an influence on the Vietnam Veteran and the social imaginary. Although Bissell commented that "heroes are uncomplicated," throughout this section (and chapter) we see how the reality of living with a war veteran upbraids such static societal images of an *uncomplicated* belief structure.

Troubling such images and narrating an alternative story of the heroic Father is a significant task that underlies these interviewees' narratives. However, the societal image of the Vietnam Veteran and history of the Vietnam War never entirely fade. Samantha, Renee, and Danny initiate us into how the past, in the context of present intersubjective relations, intercedes on their relationships with their fathers. In their narratives, the Vietnam Veteran is a complex social category that continually reminds us of the incomplete and irresolute nature of intersubjective relationships. The dominant fiction of the heroic Father is always present but never simply or purely incorporated into their narratives. Samantha, Renee, and Danny help me begin this analytical journey through the tracings of broken and fragmented inscriptions of social life, descending into the tumult of beliefs surrounding the masculine subject as imagined through the heroic Father. The Vietnam Veteran is a precarious category that necessitates the interviewees' exploration of the stress and strain that ideal categories of social existence place on our intersubjective relationships. Under this strain something emerges that is not a pure upholding of hegemonic structures nor is it an entirely new way of understanding the social world. Instead, it is a recognition of *sensuous knowledge*, "a different kind of materialism, neither idealistic nor alienated, but an active practice" (Gordon, 1997, 205) that underscores how lived experience relies on *and* departs from past trauma to open up a complex reading of social life.

Samantha and Renee: Articulating Presence

Samantha and Renee generated distinctive narratives of their father that could not sustain the ideals of the heroic warrior, even as they constructed their discussions around the deep care and admiration that they held for their father. As discussed in chapter three, these two sisters had very different ways of articulating their relationships with their father and his experiences in Vietnam. Although they shared the central facts of their father's war experiences, each woman had her own unique way of managing that knowledge. In particular, Samantha's narrative revolved around her deep pride and admiration for her father. She did not veer from that image even as she took a very critical stance regarding her father's ways of dealing with his memories of war. Renee's narrative was structured around the deep emotional connection she felt toward her father and her lucid recognition of suffering mediated by her own desire to defend him and make his dark life happier and lighter. She continually focused on this even as she held a great deal of frustration with her father for his forceful opinions and stubborn behaviors. Each woman retains an impenetrably idealistic view of her father's strengths and capacities in their narratives even as they continually negotiate this view with criticisms and questions about what those ideals have meant to their father and family.

As we learned earlier, Samantha and Renee had to watch their father's impervious Marine persona break down under the weight of the loss of their sister. More so than Renee, Samantha was uncertain how to articulate the vulnerability she saw in her father during that time without relying on the negative imagery of the Vietnam Veteran. *The crazy* image of the Vietnam Veteran allowed her a momentary respite from the incommensurability of her father's weakness with the stoic and strong masculine ideal her father represented to her throughout her life. That momentary break, while articulated as a blip in their father's typically sound and stable demeanor, is a point of focus that enables them to take a detour down the route of trauma that is so difficult to navigate in our day-to-day experiences. As they venture down this road we start to understand that the ideal Father is a problematic reality.

In their narratives, Samantha and Renee rely on notions of the heroic Father in order to explore their father's actions over the course of their lives. Samantha is particularly ambivalent to the meanings of her father's service in her life, even though she holds a great deal of respect and pride for him. Her reverence emerges out of more than his service: it emerges out of a combination of his service and the way he structured his life after he came home.

> I actually talk about my father with a great deal of pride because of the fact that he went through such hell even before he got into Vietnam and then had such a horrible time in Vietnam and has managed to have a successful career, raise three kids, [...] have a nice home, and all the rest of that.

For Samantha, the life her father built for himself and her family is what enabled her to talk about him with such honor and high regard. She knows that he had to overcome numerous obstacles to create this life, but she is unwilling to end her assessments there. She considers how his experiences in Vietnam shaped his desire to build a life that neutralized the stereotype of the socially damaged Vietnam Veteran. So rather than generate an unbending image of her father as the ideal breadwinner, she explained how he desired the perfect family life, building something better than he had experienced in his life.

> And I know when he met my mom and they dated for a while, he was so bound and determined. He wanted to get married and he just wanted to start his life. [...] They were married nine months from the day they met. That's how eager my father was to have a life and have a family. And I think that he liked the idea that she came from a big family because to him it meant stability. It meant the all–American pie dream, you know, what his life lacked.

Ultimately, his longing for a stable life put pressure on all of them to live up to his ideal of the *all–American pie dream*. As an adult with a family of her own, she was able to reflect on why he might have been such a perfectionist and held her and her sister up to nearly impossible expectations. She explained, "I think these guys [Vietnam Veterans] need[ed] stability. [...] Maybe they, they just needed something to hold on to. [...] They wanted to wake up next to someone in the morning, you know. They wanted a future because the past sucked so bad." Samantha and Renee understood that the perfect image was just that—an image—and as a result of his desire for stability they felt they had been subject to a great deal of rules and regulations that ranged from having quarters bounced off of their bed after they made it to eating their dinners in prescribed order and sequence on their plate. They had firsthand experience of the disquieting reality of maintaining an image of the perfect family.

Neither woman painted her growing up as ideal, each drawing the conclusion that her father held on to an idyllic family image so tightly that it caused problems for them. Renee emphasized how she and Samantha

> always had to be very strong. And we—that was just a given and I think that's part of his. I think that's kind of part of what's been sewn into his life but also, you know, life is not for the weak. We're not weak people. And yet, you know after [my sister] died, we had to be strong and he was the weakest person.

The strength *sewn into his life* was the result of his ability to overcome the trauma of war. Yet, that strength was not static or infallible. Although *life was not meant for the weak*, Renee saw firsthand how such strength comes at a price and is never unbroken or unflawed. Seeing her father's weakness led her to comprehend with a great deal of sensitivity the complex way he presented himself to the world. The expectations he held for his children were the same expectations he held for himself; yet, he could not live out that image any better than Renee or Samantha could. Renee realized that much of his life was filled with disappointments and that he did not want her and Samantha to experience similar pain and loss.

Renee, as mentioned above, complicates the social image of the heroic Father by engaging in a discussion of the emotional strife her father experienced when he came home wounded. Her narrative of her father, while it can be read as a disruption of the heroic Father, also can be interpreted as an attempt to separate him from the public representation of the Vietnam Veteran. She explained that she experiences "a little bit of defensiveness [...]. I think people are really quick to judge and very quick to make opinions and speak opinions without necessarily doing some background [...]. And I think a lot of it is defensiveness." Her defensiveness is, in part, a response to other's (and arguably her own) reliance on public representations of the Vietnam Veteran that she believes denies her father a more complex social existence. It is also the result of her father's adamant responses to his daughters' development of their own opinions and ideas about the war. She explained how difficult it was to talk with him about war, particularly the Vietnam War, and he made them feel like they could never understand. And if they could not understand, they had no right to formulate an opinion that diverged from his. Renee explained that

> if you went back and said, "In Vietnam they did this," [he would respond], "You don't know anything about it. You have no right. You know I thought I raised you to be a good Republican," you know. Well, no, you raised me to think for myself. [...] So there were all these contexts where suddenly he couldn't tell us what we thought about Vietnam and his experience and everything.

She was very open about talking about the struggles she and Samantha had with their father as he lost the ability to place his ideas onto his children. At the same time, Renee emphasized how even though he was/is so strong-willed and opinionated, he taught her and Samantha to be the same way. In this regard, her own protectiveness of her father and his position as a Vietnam Veteran is not unlike her father's stake in ownership of the war experience. When she states that people need to do some "background" research on the Vietnam War before passing judgment on those personally involved in the war, she is referring to formal knowledge, but she is also intimating how living with her father, a Vietnam Veteran provides an even fuller picture of the meanings of the Vietnam War than others might be capable of seeing or knowing. With greater analysis and discernment, she holds a similar stand to Tammy, who felt that being a child of a Vietnam Veteran helped her *know more about the war than anybody else would—any normal person would.* Renee, though, explores what it means in her narrative without relying on crystallized images of the heroic Father—or her father's views.

Renee explained that as she matured, she gained a broader knowledge base of the world around her than when she was a child; this created numerous tensions between her and her father that continues to underlie their relationship. There is some unwillingness on her part to maintain a perfect picture of her family life. She emphasized how he had expressed moments of weakness as they grew up. But that weakness was mediated by her recognition of the struggles she felt he has gone through in his life. Samantha also identified her relationship with her father and her existence as a child of a Vietnam Veteran as one that left her managing life issues (similar to her father's) in alternative ways from her father. While this is not unusual in any individual's desire to understand their relationship with their father and family, she particularly focused on the Vietnam War's impact on her father and subsequent layers of effects on her own life.

> He had so little control at that point in his life. You know, he had bedsores, it's unbelievable, in traction in a VA hospital. [...] They weren't rotating him enough. His leg was up in traction. It's a really bad, a really bad scene. And he had so little control that when he finally felt like it was *his* life and he could control it, he wanted control. And so that's my—as a child of a Vietnam Veteran—that's my challenge today. Making sure I can live a really good satisfying life and be happy without—control does not equal happiness. [...] Finding that happiness without feeling like I have to control things. (my emphasis)

This was a major concern for Samantha because she saw herself as so much like her father. Samantha felt she had a similar hardness in her outlook on the world in addition to her need to control all aspects of her life. While Renee focused on the inner and social complexity of her father, Samantha emphasized her father's perseverance, which had been necessitated by the numerous obstacles he faced in his life. Samantha felt she, too, had been through a lot, giving her a similar outlook on life.

> You know what's funny about my dad—and he's given me some of this. As far as, uhm, as a belief system and it's gonna sound hardcore when I say this. And maybe it is. I mean I am an empathetic person. I've been through a lot and I'm empathetic. And maybe in some ways what we've been through made me cold too. Like, there are worse things that can happen, you know, get-over-it type thing.

For Samantha, there is a sense that the world will always hand you struggles but that one must move through those obstacles and carry on with one's life. She was very practical-minded in her feelings about how the world is not a perfect place. By watching her father deal with the need to make what she identified as an imperfect world *picture perfect*, she learned this was a self-defeating way of living *her* life, and as a result could not articulate her father's life or his status as a Vietnam Veteran with blind idealism. "Yeah, so [Vietnam Veterans are] branded as the losers. They lost the war; they're the losers. Maybe that's why our fathers were so eager to do so well and have the perfect life, maybe to disprove the loser label, you know." At the same time, she does not sway in her admiration for him. "And when I describe my father to people that's—if someone asks me anything about him—that's one of the first things I say about him. You know, he's a really strong individual, he's been through a lot and he was in Vietnam, so that's how I identify him."

Throughout Samantha and Renee's narratives, a never-ending motion between managing an ideal image of their father and dismantling that ideal dominates the rhythm and flow of their articulations of their father and of presence.

> And thus we come to the core of the conceptual comprehension that is not only the structure of an affective social experience and consciousness, but also the spellbinding material relations of exchange between the defined and the inarticulate, the seen and the invisible, the known and the unknown. (Gordon, 1997, 200)

The struggle to understand the relationship between these binaristic extremes is a continual struggle for the interviewees as they work back and forth between the myriad encounters they have with both the most discernible aspects of social life and the subtler, yet no less influential, dynamics of the living present—presence.

Danny: Interrogating the Link between the Heroic Father and Phallic Identification

> There might be this heightened awareness of sort of patterns like that—that you see and you might say there is something wrong. It might be more skeptical. It might be a little more, uhm, less trusting. (Danny)

For Danny, being a child of a Vietnam Veteran is not something that he narrates with an ideal view of the honor of the military or service. More so than Renee and Samantha, Danny expresses feelings of skepticism regarding the government and its motivations for actions such as war.

To speak of masculinity in general, sui generis, must be avoided at all costs. It is as a discourse of self-generation, reproduced over the generations in patrilineal perpetuity, that masculinity seeks to make a name for itself.... It must be our aim not to deny or disavow masculinity, but to disturb its manifest destiny—to draw attention to it as a prosthetic reality—a "prefixing" of the rules of gender and sexuality; an appendix or addition, that willy-nilly, supplements and suspends a "lack-in-being" (Bhabha, 1995, 57).

An analysis of Danny's narrative of his father and his service produces many questions about masculine subjectivity and how the social monad of the Vietnam War interjects in the *manifest destiny* of the masculine subject's phallic identification. In his narrative, Danny is critical of the *patterns* the government promotes that produce uncritically patriotic views of war. His critique of these patterns can be located and analytically approached as an underlying tension between Danny's narration of his father's management of trauma and Danny's negotiation of the meanings of masculine subjectivity.

There are two major components of Danny's narrative that enable me to question the relationship between the way he articulates his father's war trauma and how issues of masculine subjectivity fold into those expressions. First are his father's frank and open discussions of his experiences in Vietnam with Danny and his sister. Second, Danny's family experienced a major transition when his mother died from a chronic disease when Danny was 16. As a result of these events and interactions, mystification of the war and constructions of the heroic Father are impossible for him to maintain throughout his narrative. Reading Danny's narrative of these experiences with his father, we can frame his articulation of his father as an attempt to recompense his father's connection to phallic identification, providing Danny with a belief in America even as he critiques aspects of the dominant fiction. Initiating the description of his family and father with similar idealism to the interviewees in chapter four, Danny states that his home life "was like the Cleavers. My mother stayed home, my father worked; we had a dog [laughs], you know. [...] I mean it was very idyllic. He was the provider for our family." As his narration of his father progresses, Danny continues to inscribe his father's personal and financial success but these aspects of his father are muted by his discussions of his father's openness about his experiences in Vietnam and the frustration Danny expresses about the way his father dealt with his mother's death.

Danny was the only interviewee to express that his father was candid in his discussions of his war experiences. In fact, Danny brought pictures to the interview that his father had given him, explaining that his father had often shown them the pictures in a slideshow presentation—much like one would show his/her friends after returning from vacation. Danny's narrative of the Vietnam War centers on his father's open and frank discussions, explaining that his father wanted to ensure his children knew about the war and that he was a part of it. It made the war an easily broached topic rather than some dark secret of his father's past. Danny said, "It sounds kind of funny to say but it's like one of those family topic discussions. Like, he sat us down to talk about sex. He sat us down and talked about cursing. He sat us down and talked to us about his war experiences." He went on to say, "And from the time we were young, some of my first conceptions of war and death came from him. And he sort of, almost, it sounds creepy but sort of bedtime story-ish, sort of family time things where he would say 'I want to talk to you kids about this stuff.'" Danny explained that his father did this because he wanted to make sure his children knew what he went through. "Again, I think he wanted to make sure that it was something that *he* talked to us about before we heard about it in other places." For this reason, Danny could not mythicize his father's service, nor could he claim his father as an a idyllic hero. In fact, this knowledge provided a means to actively critique aspects of social ideals, especially concerning the war and America's political actions.

Danny explained how he learned about the practical realities of the war experience.

> It was always a very serious thing but at the same time he wanted you to understand that it wasn't something that had been really explicitly put in a textbook, so it's not an objective date or a time or a battle per se. I don't know anything about any particular battle. Or anything about any you know time period or what he actually did there. But it, it was definitely more about the sort of the normal mundane people things. [...] For some reason it does seem mundane for history purposes but it's very much a family sense.

Again, the structure of feeling that emerges in the interactions between the static and fluid motions of the social monad develops out of a reconceptualization of the heroic Father and its relationship to intersubjective relations between father and son. Danny expressed how his father's war stories were not full of fantastic battles but addressed "mundane" daily activities. His father did not glamorize the war in his talks with his son, providing Danny with a context upon which he could build a critical view of the social world. Danny's narrative provides an analytical space to draw connections between his father's presence in Danny's life and an unromanticized image of the hero. Danny claims that he does not know the details of the war or the specificities of his father's job there, but his father's frankness about the topic of the war prevents Danny from talking about it as if it were shrouded in mystery and incomprehensibility. Instead, he told me how he would listen to audiotapes his father made while in Vietnam, listening to him talk about various actions that might appear meaningless to those who are not in intimate contact with the soldier.

> Like, the audiotape stuff just, like, he talks about buying a car; he talks about getting a stereo from the [military store] for his brother when he gets back. [...] And it's like every once in a while you'd hear this little phf-chhh!! [imitates explosion sound]. And he'd be, like, "oh, yeah, that's a flare going off. [...] That's what he was doing; he was sitting up at night on a night watch, setting off flares. Again it was one of those things that is like, yeah, it's 3 o'clock in the morning" [...]. He was keeping himself awake.

These benign insights, integrated with the reminders that his father was involved in a war, gave Danny a greater capacity to comprehend what his father did in his day-to-day life in Vietnam. Many of my interviewees would lament that they wished they knew more about those types of activities to gain a fuller picture of their fathers' lives at that time; typically, though, they were afraid to ask. But Danny had a unique experience that enabled him to make connections between that time in his father's life and his subsequent life back at home. He was able to integrate the time his father spent in Vietnam into the larger span of his father's life. His father's openness in his discussions led Danny to the assumption that his father had recovered from the war experience in a healthy and positive fashion. It *also* provided a means for him to assert his father's more critical view of society—something he admired about his father. Danny's assessment that his father had a healthy recovery from the war experience, which heightened his social awareness, generates a picture of his father as a strong and capable man, not just in his war experiences, but in aspects of his life after Vietnam as well.

Narrative Disruptions of the Dominant Fiction 169

Although Danny articulates traditional views of the Father in his narrative by talking about his father's successful career and strength of character, he focuses more on his admiration for his father's strong sense of social justice, disrupting and complicating the heroic Father. This was particularly the case when Danny explained why his father went to Vietnam. He told me how his father dropped out of college and gave up his deferment for the draft.

> But it was just one of those things where he didn't have the sense of, I'm gonna fight for my country, I'm gonna go protect, you know, do something honorable. It was just like, uhh, there's nothing—I don't want to say there was nothing else to do—but he just wasn't certain and he knew that it would provide some structure and some guidance for him in some way.

There was no guise behind his father's motivations to go to Vietnam. He was restless and did not feel like he knew what he wanted to do with his life. "Again, I think that time period [he was] discovering more of what he really wanted to do. He still didn't have direction"; it was not about going to war to fight for his beliefs. Upon his return from Vietnam he went back to college and finished his degree. Unlike Tammy and Tara, who in their attempts to uphold the dominant fiction of the Father in chapter four by describing their fathers in a very noble fashion, particularly around their service, Danny has no desire to generate such an image of his father. Instead, he sees his restlessness and forthrightness as a confirmation of his father's strength and personal integrity. While he knows the war was something that had a deep impact on the way his father saw the world, it is unnecessary for him to contextualize his father's war experiences within the social narrative of the honorable and virile warrior. At the same time, Danny's assertion of his father's well-adjusted recovery from the war experience is a way of working against the negative public representations of the Vietnam Veteran. Yet, he does not do this by upholding idyllic images of the hero. Instead, I read his narrative as a negotiation of a very different type of heroic Father who carries a more critical social consciousness, which was passed on to Danny. He explained that "I do value my family a lot. At the same time I think that every person in my family has been imbued with these idealistic goals. I don't want to make a lot of money, I don't care. I value just sort of big social justice-ish issues." For Danny, his idealism is not simply found in his father or family; it also is incorporated into his beliefs about the possibility of a just social world.

Danny's narrative relies on a different frame of idealism around which to generate a picture of his father.

At the same time, I read Danny's admiration for his father's critical social outlook as an attempt to renegotiate the masculine subject's relationship to phallic identification. Rather than simply discussing his father with preset definitions and classifications of phallic structures of identification, Danny struggles to express an alternative view of masculinity. As Williams explains about the structure of feeling, "changes in presence...do not have to await definition, classification, or rationalization before they exert palpable pressures and set effective limits on experience and on actions" (Williams, 1977, 132). As such, his narrative reflects the pressure of not just hegemonic forms of the Father and the Vietnam Veteran, but the in-formation presence of alternative constructions of masculine subjectivity that are unsettled in Danny's own sense of self in the world.

This emerged in his discussion of his mother's death and its effect on his relationship with his father. Issues of death and dying were brought up to Danny in the early conversations with his father about Vietnam, but, for him, they were coupled with the close relationship he had with his mother during her struggle with cancer. Ultimately, death and war were not taboo subjects in his life, so he spoke of all of these issues with openness much like what he attributed to his father's discussions.

> The experience of having these sort of explicit talks with my father at certain times, where I've been able to see him be, you know, a little reminiscent, a little bit emotional about things in life. The experience of really talking to him. And talking to my mother as she went through the process of dying. You know it was, I mean, it made me grow up really fast.

While we might assume that this meant Danny had a close relationship with his father, it became clear that he struggled with many realities that both his father's war experiences and the loss of his mother created in his life. It is nearly impossible to pull apart these two events in Danny's life in the context of this research, mostly because the coupling of such traumatic and life-changing events generates deep lines and layers of scripting on the palimpsest defining one's sense of self in society. The effects of the war on Danny's father cannot be neatly confined outside the perimeters of the experience of the loss of his wife; as a result, both intercede on the intersubjective relationship Danny holds with his father.

With this in mind, I now interrogate how these moments work together to generate an alternative conception of the heroic Father that disrupts and disturbs social idealizations of masculine subjectivity. Although Danny's intersubjective relationship with his father was open and intimate, this deep connection he held to his father early in life was damaged and altered after his mother's death. Danny explained how he could not understand how his father was able to deal with his grief so quickly and remarry within two years of her death; therefore, he felt a great deal of resentment toward his father for what he perceived as a betrayal of his mother. Although he explained that he now (at age 23) understood that he had a harder time grieving than his father did, the tensions remain. Danny's closeness with his father—and his admiration for him—is tempered by the irresolution he holds regarding the way that his father handled his mother's death. This is almost the opposite reaction that we saw Samantha and Renee have in their experiences with their father at the time of their sister's death. Because their father's resilience wore down in that moment, Samantha and Renee saw their father's vulnerability in the context of their own grief, which opened the door to their ability to connect with their father's trauma from the war in a more tangible fashion. The crisis of articulation manifests differently for Danny than it did for Samantha and Renee. It led Danny to see his father as stronger and impervious, rather than vulnerable and affected. Danny's father did not break down after his wife's death (at least not that could be discerned in the interview); this fortified Danny's admiration of his father's strength, which is how he links his father with strength and stoic virtues of phallic identification. Yet, at the same time, it produced a disconnect between Danny and his father (unlike the stronger connection that developed between Renee and Samantha and their father). As such, I read this part of his narrative as an articulation of the link between his father and phallic identification, which simultaneously destabilizes the qualities of masculine subjectivity that define phallic identification, *disturbing its manifest destiny* (to rephrase Bhabha). His discussion of the differences between his and his father's management of his mother's death reveals how variable masculine subjectivity is in its linkages to phallic identification.

Danny came to an impasse with his father and all the qualities of phallic masculine subjectivity that he respected in him after his mother's death. He continued to maintain how much he admired his father but it was clear he felt very different and apart from him. "Saying that I admire my father just sort of, I think that at the same time that you love somebody, and it's difficult to not have sort of mixed feelings around that. Where you're doing things that I sometimes don't like." Those *mixed feelings* about actions he did not like in his father were directly connected to his perceptions of his father's quick recovery from his mother's death. The tensions that exist in Danny's narration of the way his father recovered from Vietnam and his mother's death reflect the confrontation between constructions of masculine subjectivity and the struggle to negotiate the "self-generating" discourses of phallic identification that are, as Bhabha explained at the beginning of this chapter, *reproduced over the generations in patrilineal perpetuity.* In his narrative, Danny tries to uphold his father as an ideal masculine subject, saying that although his mother's death "hit my father very hard" and that he "dealt with my mother's death in the way he had to." He attributed his quick recovery to "one of those things that make him a tough and durable person." In fact, he told me, "Looking back on that, you know, I'm glad he did what he did. If anything else, it changed who he would have been—much more messed up [laughs]." Seeing his father's quick recovery as a sign of strength, *durability*, Danny found comfort in his father's resilient response to his mother's death (even if his father's resilience left him feeling apart from him). By emphasizing how it demonstrated that his father was not *messed up*, Danny also keeps the negative public representations of the traumatized and emotionally broken Vietnam Veteran at bay. At the same time, it creates a different set of mixed feelings from what Samantha conveyed when she talked about how difficult it was to watch her father go through a painful grieving process for her sister.

In particular, it produces a confrontation with divergent constructions of masculine subjectivity as he recognizes the differences between him and his father. Danny asserted that his own difficulty with his mother's death and his father's remarriage was a sign of his immaturity and that "a lot of it had to do with the fact that he dealt with it and I didn't." Describing his father as hardworking, successful, and sincere, he admired his father's dynamic personality and felt that he is compassionate "when he wants to be. [...] Not tough toward other people but he'll stand up to a lot." He explained how everybody in his family are overachievers with social idealism, making a passing joke at his more humble goals of being a school teacher. He says, "Again, that's like the hard work sort of thing that I meant. I don't know if it's genetic [laughs] or I might have missed out—I want to be a teacher [laughs]!" So although he holds a similar work ethic and social idealism to his father's, his negotiation of the difference between his career goals and his father's expresses the tense relationship between the lived presence of a masculine subject living out an in-formation social position and his negotiation of phallic identification. He does not hold himself to the image of his dynamic and confident father, who has worked in a variety of high-level governmental positions. He identified himself as a very compassionate person who is deliberate and worrisome. Although he is glad that his father carries the virtues of strength and stoicism that helped him with a quick recovery from difficult life events, I read Danny's discussion of his divergent personality and career goals as an expression of his reservations about the way those virtues of masculine subjectivity are a normal or singular way of being a legitimate masculine subject. He understands that the expressions of masculine subjectivity as strong, stable, and impervious are ideals with a great deal of contradiction and variability, which decenters the dominant fiction and phallic identification. Yet, his self-deprecation draws out his own ambiguous relationship to phallic identification.

The desire to realign the masculine subject to phallic masculinity, negotiating the presence of the dominant fiction in and through the lives of social subjects, is not a clear and uncomplicated process. Idealizations of the heroic Father cannot always be maintained in the complexity that exists in intersubjective relationships. There is a tension between holding on to hegemonic forms of masculine subjectivity, which value physical strength and emotional stoicism, and living out (and existing within) a very different version of those ideals that must negotiate the breaks produced by a moment such as the Vietnam War in those structures of belief. The trauma of the Vietnam War is articulated in subtle ways in these instances that cannot be easily separated and discerned from the lives that have been lived in the 30 years since its end. Still, these interviewees (and, by extension, other COVV) look to their fathers as a way of understanding not just the war, but how they see themselves actively negotiating and articulating presence as they relate to gendered social ideals.

Familial (Re)Visions: Negotiating the Ideal Father through the Crisis of Articulation

> I feel kind of sad when I think about how [my father has] just come along and just kind of gotten worse over the years. I feel awful that he's in so much physical pain all the time. I'm kind of upset, like, the way things have turned out for him. [...] He's just not the same dad we used to have.—Pam

The work involved in negotiating the confrontation between social forms and pulsating life presence, which is an essential part of intersubjective relationships, reveals numerous qualifications, reservations, and indications that there is something necessarily strained and irreconcilable about an individual's social presence. This tension is magnified under the analytical lens of a historically traumatic event because the event is never simply the possession of any single individual—or family. As previously discussed, the crises of truth and survival manifest in the second generation through their expressions of what I conceptualized as the crisis of articulation. In this section, I explore a different dimension of this crisis from the ones addressed in chapter three in order to further develop this concept. I focus here on how notions of the Father are disarticulated and then rearticulated through variegated strands of recognition of the trauma of the historical event of the Vietnam War. Through the narratives of five women struggling to make sense of their relationships to their fathers, I tell a story of the larger history of the traumatic event of the Vietnam War. I read their attempts to negotiate their experiences with their fathers and the social idealizations of the Father as a reflection of the different ways they engage with their fathers' struggles with the crisis of survival, which then structures these interviewees' expressions of the crisis of articulation. By making a causal link between the historical event of the Vietnam War and their fathers' inability to fit ideal notions of the Father (as they simultaneously renegotiate *meanings* of the Father in their narratives) these interviewees' expressions take us beyond attempts at negotiating the gap between knowing and understanding that is at the core of the crisis of articulation; they take us into the present where knowing and understanding what happened to their father in Vietnam is significant insofar as it helps them make sense of their present relationships with their fathers. This underscores the point that the crisis of articulation is as much about understanding the original event of trauma as it is about understanding its presence in current social forms and intersubjective relationships. As Caruth explains, "The belated experience of trauma... suggests that history is not only the passing on of a crisis but also the passing on of a survival that can only be possessed within a history larger than any single individual or any single generation" (1996, 71).

This is particularly salient in Pam's narrative. Through a reading of her narrative, we can link the way the ghost of Vietnam War sits down with her, intruding on her descriptions of her father's presence in her life. By emphasizing her father's deterioration and explaining why *he's just not the same dad we used to have*, we can see how her father's survival of the Vietnam War dominates her articulation of trauma. I focus my analysis on the following quote from Pam to explore how the crisis of articulation expresses *a larger history* beyond individuals, even though it is the individual story that we are reading. She explained to me,

> I think it's sad now how my dad is addicted to pain pills and has post-traumatic stress disorder and he goes to a psychologist and stuff and talks to him but they just. I kind of think that the government has just set aside all the Vietnam Vets and said okay, well you have PTSD, take this medication and they don't deal with their problems and they just give them more and more pills. And then by that time they're just hooked on pills and then they are just messed up and it's even worse than when they started.

This account of her father is quite complex. Pam has watched her father struggle over the years with the effects of physical war wounds, as well as the effects of PTSD and Agent Orange. Her frustration with *losing* her father—him no longer being the father she had when she was growing up—is expressed through the way American society has dealt with the aftereffects of the war. Similar to the way I read Samantha and Renee's father's wounded leg, I read Pam's father's addiction to pain medication as the way Pam finds a route into the crisis of articulation. The social monad of the Vietnam War is a continual presence in her and her family's lives. Her father's ongoing struggle with the crisis of survival, seen most clearly in his battle with chronic pain and drug addiction, affects the way Pam interacts with and discusses her father.

In particular, she emphasized how she does not talk to her father very often and when she does it centers on his health problems. "A lot of our talk now is because I'm in medical school and he's, like, 'well what's this medication,' because he's on so many medications now. And I talk to him about his health and then if he's gonna do this or gonna do that." Her present intersubjective relationship with her father is constituted through his illnesses and leads her to idealize her past relationship with her father. It also leads to her explicit critique of the way the government handles the ongoing effects of war trauma. Continually explaining how *they* do not help Vietnam Veterans, *they only give them more pills*, Pam looks at the larger historical context within which her father's survival exists, which shifts her individual narrative into a larger historical context. *They* must be understood as not only the government but also America and the social imaginary. Much like in O'Brien and Shafer's discussion of burden of the irreconcilable memories of the Vietnam War being placed upon the Vietnam Veteran in the social imaginary, her narrative reminds us that such images can greatly impact the way that the government deals with the larger social problems that this *imagined* responsibility carries on individual lives. It is not just the American people who can distance themselves from the memories of the Vietnam War as they look to the Vietnam Veteran, it is also governmental institutions who then react to and treat individuals in a way that marginalizes their individual trauma through the refusal (or inability) to connect individual manifestations of trauma to the larger history within which those social images of the troubled and traumatized Vietnam Veteran rest. In her narrative, Pam was less concerned about understanding her father's experiences in Vietnam than she was about making sense of the present condition of his mental and physical health and the way those conditions were being treated. As such, Pam's narrative is an expression of the crisis of articulation as she tries to connect her father's present suffering with the trauma that he experienced in Vietnam. In this manner, she and the other interviewees in this section articulate their relationship with their fathers through an imbricated discussion of their father and the Vietnam War.

More so than Pam, the following interviewees disarticulate the Father through their narrations of the presence of the trauma of the Vietnam War dominating their father's social life (his survival)—and their relationship to him. At the same time their narratives rearticulate the Father, negotiating what this idealized social form means to their lives, drawing on the trauma of the Vietnam War as they articulate their fathers' failures *and* successes as a father. Their expression of the crisis of articulation reminds us that *the belated experience of trauma is not only the passing on of a crisis but also the passing on of a survival that can only be possessed within a history larger than any single individual or any single generation.* The trauma of the Vietnam War can be felt individually, but their narratives collectively intrude on the larger historical ramifications of this event on social imaginings of the Father and family.

Tricia and Sandy: Idealized Expectations, Contested Explanations

I, I don't have—not knowing, like, being very studied on the subject I can't, like, I don't have a good opinion. I mean I know I have a lot of anger toward [the Vietnam War] just because of the—I, you know, have expectations of who a father should be and [my father] wasn't and I blame that on whatever experiences he had there but I don't know much about it. (Tricia)

For Tricia and Sandy, their fathers were often a disappointment and source of painful and frustrating memories. Their narrations of their estranged and tense relationships with their fathers leave them negotiating between the ideal Father and their fathers' failures and limitations in their lives. But they do not stop there. Navigating their fathers' survival as a Vietnam Veteran, their narratives express the crisis of articulation as each woman links her father's problematic existence to her own personal struggles with her father's problematic presence in her life. The remnants of the lacks that their fathers amassed in their war experiences move into Tricia and Sandy's narratives and leads each woman to focus her narrative on how the Vietnam War affected her relationship with her father. Whatever they do or do not know of their fathers' war experiences did not deter their adamant assertions that their fathers have been profoundly affected by their experiences in Vietnam. When I asked about her knowledge of the Vietnam War, Tricia stressed that she avoided learning about the war and felt a great deal of resentment toward what it did to her father and, as a result of that, to her. She pointedly blames the Vietnam War for her father's inability to be the father she felt he should have been. Unlike Stacey, who also claimed to have very little knowledge about the war, Tricia does not do this to maintain a clear demarcation between whatever difficult experiences her father went through in Vietnam and his subsequent experiences as a father. Instead, she, and the other women in this section, used their limited knowledge of the Vietnam War to discuss the meanings of this dark moment in American history through the damage it did to her father and how it left her without an emotionally healthy and stable father. As Tricia commented,

> From this last period of war [in Iraq] I most definitely support the troops, you know, the fact that they're there, but. You know I recognize that none—they won't come back the same. They'll have experiences that I would never understand and I think that's sad. And I think that it's unfortunate.

It is sad because she feels the effects of the disconnection that develops in a soldier between his traumatic experiences in war and his subsequent home life, making her believe that the potential for any *normal* family life is impossible.

Tricia and Sandy struggled deeply with understanding their relationship with their fathers. Both had made the conscious decision to cease having any communication with their fathers at the time of their interviews. At the same time, they held on to their fathers as an essential and important part of who they have become as women. Their narratives are structured around an intense ambivalence, which alerts us to the structure of feeling within which their narratives reside. Each tells the story of her father's failings with mixed emotions, going back and forth between identifying his failures and anger toward him and harboring a great deal of anger and criticism for the Vietnam War. Interestingly, they rely far less on the public images of the Vietnam Veteran than other interviewees and do not try to protect their fathers from that image. In their narratives, they focus more on defending and explaining their fathers as *fathers* rather than protecting his status as a Vietnam Veteran. Instead, each woman uses the war and his status as a Vietnam Veteran to explain his failings, upbraiding meanings of the ideal Father. Rather than seeing the honor in his service, they point their blame at the war and its effects. As Sandy commented, when asked if she felt there was anything unique about being a child of a Vietnam Veteran, "I think the fact that I can't depend on [my father] as much as a lot of other people depend on their fathers." As a way of making sense of the presence of the trauma of the Vietnam War in their current relationships with their fathers, these women engage with the crisis of articulation by sliding between their anger toward the event of the Vietnam War and their disappointment in their fathers' ability to be fathers. Yet, the causal link they make between the war and their father's failures as a father never fully mends the gap between knowing and understanding what the trauma of the Vietnam War means to their lives as women who have been unable to establish a strong relationship with their fathers.

Tricia's anger and resentment toward her father is continually mediated by his status as a Vietnam Veteran. She told me that she had been coming to terms with her father's limitations, but she clearly was still looking for some way of articulating the losses she felt that had plagued her as she grew up with an emotionally detached and depressed father. As she described her father, she focused on his emotional indifference and his inability to communicate with her, which left Tricia intimidated by him. When she was asked about ever bringing up the topic of Vietnam with her father, she said, "Uhhm. No. It's not something that I would tempt fate with." She was aware that the Vietnam War was a source of pain for her father, and his intimidating stature and intense demeanor left her too scared of him to attempt to engage with him on such topics. She explained why he was such a threatening presence to her:

> He's a very, uhm—6 foot 3—very broad man. Very stern looking. I mean he was never particularly mean in that sense but very— he always intimidated me because I didn't. As a child I couldn't communicate with him very well. And while trying to establish a relationship with him throughout my high school time, he, he just wasn't—it's not something I would broach.

She also stressed how critical he was of her choices of activities and academics, feeling that he undermined her confidence. When she told him she was applying for a scholarship to go to a private school he warned her that she would never fit in and when she tried out for the softball team he asked her why she would ever do a sport. She felt all of his doubts in her and his inability to show her any form of support led her to feel more dislocated from him as well as determined to succeed in her life choices. Over and over again, she felt there was a huge gap in their ability to communicate and for him to understand the needs of a girl growing up.

So, although Tricia touched on her father's economic absence, she was more troubled by his inability to invest himself in her life. As she explained, "I remember asking my mom can you please have him not live here anymore. But more because he was never a friend to me. Never really had the ability to understand me." The support and understanding she believed a father should express to his children demonstrate how she negotiates the ideal Father within her own experiences with her father. It is important to recognize these reified abstractions even as they reference a tenuous existence in these interviewees' narratives; these abstractions remind us of how their presence impacts our sense of grounding in the social world even if they are highly constraining and problematic to the actual lived experiences in which social actors engage. As Williams tells us, "Social forms are then often admitted for generalities but debarred, contemptuously, from any possible relevance to this immediate and actual significance of being" (1977, 130). What we see when we focus on the contradictory coexistence of generalized abstractions and the lived impossibility of those ideological forms constituting the dominant fiction is an ambiguous presence. As such, Tricia moves in and out of the *mythicized* ideal of the Father and family as she tries to explain her intersubjective relationship with her father; as much as she tries to render her father absent from her day-to-day living, he is a significant presence in her thinking and feeling about the social world she inhabits. Her father as Vietnam Veteran is symbolic of the loss she feels marks her life and the emotional void his absence created in her life. She explained at length how being a child of a Vietnam Veteran left her without the ability to see a healthy and loving relationship. "I missed not having two healthy parents." By this she meant,

> I never learned that—not having that around all the time I think I missed out on something that's caused a lot of trust issues with me. Like I'm very much a reserved person. Physical contact for me is very difficult, like even hugging family members. [...] I think that a lot of that has to do with not having a father figure just there. I've always had a lot of trouble with men. Male voices—like from teachers. I've been intimidated and it's been something I've had to overcome and I think that if he was a healthier person I'd have a lot less trouble with that.

She connected the problems that developed around the lack of a healthy, stable, and supportive father in her life to the Vietnam War. The image of the damaged Vietnam Veteran in conjunction with the Vietnam War provides her with a means of reflecting upon and articulating her own loss of a healthy father. The need to understand the war in these terms was one of the reasons she decided to participate in my research.

> It's unfortunate—I wish I knew more about my father's experiences. I mean, I found pictures. I would know nothing about them and I think it's unfortunate that I don't. You know I'm very naive and I think one of the reasons I wanted to help you—I mean I'm not totally naive to it. And it's—I could go read a book, but I don't. I don't necessarily want to.

In this fumbled comment, the crisis of articulation presses through her discussions of her limited knowledge of the war and her assertion that she still feels that she has something to offer to my research. Specifically emphasizing how the war has taken away vitality and possibilities in this man who is her father, her narrative reminds us of Pam's discussions of her father's chronic pain and drug addiction through the similar way it addresses the larger story of the Vietnam War. By linking her father's emotional distance to the experiences he had in Vietnam *and* tying his emotional distance back to her own experience of the loss of an active and involved father, the echoes of the intergenerational transmission of trauma can be heard. Ultimately, Tricia wanted to make sure people understand how the traumatic effects of the war become part of family life, explaining that it is with sadness and remorse that

> I can look back now and in interactions with him you can see the pain that he feels that he, like—it's almost a shell of himself as he gets older and doesn't have the opportunity. Like there are times when he really wanted to be a normal human being and he just would get kicked right back—couldn't get control of it.

Ultimately, the trauma of war finds articulation through her relationship with her father—the man she harbors both love and resentment toward. The strength of the dominant fiction and the *mythicized* ideals of the father mediate her explanations of her father's failures. In a sense, she articulates the trauma he experienced in Vietnam as that which imposed itself onto his sense of self in the world, making it impossible for him to *be a normal human being*, that is, to be the father—masculine subject—she felt he was *supposed* to be.

This is not unlike Sandy's experiences with her father. Although she continually asserted that she was the one to defend her father to her family, she held a great deal of resentment toward his inability to *be* a father, using language that implied that her father is a victim of the trauma of war. As she explained,

> I feel that I'm kinda defensive of my dad. A lot of people in my family don't like him—for many reasons [laughs]. I kind of—I don't really stick up for him but I kinda can see a relation as to why, like, so much has gone on in his life. That I, like, not that I don't—I don't give him an excuse—but obviously there's reasons behind why he's chosen the way he has in life. That a lot of times things happen you don't really have control over.

Her narrative generates mixed feelings about her father's emotional, physical, and financial absence. While she feels she understands that her father has faced many difficult experiences—most significantly, the Vietnam War—she still knows she cannot allow him to be a part of her life. At age 22, she had not seen her father in almost seven years, only occasionally talking with him on the telephone. Like Tricia, Sandy was afraid to emotionally invest in her father. Although she was very close to her father as a young girl, her parent's divorce and the abuse he inflicted on her family left her angry and disappointed in her father. Moving through extremes in her feelings for her father she described her current feelings for him as "complacent," but that emotion is filled with the residue of her struggle to come to terms with who he is and what he did to her family. She felt "almost like I *have* to deal with him. Then sometimes it's like I care about him. Obviously, like, I know—as much as I say, gosh, I wish he would die and I wouldn't have to deal with this. I mean, I know if he did, I would be really upset." Throughout the interview she could not decide where her feelings for her father rest.

Her father's status as a Vietnam Veteran ultimately provided her with a socially grounded means of explicating her father's failings. At the same time, it enables us to understand how her father's individual experience with trauma, and her subsequent feelings of loss generated from that trauma, come together in a larger history of the Vietnam War that is tangled in personal suffering. The experience of a traumatic event, for the second generation, hinges on understanding how the event intrudes upon the present. Unlike the generation experiencing the trauma, they are not focused on articulating the actual event. Watching her father go in and out of VA hospitals for treatment of his emotional problems, she worked in and through the reified abstractions of the traumatized Vietnam Veteran as a way of understanding her own losses and frustrations with her father. She in no way excused his behaviors or contradicted the pain he inflicted on her family. Instead, the trauma of the war and her father's experiences there enabled her to access an understanding of her father, albeit with a great deal of ambiguity. Never did she claim that there was a clear causal relationship between her father's status as a Vietnam Veteran and his abusiveness; yet, her father's status as a Vietnam Veteran ultimately provided the grounding for her narration of how, rather than holding together the family and being a mainstay of its continuation, her father destroyed her experience of the traditional family and the world as she knew it. At the same time, by defending her father to her family and asserting that there are things people face in their lives that they have little control over, she created a way of justifying his actions and struggles; specifically, she identified the experiences her father had little control over as what he went through in Vietnam. By relying on his status as a Vietnam Veteran, Sandy negotiated the effects of the ideal Father, moving between her understanding of that fixed social form and how *her* father undermined the reality of those structures of belief. She expanded on how she felt the loss of not having a father she could depend on, like *a lot of other people*, by saying,

> Just seeing a lot of people in school—a lot of them—the person that they depend on the most is their father. And they call—like I have to find other ways around that. Just simply because of that, like, he isn't—he can't even take care of himself. So, there's no way he can really take care of me or give me advice.

Sandy believed that other people can depend on their fathers and that the *typical* father is the symbol of strength and social cohesion. Unable to idealize her own father, she focused on assumptions regarding what she perceived other people experienced. At the same time, she idealized the life she had before her parents' divorce and her discovery of her father's abuse. She explained how

> Our life totally shattered when that happened. I mean we went from upper middle class family to like dirt poor. And it was a big change and I think the fact that my mom's friends and my church, our relationship with the church. I'm very close with my pastors. They're like family.

Ultimately, these experiences disrupt the idyllic image of the family and forced her to look elsewhere for the support she needed in her life.

Like Tricia, Sandy identified many of her struggles with trusting men to problems she had with her father. Explaining that she does not "really trust men. I mean I'm very skeptical when it comes to relationships. [...] Not that I'm a man-hater but I just [pause]—I'm just afraid I'm gonna marry [someone like] my father." Having to deal with her father's absence and the subsequent fears around trusting men and relationships are a continual struggle for Sandy, as well as for Tricia. Rather than outright negating the normalcy of such family structures and idealized notions of the Father, these women oscillate between trying to locate their fears and insecurities within the lack of a *normal* family life and emphasizing how lucky they have been to develop an extensive social network that expands beyond biological family relationships. In a sense, their narratives reflect the contradictory existence of social forms in the lived experiences of individuals. Tricia identifies her family as her "first priority" in her life, but it is not a family in the normative sense. "I mean—family means—since my family moved here we don't have actual gene—like, blood-related relatives but we have a lot of family [friends]. And I really value the support system they provided for me." She adds, "I think [my success in school and graduation from college] was a collaborative effort. [...] I feel that it's—it was definitely a village effort." The void that her father's absence created in her life was countered by the far-reaching extended family found in the adults who were there for her emotionally and financially. Similarly, Sandy felt that the positive aspects of being a child of a Vietnam Veteran led her to looking outward for support and trusting in her church and community. "I think that [being a child of a Vietnam Veteran] also helped me build up other—the structure of friends and family and emotional support that I have. So I'd say both negative and positive [effects of being a child of a Vietnam Veteran]—like, obviously it'd be great if I had a father who could be there for me." In this regard, these two women were able to find alternative narratives of family life that counter hegemonic images of the family and the Father. At the same time, though, they uphold idyllic images of the father even as they lamented that there is a significant void that will not be filled. It is that continual awareness of the fixed forms of family and the Father that leaves these women negotiating the ideals of these fixed forms within the context of their fathers' precarious presence in their lives.

This is slightly different from the Vietnam Veterans like Kovic navigated their personal feeling of failure in gaining identification with phallic masculinity, but intimately related. While Kovic felt that the possibility of a *real* family ended with his paralysis, he finds a new family to recoup those losses in relationships with fellow Vietnam Veterans. Sandy and Tricia felt the possibility of a *real* family was thwarted by their father's status as a Vietnam Veteran. This leads them to develop ties outside of their families—looking to friends and institutions such as the church and school for support. In both cases the feelings of loss are never overcome and there is still the need to hold to a belief in the phallic masculine subject and traditional family structured around the ideal Father, even as they defy the reality of those structures. The residue of the lacks that men accrued in their war experiences move into the world of their children, leaving them managing what the war left behind for them within their fathers. What is left behind for Tricia and Sandy is a desire to maintain belief in the dominant fiction even as their intersubjective relationship with their fathers continually renders that story of America and the traditional family impossible. Navigating their father's survival through their own expressions of loss, we can hear the resonance of the ongoing effects of the traumatic event of the Vietnam War. Although it is not a war story in the traditional sense, it underscores how the social monad takes on different dimension for the second generation. Let us now turn to hear what happens in the interviewees' narratives that further destabilize the dominant fiction.

Absence as Presence: Dominique and Montana

At 22 and 24, respectively, Dominique and Montana were in search of their fathers. They were not looking for the men themselves so much as they were looking for a way of retrieving an image of their fathers from the ashes of their fathers' traumatic pasts. Their fathers' status as Vietnam Veterans figured largely in these women's family lives and came to define their relationships with their fathers. Unlike Tricia and Sandy, they did not have the *luxury* (if we can call it that) of severing ties themselves, because their fathers did that for them, rendering themselves as an absent presence in their daughters' lives. These men's survival has been precarious, to say the least. Their narratives reflect the unstable and in-formation relationship they have with their fathers, negotiating and renegotiating the presence of the trauma of the Vietnam War. As they seek meanings to their fathers' absence, these two women remind us that there is no simple resolution to trauma's reverberations in individual and social life. As we learned about Montana's father in chapter three, he recently passed away from liver disease. Like Montana's father, Dominique's father struggles with alcoholism, as well as other drug problems. In a similar fashion to Montana, Dominique believed much of the reason behind her father's addictions is the pain and suffering he experienced in Vietnam. As she explained, "My dad isn't—is. I don't want to say he's a bad dad, but he's always in and out a lot. [...] He's very heavily into drinking and drugs. And I think a lot of that has to do with the Vietnam War. Like I blame a lot of that on the war, because he wasn't like that before." For her, the Vietnam War is the reason for her father's problems and the source of his absent presence as a father. She identified his status as a Vietnam Veteran as the experience that dominates his life. She emphasized how "that's all he discusses—is just Vietnam and we won't discuss about, you know, how I'm doing or what's going on, so."

In her descriptions of her interactions with her father, Vietnam is always present. Vietnam absorbs his life, not only through his direct discussions with Dominique, but also in the way he navigates his survival. Specifically, Dominique links his substance abuse and emotional dislocation to his experiences in Vietnam, which then go on to shape the narrative of her own losses. She expressed intense frustration with her father as she simultaneously demonstrated deep love and connection to him. Yet, her critiques were pointed:

> He's an absent father. I go to see him and he—it—he's an alcoholic. And drugs—that overcomes his girls. He'll choose that any day over his three girls. I go and see him and he'll be sittin' there and he's drunk and he's high. So, you're talkin' to him, but you're really not because it's not him.

She went on to tell me how he continually disappointed her by refusing to come to important life events, such as her graduation from college.

> And he promised that he'd be there and he never showed up. And when he called me [begins to cry]. When he called me he said that he didn't have a sitter for the dogs. [...] He won't show up for a lot of family functions and he won't show up to things that are going well in a person's life. [...] And he always has these ridiculous excuses [...].

Over and over again she asserted that her father was not truly a father to her, yet that does not prevent her from seeking out a relationship with him—even if it did not fit her imagining of what a father-daughter relationship should be. She told me how she continually tried to enter her father's world by talking with him about his experiences in Vietnam, explaining "I've wrote poetry for him and stuff. Like, I've really been into it." In a sense, she made due with this form of engagement with her father but it did not provide a long-term foundation for their relationship. "I wanted to be a lot closer to him. I wanted to—but he pushed. [...] I wanted to be sure he was okay. And he went the opposite way and kinda pushed me away after he talked to me about [his experiences in Vietnam]." Ultimately, her attempt to create a different type of relationship with her father through his Vietnam experiences broke down and although she had not seen or spoken with her father in almost a year, she had every intention of visiting him and trying to establish ties with him once again. She asserted, "I try to be daddy's little girl. And it doesn't work. With him it really doesn't [laughs]." Yet it was clear that this did not inhibit her attempts or desire for that connection.

In her narrative she continually works through the process of disarticulating and rearticulating the relationship between her father and notions of the ideal Father. As she disarticulates his presence in her life she shifts back into a rearticulation of her father's connection with the ideal Father by talking about the brief time her father was sober. Seeing what her father *could be* enabled her to generate a narrative that was full of hope for his resurrection as a father even as she then turned back into disarticulations of her father throughout the interview.

> I know the person that he can be off of the drugs and that Valium that they still have him on and stuff. I know what he can be like when he's getting help and he's talking to somebody about the war and his issues. He's a whole other person. He's friendly and he's caring. He just is like, I don't know, he's a dad and he—he likes to talk about you and what you're doing.

He's a dad. Dominique holds an imagined vision of her father sober that facilitated her hopes that her father could *be* a father to her. Like Tricia, she wants a father who will care about her and her life, something her father has been unable to do because his own struggles so completely dominate his existence. For her a father is loving and caring. It matters little to her that he is unable to financially provide for her; she is more concerned about him having the capacity to emotionally invest himself in her life. And while she holds on to that hope, she is exceptionally aware that it is a distant and remote dream.

> And I think a lot of it, like I said, has to do with the Vietnam War. I think he just, he's afraid to get close to people now. [...] My dad never really showed love and compassion and never. He bought his kids. Like every time we'd see him. I mean, I was 5 years old being handed a $50, so it was like.

Monetary support did not capture what she felt was missing in her relationship with her father. In some regard, explaining her father's failings through his status as a Vietnam Veteran allowed her to hold on to the dream of her father being a more loving and caring person to her (supporting her belief in aspects of the social form of the Father), even if that narrative is layered with doubts and reminders of her father's absence in her life.

Montana constructed a narrative of ambiguous optimism as she retold the life and death of her father. Working through the structure of feeling, her narrative looks to bittersweet lessons her father's death has taught her. She explained that it is his death that initiated his resurrection into her life. At this point in her life her father is literally an absent presence—his memory holding a dominant place in her memory and narrative despite his bodily absence. She explained that "I didn't realize how much he was a part of my life until he died. I used to think that my dad didn't mean a whole lot to me. I used to think that he wasn't really a part of my life." Because she did not see her father that often and her interactions with him were contained to yearly visits in the summer, her relationship with him "seemed so disjointed always and then I thought because of that he wasn't really part of my life and when he died I had no idea how much he was. And he's oddly more in my life now than when he was alive." Ironically, it was his death that enabled Montana to look at her father's life with greater sensitivity and perspective. His death, the final expression of his painful survival, transfers into Montana's narrative as an expression of the crisis of articulation. Through her father's death, she found a voice for articulating his limitations as a father. Yet she makes peace with those limitations by contextualizing their relationship within the historical event of the Vietnam War. As she told us earlier, "My father lived a very sad life. And most of that was the result of his experiences in Vietnam."

Through his death, she explained that she was finally able to see what her father meant to her life. In particular, it is through his death that she builds connections between her father's life and the trauma of the Vietnam War. At the same time, these linkages affect her personal struggle with her distant relationship with her father and meaings of the Father in her own life. Not understanding the meaning her father held in her life until he was gone left her picking up the pieces of his life and trying to fit them into a narrative that could heal that past and make sense of her own anger and feelings of loss. As she explained,

> The reason I'm not as angry as I was is because my father's death sparked a lot of healing for me and I've been able to come to terms with his life and my place in it. And I think if he hadn't died, I'm not sure I could have done that healing and that's hard to say but true. There's just a lot of stagnation with him. And when he died it allowed me to free a lot of that up.

At the same time, her narrative contains numerous contradictions and unresolved issues regarding her father's absent presence in her life. Ultimately, many of the unresolved issues she identifies in herself come back to the irresolution she carries about her father. In a sense, she felt that by working through the space her father created in her life she would find a way of mending the breaks and rough edges of her own life. As she explained,

I'm surrounded by good people. I have good faithful loving friends and I have a very supportive family and I'm with a man that I love very much and who is also very supportive. So I feel that my life is extremely positive. But it's still marked by a lot of internal negativity that I haven't been able to dispose of yet. I'm very happy with my life and where it's going, the people and my experiences but I still have a lot of negative emotion that doesn't always fit with that.

Part of what does not fit is the way lived experience can never be contained within fixed social forms like the Father and family that attempt to fix our social experiences. She struggled to reconcile social ideals of the family and father, yet her father has forced her to confront a contingent reality in which his death has turned him into a more dominant presence than he was when alive. Montana demonstrates how *perhaps the dead can be reduced to fixed forms, though their surviving records are against it*. As a *surviving record*, Montana is living in and through her father's memory—a living record, rendering her relationship with him continually in-formation. This prevents her from reducing her father to a fixed form. She is hesitant, though, about how to navigate the complexities of his life within her own insecurities and struggles.

The dynamic and shifting reality of our intersubjective relationships leave many unresolved issues that cannot be reduced into neat and tidy categories of social life. The work of COVV within the social monad—much like the survivor's struggles with the original moment of trauma—is in continual flux. And while meaning is frequently sought in their narratives, these interviewees cannot easily resolve questions regarding their relationships with their fathers within the confines of fixed social form such as the Father and Vietnam Veteran. What results is a story of the trauma of the Vietnam War structured around a lived experience as it confronts a past that is without resolution. This comes through Montana and Dominique's narratives as they negotiate their fathers' absence in their lives, which is not really an absence at all. In a sense they are articulating the social monad with the crisis of articulation. Trying to fit their experiences into a social world of fixed forms and ideals about what a father and family mean, these women (and the other interviewees, for that matter) are left with the task of making sense of the variability in their relationships with their fathers; the relationship never seems complete or fully formed, though, because the unfinished business of trauma from which their fathers struggle to survive is outside the context of what most people can comprehend in their daily social lives.

Without a clear way of expressing what it is that is unique about being a child of a Vietnam Veteran, Montana tries to explain what her relationship with her father has generated within her own sense of self. "I think that my experiences may have been marked by a lot more anger and sadness and bitterness as a result of my father's experiences. I think I'm more of those things and I think he was more of those things." At the same time, Montana also explained why articulating her feelings and relationship is so difficult. "I think there has been a lot more I've had to piece together about my life on my own than maybe some of my friends growing up that didn't have a father—a veteran for a father." Because her father was not there to provide a stable view and experience of the social world through a normative family life, she feels that her father's absence as a father has left her seeking other routes of explanation as she pieces together fragmented social experiences that constitute a life working in and between a historically traumatic event.

> It is about going beyond what you already know just so. It involves being taken beyond a dull curiosity or a detached know-it-all criticism into the passion of what is at stake. It is not individualistic, but it does acknowledge, indeed it demands that change cannot occur without the encounter, without the *something you have to try for yourself*. (Gordon, 1997, 203—emphasis in the original)

Exploring the social monad of the Vietnam War requires attention to what lies beyond what society knows—or thinks it knows—and explore the possibilities of change and transformation that exist in the world for those who cannot hold fast and tight to fixed forms of social structures. This process also requires society to look at the way individual and historical trauma intersect in these interviewees' expressions of the crisis of articulation.

(Familiar) Father Narratives and the Elusive Masculine Subject

Examining the narratives of COVV through the structure of feeling reminds us of the immense fluctuation that exists within hegemonic structures of society. When we look closely at the Father and the Vietnam Veteran, the layers of articulation complicate our understanding of masculine subjectivity. Their intersections reveal the density of our gendered selves. The men and women I interviewed long for clear social forms of recognition even though (or maybe because) their lives belie the reality of such certitude. Journeying through the different narrative layers of my interviewees, we understand how the historically traumatic event of the Vietnam War takes form in Vietnam Veterans' lives as fathers—as men. The interviewees dislodge normative notions of masculine subjectivity as they discuss their fathers' successes and failures. They try to explain and justify their fathers' lives by incorporating facets of the trauma he lived through. In doing so, they develop an image that is far more complicated than that of the Vietnam Veteran as traumatic subject. Yet he still embodies the effects of trauma. All these images reflect back on to the lives of the second generation. The images may be diffused and distorted but they linger on. The Father is the progenitor of social life—the arbiter of a national (in this case American) ethic. Yet, in the stories and visions that my interviewees tell about their fathers and themselves, the masculine subject is not as solid, ossified, unbroken, unaffected as the dominant fiction imagines. Although my interviewees have no intention of disturbing the masculine subject's manifest destiny, they do. Their intersubjective relationships with their fathers draw attention to the masculine subject's *prosthetic reality* (to re-invoke Bhabha). The masculine subject's *innate invisibility* is exposed. This particular traumatic break in the dominant fiction, which my interviewees intimately relate to, leads to a spectrum of narrative reactions. Through the lens of the structure of feeling, what is often thought to be solid and impenetrable becomes murky and porous.

What statement do these interviewees and my analysis make about Bhabha's comment on the complex "relation between historical needs, political desires, and the destiny, even density, of our gendered selves"? While we may need to remember how the past affects us in the present— how war affects us as social subjects— how do such needs intercede on the political (desires?) actions of war? The dominant fiction of America and the existence of patriarchal structures seek out our belief in the illusion of moral certitude and the honor of war. But to what end? I suppose this is a rhetorical question on my part but one that needs to be asked in light of our present political trajectory, in light of our presence in Iraq. Existing in such a present, it is easy to assess the imperviousness of the illusions the dominant fiction creates. Although these 25 people constituting my research may counter that illusion through their intersubjective relationships, the larger story continues. The masculine subject moves through generations in *patrilineal perpetuity*. "'He,' that ubiquitous male member, is the masculinist signature writ large—the pronoun of the invisible man; the subject of the surveillant, sexual order; the object of humanity personified" (Bhabha, 1995, 57). *He* still lingers on in the story of America, however mutated and diffuse. The intergenerational transmission of trauma may expose the vulnerabilities between lived experiences and the dominant fiction, but that does not mean the fiction ends. It remains a powerful force in the lives of these individuals. It is what causes much of the uncertainty and anxiety in their own lives. The dominant fiction works together with lived experience tensely and sometimes painfully. Much like the dominant fiction of America, the traumatic event of the Vietnam War is a moment laden with explosions of memories that insinuate themselves into the lives of the second generation—COVV —in ways that they cannot fully negate, or readily accept, as their own memories and lives. What they do understand as their own is the work necessary to rebuild continuity between the dominant fiction and the traumatic break they so intimately know. Perhaps it is in that space we can begin to imagine and believe in the strength and possibility of something else.

THOUGHTS AND CONCLUSIONS
Stretching toward and beyond the Horizon

Bissell writes, "The war had not ended for [my dad], and now it is in me" (2004, 64). His comment conveys the subtle density that the gift of trauma hands to the second generation. Vietnam is *in* Bissell as it is *in* my interviewees, but its specific mass and weight is felt in a variety of diverse ways. The fractured pieces of the traumatic history of the Vietnam War cannot be read as a linear series of events that progress into a cumulated story of the past. There is no clearly marked beginning, middle, and end. Instead, in this research, we have moved through a social monad that resembles a palimpsest of layered narratives merging and separating to reveal an incomplete and shifting story of a history of the present. The layers I explored in this research remind us that the historically traumatic event of the Vietnam War is still being lived out, is still in-formation. The tangled intersections of the Vietnam Veteran Narrative, individual Vietnam Veteran narratives, and the narratives of my interviewees remind us that the social world is founded on the continual negotiation and renegotiation of social forms and intersubjective relationships. For the second generation, the gift of trauma passed on to them is not founded solely in the historical event of the Vietnam War; it is a lived presence animated by their fathers' lives, not only as Vietnam Veterans but as men—fathers—who live their own unique social existence. As such, the traumatic event finds its expression in the Vietnam Veteran—symbolically and literally—for children of Vietnam Veterans (COVV). The second generation of trauma articulates the moves and shifts of the transmission of trauma through their personal recollections of and intersubjective relationships with their fathers.

My interviewees' narratives convey a story of traumatic resonance that works within the layered social inscriptions of the event of the

Vietnam War. This process is a telling reminder of why sociologists should be concerned with the way social research often converts *experience into finished products* (in the words of Williams). Social analysis can lose its strength and veracity when it is only "centered on relations between these produced institutions, formations, and experiences, so that now, as in that produced past, only the fixed explicit forms exist, and living presence is always, by definition, receding" (Williams, 1977, 128). Losing that *living presence*, or at least a *recognition* of its presence, diminishes the power of social life on social forms—something of utmost concern in my research. This leads me to an ending that is not a final assessment of trauma's fixed form in the second generation, but to an ending that *stretches toward and beyond the horizon* (drawing once again on Gordon), recognizing the intrusion of life presence on the social forms of American society. In his article, which I have been weaving in and out of my analyses, Bissell (like my interviewees) tries to transform the shadowy and stammered articulations of the trauma of Vietnam that reside in his father into an *undiminished life* that reminds America of the formidable effects of the history of war, not only upon his life but upon our society. "War necessarily wounds everyone right down the line," writes Bissell. "A body bag fits more than just its intended corpse. Take the 58,000 American soldiers lost in Vietnam and multiply that by four, five, six—and only then does one begin to realize the damage this war has done" (Bissell, 2004, 64–5). The human legacy of the Vietnam War that fills those body bags belongs to more than the individual soldiers who fought in Vietnam, but it is not simply a burden for the children of Vietnam Veterans to bear. To rephrase Felman's comments, which opened this work: *the real problem of trauma may be that of the second generation,* but it is not they alone who live with its presence. The problem my interviewees face is how to receive the stammered articulations of the post-narrator and transform that broken story into *an undiminished life whose shadows touch softly in the spirit of a peaceful reconciliation.* But this is, ultimately, a *collective undertaking that belongs to everyone.* The gift of trauma that my interviewees carry includes the burden of trying to make the echoes of a painful and irresolute past, that is at once personal and social, audible. This is by no means an easy task in light of its broken and fractured manifestation in social life. The insights that my interviewees bring to this gift of a traumatic history are subtle reminders that the Vietnam War has a rich and complex social existence, the implications of which blur the boundary between individual and social life. Confronting the trauma of the Vietnam War and its human legacy in this fashion is a fundamental component of a history of the present.

As such, a history of the present takes shape under the weight of the things we carry as individuals and as a society. I utilized O'Brien's stories in *The Things They Carried* throughout my research, because they remind us of the post-narrator's complicated presence in the narratives of my interviewees. His stories are a consummate reminder that the Narrator of social trauma is also a narrator of individual trauma; the *I* and *we* of the story intersecting and shifting. O'Brien's stories of the things *he* carries in and out of Vietnam is framed by the story of the things *America* carries. As he reminds us, "and for all the ambiguities of Vietnam, all the mysteries and unknowns, there was at least the single abiding certainty that they would never be at a loss for things to carry" (O'Brien, 1990, 16). The traumatic memories he carries may not be able to provide answers or clarity to the breaks incurred in Vietnam, but they do promise to be a demanding social presence. Those *things*—traumatic memories—that Vietnam Veterans carry spread into their children and society through seemingly innocuous and mundane ways, leaving the truth of the past felt in and through the *engagement with others and with the world* (to re-invoke Prager). As such, my interviewees initiate their own stories from a place of linguistic faltering, picking up and leaving behind various pieces of the story of the Vietnam War that allow them to add another layer to the palimpsest that is the story of the Vietnam War.

To speak of trauma is one thing but, as my interviewees demonstrated, to speak of its echoes is quite another. As Montana told me,

> No one ever asks what it's like [to be a child of a Vietnam Veteran]. Most people don't care it seems. And the people that maybe do, it seems that they're too uncomfortable to ask and deal with the things they hear. It's been really nice to have someone ask that's not a counselor.

In her comments, I hear the struggle to find a way to be listened to that extends beyond the personal psychological effects of trauma, to speak of trauma's sociality. The search for a social voice that can speak with and between the individual and society is part of the work of conducting a history of the present. "Perceiving lost subjects of history—the missing and lost ones and the blind fields they inhabit—makes all the difference to any project trying to find the address of the present," Gordon tells us. "And it is the writing of the history of the present that is, I think, the sociologist's special province" (Gordon, 1997, 195). For Gordon, the sociologist is the one that must find linkages between the past and present and between the personal and the social in order to engage with the ghosts of the past that haunt our present social life. In telling the history of the trauma of the Vietnam War, society's burdens are reckoned with through the lives and images of Vietnam Veterans. But that reckoning is *inscribed affectively* in the in-formation and interactive relationship with individuals and social forms, reminding us that "to imagine beyond the limits of what is already understood is our best hope for retaining what ideology critique traditionally offers while transforming its limitations" so that it can address the pressing existence of the shadowy, *embryonic*, forms of social life (Gordon, 1997, 195).

Much of embryonic forms of social presence that complicate my interviewees' narratives emerge out of the crises that trauma provokes in the survivor. O'Brien's work demonstrates aspects of these crises and the movements within the Vietnam Veteran Narrative. Transgressing the boundary between individual and social, O'Brien's work in *The Things They Carried* reminds us of the way the Narrator tells the story of his idealized innocence as he went into Vietnam and the breaks that occurred in both his war experiences *and* his homecoming. Specifically, O'Brien demonstrates how individual Vietnam Veterans hang their personal narratives upon the bones of the Vietnam Veteran Narrative, providing textured contours to the social frame that moves us between the dynamics of belief in the dominant fiction of America and the break of those beliefs under the weight of war combat and homecoming. O'Brien's stories underscore the complexity involved in transforming lived experience into a story and that story- and happening-truth are complementary inscriptions on the palimpsest. The crises of truth and survival emerge as the Narrator tries to explain the losses and fragmented memories that still continue to haunt his social presence. For O'Brien, telling stories is the way *he* survived trauma—it is not simply a tidy representation of the Vietnam War. This is necessarily a key point in the Vietnam Veteran Narrative. "Telling stories seemed a natural, inevitable process," writes O'Brien,

> like clearing the throat. Partly catharsis, partly communication, it was a way of grabbing people by the shirt and explaining exactly what had happened to me, how I'd allowed myself to get dragged into a wrong war, all the mistakes I'd made, all the terrible things I had seen and done. I did not look at my work as therapy, and still don't. Yet... it occurred to me that the act of writing had led me through a swirl of memories that might otherwise have ended in paralysis or worse. By telling stories, you objectify your own experiences. You separate yourself. You pin down certain truths. You make up others. (1990, 157–8)

O'Brien's stories work with the imbricated layers of individual and social memory that comprise the story of the Vietnam War. His stories touch upon the uncomfortable overlap between happening- and story-truth that objectifies personal experience as it reminds us of the limitations of social forms. At the same time, his stories reaffirm and fortify public representations of the Vietnam Veteran as they tell a social story of the broken structures of belief America experienced in the traumatic event of the Vietnam War. This is similar to Oliver Stone's work, which negotiates the boundary between *I* and *we* as he moves between his and Kovic's experiences of trauma, creating an amalgamation of the Narrator/narrator.

Writing war stories has been Stone and O'Brien's way of reconciling the traumatic memories of the past that plague their present lives. It is the way they manage the crises of truth and survival. The stories that save the survivor affect the second generation, shaping my interviewees' understanding of their fathers and the traumatic event of the Vietnam War. My interviewees' distance from the original event of trauma and reception of its effects through their fathers' and society's stories leave them uncertain about their own understanding of the event and its presence in their lives. Bissell may recognize that the war is *in* him, but the ways it intrudes on and becomes part of his own narrative are ambiguous and difficult to articulate. This struggle reflects COVV's engagement with what I have identified as the crisis of articulation. The interviewees try to articulate the echoes of a stammered articulation but their expressions are fraught with anxiety. This uneasiness manifests itself in the experiences they narrate to me about their relationships with their fathers. Telling stories of hopes, disappointments, love, and sadness, we can hear the event of the Vietnam War rise to the surface; they negotiate the inscribed narratives that reside on the palimpsest as they add another layer to this complex history of the present. Individually they told me their stories; together, these 25 men and women make the presence of this traumatic history audible. Their narratives address hegemonic structures such as the Father and hero, which shed light on the way the trauma of the Vietnam War fractured American masculine subjectivity, opening up larger questions about how America has recovered from the traumatic break in the dominant fiction. Looking at my interviewees' narratives as both collective and singular stories that are incomplete and in transition, a history of the present emerges. As Gordon explains, "to write a history of the present requires stretching toward the horizon of what cannot be seen with ordinary clarity *yet*" (1997, 195—my emphasis). This work, for me, is not intended to pick at the old wounds of the Vietnam War but to remind us that there are wounds that have not been accounted for and that are still being lived out, affecting the social memories of America. A history of trauma is not a fleeting or passing series of moments and events; it is an active presence that compels us to engage in the more difficult task of looking at the reverberations of societal breaks with its dominant fiction. In this research, that has meant that I must look at the way my interviewees address the effects of fractured social forms such as the phallic masculine subject and the Father to understand their own social position and gendered subjectivity. Although it can be painful and uncomfortable to take a closer look at some aspects of America's difficult past, the voices of my interviewees remind us that we are anything but doomed to a sealed fate. We can see how the presence of the past advances our ways of seeing and thinking about the world. We can see how individuals creatively work between fixed social forms and fluid life experiences, demonstrating the possibility of social transformation. Their stories do not center on the world of combat and Vietnam and its traumatic repetition; instead, these men and women tell stories of hope that show that lives can be rebuilt and new hope can enter in surprising and unexpected ways. And while we may know on a base level that the world is complex and full of dynamic individuals negotiating the stories—myths, dominant fictions—and other reified tales of our national past, it is too easy to speak of *the* story as if it were the *only* story of our lives. It is too easy to assume that we all receive history as the same story. I do not want to pretend that national myths are not powerful and that individual expression alone can conquer the oppressive aspects of America's dominant fictions, but it is important to be aware that myths do not always win our hearts and minds. And this is one way of trying to touch the pain of the past *softly in the spirit of a peaceful reconciliation.*

In the process of *dragging our stories out into the ditches of shared human memory,* our stories cease to be ours. At the same time, they remind us of how we are part of the story—for better or worse. It is important to remember, as Olick explained in chapter one, that social memory is *both* collected and collective. It comprises both the individual recollections and the social configurations that organize how we as individuals and a society put our memories into words. These stories are intimate and personal for Vietnam Veterans struggling to find a voice of their survival from trauma that are beyond what many of us in America could ever comprehend. The breakdown that many Vietnam Veterans experienced in their lives as a result of their combat experiences took them

Thoughts and Conclusions

out of their comfort zones as human beings, American citizens, and masculine subjects, turning a familiar, safe, and comprehensible world into something distant and dangerously out of their control. Coming home, some tried to reestablish their beliefs in a number of ways, not the least of which was starting a family and rebuilding the American dream that seemed so real to them before they left. This is where my interviewees' narratives begin.

In particular, their intersubjective relationships with their fathers generate an even more complex relationship with the event of the Vietnam War than the Vietnam Veteran Narrative and the narratives of Vietnam Veterans. In my interviewees' discussions of their fathers, they touch on important aspects of the Father, the Vietnam Veteran, and hero, which enabled me to interrogate how these crystallized structures work as interlocking identity categories defining the masculine subject's position in the dominant fiction of America. Providing greater texture to the palimpsest of the Vietnam War, the narratives of the second generation remind us that objective and subjective experiences are not mutually exclusive. Tangled into a sensuous knowledge that cannot be categorized or inserted into binaristic structures of social analysis, my interviewees' narratives remind us that the layers constituting the event of the Vietnam War are deeply intertwined. The intersubjective relationship my interviewees have had with their fathers animate these social forms to help us better understand how the intergenerational transmission of trauma shifts our concerns beyond the original event of trauma and into the way that event shaped (and was shaped by) these interlocking identity categories. Such a perspective has the potential to dislocate the traumatic events of the Vietnam War that are so deeply secured in the Vietnam Veteran Narrative and Narrator in order to look into the way this traumatic event touches the structures of American society.

In these pages I have tried to understand how the complexity of our lived experiences shed light on a history of the present that struggles to reach for an ever-out-of-reach horizon. The ruptures emerging from the breakdown of articulation is what makes trauma visible; the pieces being the gift handed to the next generation. For COVV, piecing together the fragments of remembrance is fraught with uncertainty. Yet, in their discussions of their fathers, we see how this gift filters into their daily lives, prompted by their intersubjective relationship with their fathers. History *does* get under our skins; Bissell feels this as he tells us that Vietnam is *in* him. To say that Vietnam is in my interviewees, as it is in me, does not make it something easily articulated to a society that struggles to understand the presence of war. The struggle to speak, to articulate, and to be heard are crucial reminders that "War, when necessary, is unspeakable. When unnecessary, it is unforgivable. It is not an occasion for heroism. It is an occasion only for survival and death. To regard war in any other way only guarantees its inevitable reappearance" (Bissell, 2004, 65). Bissell's words provide me with the ability to cautiously conclude that Benjamin's project of historical materialism is a necessary project that promotes the utility of a theory of history as trauma, which has the capacity to convert trauma into insight. And it is with optimism that I look toward the horizon for further insights into this still in-formation presence.

METHODOLOGICAL APPENDIX

When children of Vietnam Veterans tell their stories of the trauma of the Vietnam War, whose story are they relying upon? A related and even more problematic question also remains: are the stories they tell based on reality or some mythologized story of the past? How can I tell the *difference* between fact and fiction? How can I *tell* the difference between my interviewees' stories and social narratives? More importantly, how do these questions take my research to a productive place? In this appendix, I briefly discuss my methodology, explaining how analyzing narratives is never about isolating a nugget of truth or staking a claim on the possession of pieces of stories of the past. Analyzing narratives is about recognizing the contradictory existence of two equally powerful and integral aspects of social life: the hardened structures, dominant fictions we might call them, that provide grounding upon which most of us construct our lives; and the dynamic, fluid, nearly impossible to articulate, affectual life we all live. The narratives my interviewees tell me are guided by both of these parts of social life. Some move between them more successfully than others and some depend on one far more than the other but they always recognize the existence of some larger story at work in their struggle to talk about the trauma they recognize (even at its most imperceptible level) in their fathers. This appendix is a series of meditations that explores what it means to develop a method of inquiry into traumatic impulses and the subtle transmissions of social life. As Gordon states, "method is everything and nothing much really" (1997, 24). It structures, limits, contains how we look at the data; it is the data that breathes life into the structures; it is the lifeblood of research.

My data are comprised of two co-constitutive layers: the primary layer consists of the interviews I conducted with children of Vietnam

Veterans (COVV) and the secondary layer is a combination of selective social artifacts considering the Vietnam Veteran and Vietnam War.

In the fall of 2002, I was introduced to a Vietnam Veterans organization (servicing the Western New York region[1]) that was willing to help me initiate contact with potential subjects. The men and women belonging to this organization distributed information on my research to their sons and daughters. Within a month of my initial contact, I began receiving calls and e-mails from men and women willing to participate in my research. The positive (albeit conservative) response snowballed for me and within several months I had conducted approximately 12 interviews. At the same time, the members of this organization put me in contact with several other resources that helped me do a second round of interviews beginning at the end of the summer of 2003. Through this second phase of my search for subjects I gained the remaining 13 interviewees who comprise my sample of 25 men and women.

The interviews were semi-structured and lasted from one to three hours. The length of the interview was dependent upon the individual subject's desire and ability to elaborate on the questions I asked him/her. Specifically, the interview was divided into three sections: first, I questioned the subject's knowledge of the Vietnam War and the ways s/he gained knowledge of the war; second, I probed the subject's relationship with his/her father, asking questions about the way he discussed the war with the subject; and third, I asked the subject to talk about him/herself and what s/he thought it meant to be a child of a Vietnam Veteran. The subjects also filled out a biographical information sheet for general information about themselves as well as their knowledge of their fathers' service in Vietnam. Each interview was recorded and later transcribed by me for analysis. In addition, specific personal details were changed and pseudonyms were given in order to protect the identity of each subject.

I sought out respondents whose *father* served in the Vietnam War and *returned home*. I isolated my sample to respondents whose father returned from the war (rather than including men who were killed or missing in action) because I am interested in the intersection of intersubjective relationships between father and child and collective memory of the Vietnam War and images of the Vietnam Veteran. The sample consisted of primarily white working/middle-class adults between the ages of 19 and 35 (see table A.1). It also was comprised of over twice the number of women than men. All the respondents had some level of college education even though their parents did not necessarily go to

Table A.1 Interviewee details

Pseudonym	Age	Race	Sex	Marital status	Occupation
Samantha[a]	34	White	F	Married	Homemaker
Ted	35	White	M	Single	Manager
Mark	28	White	M	Single	Director
Dominique	22	Puerto Rican	F	Single	Student
Stacey	19	White	F	Single	Student
Stan[b]	34	White	M	Married	Attorney
Greg	32	White	M	Single	Director
Renee	31	White	F	Married	Yoga Instructor
Tammy	27	White	F	Married	Student/Teacher's aide
Sandy	21	White	F	Single	Student
Tricia	22	White	F	Single	Student
Pam	25	White	F	Single	Pharmacy intern
Montana	24	White	F	Single	Student
Ashley	20	White	F	Single	Student
Tara	27	White	F	Married	Student emp. coordinator
Danny	22	White	M	Single	Educator assistant
Holly[c]	27	White	F	Single	Staff assistant
Jenna	20	White	F	Single	Student/Staff supervisor
Melanie	21	White	F	Single	Student
Trevor	23	White	M	Single	Student/Personal trainer
Beth	23	White	F	Single	Student
Lesley	25	Black	F	Married	Student
Linda	35	White	F	Married	n/a
Dana	22	White	F	Single	Student/Student assistant
Kelly	34	White	F	Married	Homemaker

[a] Samantha and Renee are sisters.
[b] Stan and Greg are brothers.
[c] Holly and Jenna are sisters.

college. It is important to note that less than half (11) of the respondents claimed that their fathers were diagnosed with post-traumatic stress disorder (PTSD). Some were not sure if their fathers had been diagnosed while several believed that their fathers have PTSD but had not bothered to go to a mental health facility to be diagnosed and treated.

NOTES

Introduction The Traffic in Memories

1. Greg and Stan are brothers, who I interviewed individually. I return to these aspects of their narratives in later chapters. I introduce them here to provide an abbreviated example of the complexity of reading my subjects' narratives.
2. Marianne Hirsch, whose research is on the Nazi Holocaust, has coined the term "postmemory" to describe the phenomenon of the absent presence of trauma for the second generation of the Holocaust in her book *Family Frame: Photography, Narrative and Postmemory*. "Postmemory," Hirsch writes, "characterizes the experience of those who grow up dominated by narratives that preceded their birth, whose own belated stories are evacuated by the stories of the previous generation shaped by traumatic events that can be neither understood nor recreated" (Cambridge, Harvard University Press, 1997, 22).
3. The methodological appendix has a detailed description of the interviewees and the interview process.

1 Exploring Trauma and Memory through the Social Monad

1. I am not asserting that these concepts all carry the same meaning. Each is a complex concept. My point for conflating them in my research is to emphasize the relationship between individual and social memory.
2. The practice of leaving objects at The Wall has become a ritualized phenomenon. Compared to The Wailing Wall in Jerusalem, the Vietnam Veterans Memorial has become a site of commemoration with affective personal exchanges. "The Vietnam Veterans Memorial has been the subject of an extraordinary outpouring of emotion since it was built. More than 150,000 people attended its dedication ceremony, and some days as many as 20,000 people walk by its walls.... The

memorial has taken all of the trappings of Lourdes and the Wailing Wall in Jerusalem. People bring personal artifacts to leave at the wall as offerings" (Marita Sturken, *Tangled Memories: The Vietnam War, the AIDS Epidemic, and the Politics of Remembering* [Berkeley, University of California Press, 1997, 74]).

3. As a sociologist and psychoanalysis, Jeffrey Prager has written extensively on the intersection of social memory and psychoanalytical theory. His book, *Presenting the Past*, deals with the complexities involved in individual processes of memory and the importance of locating individual memory in the social and historical contexts within which their memories develop through the case study of one of his patients. He has also written about this relationship in articles such as "Lost Childhood, Lost Generations: The Intergenerational Transmission of Trauma." His work sits alongside Barry Schwartz and Jeffrey Olick in terms of its contributions to the sociological study of social memory.

4. Ann Cvetkovich has done extensive work on lesbian experiences of sexuality, trauma, and abuse in literature, focusing largely on the work of Dorothy Allison. The work I cite here, *Archive of Feeling*, provides a unique analysis of social and individual memory, as it combines literature, in-depth interviews, and historical analysis to develop a history of the AIDS activist group, ACT UP. I utilize her work in my project, because she is interested in the way personal emotions and feelings work to shape the way events are remembered and memories are articulated, which is particularly important to the overall framework of my project.

5. A performance artist and activist, Lisa Kron provides important insights into alternative ways in which personal and social memory are articulated. Cvetkovich utilizes Kron's work to discuss generational transmissions of trauma. I use her work in a similar fashion, as it opens possibilities and surfaces questions about how a person's experiences with trauma move through social structures such as the family. Such flows of experiences and memories highlight the complicated and often unpredictable ways in which memories of historical events are embodied through dynamic emotional relationships.

6. It is important to note that I focus on the male Vietnam Veteran in this research. The experiences of men who fought in the Vietnam War differ dramatically from women (e.g., see Keith Walker, ed., *A Piece of My Heart: The Stories of 26 American Women Who Served in Vietnam* [Novato, CA, Presidio Press, 1985]). In addition, the social images of the Vietnam Veteran focus on the men's experience in combat, rendering women mute in much of the imagery of the Vietnam War. It is not my intention to do the same. Because I am interested in masculine subjectivity and tensions within it that the trauma of the Vietnam War produced, women's experiences fall outside the perimeters of my research.

7. I am referring here to discussion surrounding Haditha and Abu-Ghraib. To read headlines such as "Haditha: The My Lai of our Time?" or read Seymour Hersh [one of the reporters who broke open the events of My Lai] pursue the events of Abu-Ghraib reminds us that memories of the past hold deep presence in a variety of contexts.

2 Conceptualizing the Vietnam Veteran Narrative as a Narrative of Trauma

1. My focus is a slight departure from Susan Jeffords work in her book *The Remasculinization of America: Gender and the Vietnam War* (and other articles); her work is far more comprehensive and ambitious in scope with regard to the cultural forms she analyzes within the category of *the Vietnam narrative*. Because the focus of my research is on the way the Vietnam Veteran Narrative carries into the children of the Vietnam Veteran, I am more interested in how this narrative conveys and articulates trauma within personal reflections and societal images of combat, ultimately generating an enunciative site of trauma.
2. I want to make clear that I recognize that there is a body of work dedicated to film studies and analysis. My analysis of these films does not always stay within the boundaries of film theory and study because my focus is on the narratives being told of the Vietnam Veteran. I infiltrate the boundaries between written and filmic narratives for the purpose of understanding this larger social narrative. In this respect, my analysis is not a faithful film analysis.
3. This assessment is from my readings of Vietnam Veteran Narratives (see Christina Weber, "Conceptualizing a Vortical History: Narrative Negotiations of Vietnam Veterans," Department of Sociology, Buffalo, SUNY—University at Buffalo, 2001), but can also be found in works such as Lloyd Lewis's *The Tainted War: Culture and Identity in Vietnam War Narratives* (Westport, CT, Greenwood Press, 1985) and Jeffrey Loeb's unpublished dissertation, "After the Flood: Survivor Literature of the Vietnam War" (Department of English, University of Kansas, 1995). In Lewis's book, he organizes his analysis around the following themes. He first looks at the initiation process and the idealism instructing the boys' worldview as they entered the war. He then looks at the war experience and the way it breaks that worldview, ending the book with the way that break affected their return home.
4. As Kaja Silverman explains,

    The dominant fiction neutralizes the contradictions which organize the social formation by fostering collective identifications and desires, identifications and desires which have a range of effects, but which are first and foremost constitutive of sexual difference. Social formations consequently depend upon their dominant fictions for their sense of unity and identity. Social formations also rely for their continued survival upon the dominant fiction; both the symbolic order and the mode of production are able to protect themselves from interruption and potential change only so long as that ideological system commands collective belief—so long, that is, as it succeeds in defining the psychic reality of the prototypical subject. (*Male Subjectivity at the Margins* [New York, Routledge, 1992, 54–5])

    The dominant fiction relies on the ability to maintain belief in the prototypical masculine subject, which is defined by the correlation to phallic masculinity. In

particular, the dominant fiction relies on the ability to maintain belief in the gender order, which privileges the masculine subject as the holder of social power.
5. For example, Tim O'Brien writes in his memoir, *If I Die in the Combat Zone*, "Unlike the dreamy, faraway thoughts about returning alive to *the world…*" (New York, Random House, 1975, 172; my emphasis). Lewis explains this disconnection further by writing, "The returning warriors' experience in Vietnam had been located in a specific socially constructed world very unlike the world they were reentering. As their own linguistic categories indicate, 'the Nam' and 'the World' were apprehended as disparate social universes" (*The Tainted War*, 1985, 135).
6. As Michael Klein comments in his article, "Historical Memory and Film," in *From Hanoi to Hollywood: The Vietnam War in American Film*, ed. G. M. Linda Dittmar (New Brunswick, Rutgers University Press, 1990, 24), "The advertisements for *Platoon* stressed that the film was authentic as its director was 'a decorated infantryman who spent fifteen months in Vietnam.'" Richard Corliss's review of the film in *Time* magazine is titled "*Platoon*: Viet Nam, the Way it *Really* Was, On Film." (January 26, 1987, 55–61; my emphasis). The liner notes on the DVD state, "*Platoon* is the Vietnam War as it *really* was: mean, ferocious, deadly, real. And, in the hands of filmmaker and Vietnam combat veteran (decorated with a Bronze Star) Oliver Stone, it is…a landmark of battle *authenticity* seen from the viewpoint of ordinary foot soldiers." *The Motion Picture Guide* writes, "*Platoon* has no equal when it comes to capturing the *reality* of men in combat." Sheila Benson in the *Los Angeles Times* writes, "War movies of the past, even the greatest ones, seem like crane shots by comparison. *Platoon* is ground zero" (cited in DVD liner notes—my emphases).
7. It is important to note that many critiques of *Platoon* argue that the film is ahistorical in its representation of the Vietnam War. Klein states "*Platoon* does not problematize or clarify the experience of the Vietnam era. It fails to situate the American military presence in Vietnam in political or historical perspective" (Klein, "Historical Memory and Film," 1990, 25).
8. Again, this does not mean that *all* the men who served in Vietnam held these beliefs to the same degree as the prototypical narrator. In fact, Stone continually shows us how the black soldiers were not nearly as naïve about their actions in Vietnam. King, a southern black man, cannot understand why Taylor would volunteer to come to Vietnam if he did not have to. It is important to reiterate that the dominant fiction is a societal story and that white, typically middle-class men were the ones telling the story and hoping to claim the benefits of it—not black and/or poor men. Consider this exchange between Taylor and King (and a third man) as they are cleaning the latrines:

> *King*: "Now Taylor, how in the fuck you get here, anyway? I mean you look educated."
> *Taylor*: "I volunteered for it."
> *King*: "You did what?"
> *Taylor*: "I volunteered. I dropped out of college. Told them I wanted the infantry. Combat. Vietnam."
> *Third Man*: "You volunteered for this shit, man?"

Taylor: "Yeah. You believe that?"
King: "You is a crazy fucker. Givin' up college?"
Taylor: "It didn't make much sense. I wasn't learnin' anything. I figure why should just the poor kids go off to war and the rich kids always get away with it."
King: "Oh, I see. What we got here is a crusader."
Taylor: "No."
Third Man: "Sounds like it."
King: "Shit. You gotta be rich in the first place to think like that. Everybody knows, the poor always being fucked over by the rich. Always have, always will."
Taylor, the Narrator, learns this for himself through the war experience.

9. When I write *Born* I am referring to the film, not the book, *Born on the Fourth of July*. I do discuss the book and make it clear when I am talking about the book rather than the film. I primarily refer to the book in order to complement and clarify sections of the film where specific points are not as clearly articulated.

10. Steve Butler is a fictional character Stone created for the purposes of the film *Heaven and Earth*. The film's narrator is Le Ly Hayslip, not Butler. Stone used Hayslip's memoirs, *When Heaven and Earth Changed Places* and *Child of War, Woman of Peace*, for the film. Butler is an amalgam of the American men Hayslip has been involved with—both during the war and after coming to the United States. As Stone explains, "I cut that down to one man—played by Tommy Lee Jones—only because of time, as the film was already two hours and twenty minutes long. Ultimately, in my opinion, there were not sufficient differences among these men to warrant different characters" (Stone, quoted in Hixson, 2000, 242). I conduct my analysis of the film with a focus on Butler and the second half of the film (when they have come to the United States after the war), not to diminish the story or experiences of Hayslip, but to further my argument about the Vietnam Veteran Narrative. The lack of differences in Stone's view between the men points to his vision of a central masculine subject to juxtapose with Hayslip's character of Vietnamese feminine subject, which enabled Stone to further explore the problem of homecoming in the Vietnam Veteran Narrative.

11. Tracy Karner did extensive research at a VA clinic in Kansas City, Kansas. There she was a participant observer in the treatment of a group of men for PTSD. Her research relies on the narratives these men constructed while in treatment for PTSD at the VA. I utilize her unpublished dissertation and several published articles.

4 The Vietnam Veteran Father: Reconfiguring Hegemonic Discourses of Masculine Subjectivity

1. Much like the research on the category of man and the masculine subject, which came to fruition only in the last 20 years, the work on fatherhood often is overlooked as a category of analysis, even within the field of masculinity studies.

2. There are a few exceptions to this. Marsiglio did publish an edited volume on fatherhood for Sage's Research on Men and Masculinities series. Yet, even these articles take the connection between fatherhood and masculinity for granted. While the articles focus on a variety of social contexts in which the father exists, there is a noticeable absence of research that interrogates fatherhood as a social category and that conducts analysis of the links between the changing meaning of fatherhood and masculinity. The articles do not explicitly address the way shifting ideas of masculinity affect how society conceptualizes fatherhood. It is often an underlying assumption and tension—but it is rarely fleshed out. It sits in the book like a white elephant. The index in Marsiglio's book logs only two pages where "masculinity" is directly addressed and one page where "manhood" is addressed. While we might assume that the topic is so prevalent that it would be redundant to index it, it is clearly a connection ridden with anxiety for researchers in the field of masculinity. In one of the places where masculinity is directly addressed, Hawkins et al. make the following comment: "Moreover, sharing daily family work may be a more pragmatic course for changing men's lives within the family than strategies advocated by some men's movements. The painful emotional work to reconceptualize masculinity...is probably more threatening to men than changing diapers and bathing children" (1995, 53). This alludes to the fears involved, not in calling for a more active and involved father, but in addressing the more profound structural realities reinforcing not only gendered relationships, but the very basis of masculine subjectivity. The other mention of masculinity is by Marsiglio in his discussion of the way fatherhood is impacted by "hypermasculine" views held by black urban men. The focus on the limitations of minority men being able to be good fathers effectually dances around the limitations they face in the economic world. There is only passing and assumptive mention of how economically marginalized men develop meanings of fatherhood when one of the most powerful prerequisites for identifying a good father is his ability to be a breadwinner (discussed below). In many ways, this makes the *white* elephant a fitting metaphor for the ever-present, yet unspoken, struggle masculinity studies has in addressing the role white middle-class expectations of masculine subjectivity and fatherhood affect our understanding of family and gender relationships within a broader social context.

3. Pierrette Hondagneu-Sotelo and Michael Messner, in their article, "Gender Displays and Men's Power: The 'New Man' and the Mexican Immigrant Man," define this "new man" (new or modern masculinity) in the following way: "He is a white, college-educated professional who is a highly involved and nurturant father,'in touch with' and expressive of his feelings, and egalitarian in his dealings with women" (*Theorizing Masculinities*, ed. H. Brod and M. Kaufman [Thousand Oaks, CA, Sage, 1994, 202]).

4. This could be accounted for by my sample being raised in primarily working- and lower-middle-class homes. Regardless, it raises questions about the dominance of the progressive images of the new father and masculinity in practice (rather than in theory). It also provides insight into how those fathers who do not fit into this image can still be identified as successful and good fathers by their children.

5. *Without a Trace* is a crime series about a group of FBI agents who are part of the missing persons unit. Each episode revolves around their search for a missing person, leading them through the person's life and the various dramatic interactions they have with others.
6. *Cold Case* revolves around a group of detectives in Philadelphia who revisit old murder cases that have not been solved—cold cases. The show weaves together the past and the present in a visually dynamic fashion by reconstructing the traumatic moment—the murder (and the era in which it took place)—as it looks in the present lives of those involved in the victim's life. The show literally flashes between the image of the person in his/her past incarnation and his/her present bodily form. Going through the necessary drama of pointing to different suspects, the detectives uncover a variety of aspects of the victim's personal life, along with those of the other people involved in the murder case.
7. The My Lai Massacre was one of the most notoriously heinous actions of the American military during the Vietnam War. On March 16, 1968, Charlie Company First Battalion went into the village of My Lai and killed 504 unarmed Vietnamese civilians (mostly women, children, and elderly). The only American injury was a self-inflicted gunshot wound in the foot. Ultimately, *individuals* were tried for their actions but there was only one conviction (US Army Lieutenant William L. Calley).
8. This is beyond the scope of my work but it is important to point to how the unfinished business of the Vietnam War is revisited as the United States embarked on a new war—perhaps hinting at a far deeper traumatic repetition that links the broken masculine subject to larger issues of national military efforts. As such, one can look at Anderson's comments above as prescient of the events that took place at Abu-Ghraib and Haditha in Iraq.
9. It is important to note that at the time of Eleanor's murder Terry had only been drafted. The show clearly makes it known that Terry ultimately never went to Vietnam or experienced combat. By his own admission he told the detectives he was fortunate enough to be stationed in Korea.

Methodological Appendix

1. I have removed specific details about the organization in order to maintain the confidentiality of my subjects.

BIBLIOGRAPHY

American Psychiatric Association. 1997. *Diagnostic and Statistical Manual of Mental Disorders:DSM- III-R*. Washington, DC: American Psychiatric Association.
Ancharoff, Michelle, James Munroe, and Lisa Fisher. 1998. "The Legacy of Combat Trauma: Clinical Implications of Intergenerational Transmission." In *International Handbook of Multigenerational Legacies of Trauma*. Edited by Y. Danieli. New York: Plenum Press.
Anderson, David L. 1998. *Facing My Lai: Moving Beyond the Massacre*. Lawrence: University Press of Kansas.
Antze, Paul, and Michael Lambek. 1996. *Tense Past: Cultural Essays in Trauma and Memory*. New York: Routledge.
Appy, Christian. 1993. *Working-Class War: American Combat Soldiers and Vietnam*. Chapel Hill: University of North Carolina Press.
Baker, Mark. 1981. *Nam: The Vietnam War in the Words of the Men and Women Who Fought There*. New York: William Morrow.
Baritz, Loren. 1985. *Backfire: A History of How American Culture Led us into Vietnam and Made us Fight the Way We Did*. New York: William Morrow.
Benjamin, Walter. 1968. *Illuminations*. New York: Harcourt, Brace Jovanovich.
Benson, Leonard. 1968. *Fatherhood: A Sociological Perspective*. New York: Random House.
Berkhofer, Robert F. 1995. *Beyond the Great Story*. Cambridge: Harvard University.
Bhabha, Homi K. 1995. "Are You a Man or a Mouse?" In *Constructing Masculinity*. Edited by M. Berger, B. Wallis and S. Watson. New York: Routledge, 57–65.
Bissell, Tom. 2004. "War Wounds: A Father and Son Return to Vietnam." *Harpers Magazine* (December): 57–65.
Bordo, Susan. 1999. *The Male Body: A New Look at Men in Public and in Private*. New York: Farrar, Straus, and Giroux.
Boyarin, Jonathan., ed. 1994. *Remapping Memory: The Politics of TimeSpace*. Minneapolis: University of Minnesota Press.
Bruzzi, Stella. 2005. *Bringing Up Daddy: Fatherhood and Masculinity in Post-War Hollywood*. London: British Film Institute.
Butler, Judith. 2003. "Afterword: After Loss, What Then?" In *Loss*. Edited by D. Eng and D. Kazanjian. Berkeley: University of California Press.

Caputo, Philip. 1977. *Rumor of War*. New York: Ballantine Books.
Card, Josefina. 1983. *Lives after Vietnam: The Personal Impact of Military Service*. Lexington, MA: D. C. Heath.
Caruth, Cathy. 1995. *Trauma: Explorations in Memory*. Baltimore, MD: Johns Hopkins University Press.
———. 1996. *Unclaimed Experience: Trauma, Narrative, and History*. Baltimore, MD: Johns Hopkins University Press.
Corliss, Richard. 1987. "Platoon: Viet Nam, the Way it Really Was, On Film." *Time* (January 26).
Cvetkovich, Ann. 2003. *An Archive of Feeling: Trauma, Sexuality, and Lesbian Public Cultures*. Durham: Duke University Press.
Danieli, Yael., ed. 1998. *International Handbook of Multigenerational Legacies of Trauma*. New York: Plenum Press.
Davidman, Lynn. 2000. *Motherloss*. Berkeley: University of California Press.
Deleuze, Gilles. 1991. *Bergsonism*. New York: Zone Books.
Deleuze, Gilles, and Félix Guattari. 1987. *A Thousand Plateaus: Capitalism and Schizophrenia*. Minneapolis: University of Minnesota Press.
Dittmar, L., and G. Michaud, eds. 1990. *From Hanoi to Hollywood: The Vietnam War in American Film*. New Brunswick: Rutgers University Press.
Dowd Hall, Jacquelyn. 1998. "'You Must Remember This': Autobiography as Social Critique." *Journal of American History* (September): 439–66.
Faludi, Susan. 1999. *Stiffed: The Betrayal of the American Man*. New York: HarperCollins.
Felman, Shoshana. 2002. *The Juridical Unconscious: Trials and Traumas in the Twentieth Century*. Cambridge: Harvard University Press.
Felman, Shoshana, and Dori Laub. 1992. *Testimony: Crises of Witnessing in Literature, Psychoanalysis, and History*. New York: Routledge.
Figley, Charles R. 1995. *Compassion Fatigue: Coping with Secondary Traumatic Stress Disorder in Those Who Treat the Traumatized*. New York: Brunner/Mazelm.
Gergen, Kenneth, J. Stanford Gergen, and Chase Martini. 2002. "Blessed Be the Name of the Father: Generational Echoes." In *Between Fathers and Sons*. Edited by T. S. Robert Pellegrini. New York: Haworth Press, 125–39.
Gilberg, Gail Hosking. 1997. *Snake's Daughter: The Roads In and Out of War*. Iowa City: Iowa City Press.
Gillis, John. 1996. *A World of their Own Making: Myth, Ritual, and the Quest for Family Values*. New York: Basic Books.
Gordon, Avery. 1997. *Ghostly Matters: Haunting and the Sociological Imagination*. Minneapolis: University of Minnesota Press.
Griswold, Robert. 1993. *Fatherhood in America: A History*. New York: Basic Books.
Halbwachs, Maurice. 1992. *On Collective Memory*. Chicago: University of Chicago Press.
Hawkins, Alan. 1995. "Rethinking Fathers' Involvement in Child Care." In *Fatherhood: Contemporary Theory, Research, and Social Policy*. Edited by William Marsiglio. New York: Sage Publications, 41–57.
Hayslip, Le Ly. 2003. *When Heaven and Earth Changed Places*. New York: Penguin Books.
Herman, Judith. 1992. *Trauma and Recovery: The Aftermath of Violence—from Domestic Abuse to Political Terror*. New York: Basic Books.

Hirsch, Marianne. 1997. *Family Frames: Photography, Narrative, and Postmemory.* Cambridge: Harvard University Press.

Hixson, Walter, ed. 2000. *Historical Memory and Representations of the Vietnam War.* New York: Garland Publishing.

Hondagneu-Sotelo, Pierrette and Michael Messner. 1994. "Gender Displays and Men's Power: The 'New Man' and the Mexican Immigrant Man." In *Theorizing Masculinities.* Edited by H. Brod and M. Kaufman. Thousand Oaks, CA: Sage, 200–18.

Hunt, Andrew. 1997. *The Turning: A History of the Vietnam Veterans against the War.* New York: New York University Press.

Huyssen, Andreas. 1995. *Twilight Memories: Marking Time in a Culture of Amnesia.* New York: Routledge.

Jeffords, Susan. 1989. *The Remasculinization of America: Gender and the Vietnam War.* Indianapolis: University of Indiana Press.

———. 1990. "Reproducing Fathers: Gender and the Vietnam War in U.S. Culture." In *From Hanoi to Hollywood: The Vietnam War in American Film.* Edited by L. Dittmar and G. Michaud. New Brunswick: Rutgers University Press.

Karner, Tracey X. 1994. "Masculinity, Trauma, and Identity: Life Narratives of Vietnam Veterans with Post Traumatic Stress Disorder." Department of Sociology: University of Kansas.

———. 1995. "Medicalizing Masculinity: Post Traumatic Stress Disorder in Vietnam Veterans." *Masculinities* 3(4): 23–65.

———. 1996. "Fathers, Sons, And Vietnam: Masculinity and Betrayal in the Life Narratives of Vietnam Veterans with Post Traumatic Stress Disorder." *American Studies* 37(1): 63–94.

Kilby, Jane. 2003. "The Writing of Trauma: Trauma Theory and the Liberty of Reading." *New Formations* 47: 200–12.

Klein, Michael. 1990. "History, Memory, Film, and the Vietnam Era." In *From Hanoi to Hollywood: The Vietnam War in American Film.* Edited by G. M. Linda Dittmar. New Brunswick: Rutgers University Press, 19–40.

Knijn, Trudie, and Ann-Claire Mulder. 1987. *Unravelling Fatherhood.* Providence, RI: Foris.

Kovic, Ron. 1976. *Born on the Fourth of July.* New York: Simon & Schuster.

Kraus, Natasha. 1996. "Desire Work, Performativity, and the Structuring of a Community: Butch/Fem Relations of the 1940s and 1950s." *Frontiers* 17(1): 30–57.

Langer, Lawrence. 1999. *Holocaust Testimonies: The Ruins of Memory.* New Haven, CT: Yale University Press.

Lessing, Doris. 1994. *Under My Skin: Volume One of my Autobiography.* New York: HarperCollins.

Lewis, Lloyd. 1985. *The Tainted War: Culture and Identity in Vietnam War Narratives.* Westport, CT: Greenwood Press.

———. 1995. "After the Flood: Survivor Literature of the Vietnam War." Department of English, University of Kansas.

Loeb, Jeff. 1996. "Childhood's End: Self Recovery in the Autobiography of the Vietnam War." *American Studies* 37(1): 95–116.

Lupton, Deborah, and Leslie Barclay. 1997. *Constructing Fatherhood: Discourses and Experiences*. Thousand Oaks, CA: Sage.

Mason, Patience. H. C. 1990. *Recovering From the War: A Woman's Guide to Helping Your Vietnam Vet, Your Family, and Yourself*. New York: Viking.

Matsakis, Aphrodite. 1988. *Vietnam Wives: Women and Children Surviving Life with Veterans Suffering Post Traumatic Stress Disorder*. Kensington, MD: Woodbine House.

Moser, Richard. 1990. "Talkin' the Vietnam Blues: Vietnam Oral History and Our Popular Memory of War." In *The Legacy: The Vietnam War in the American Imagination*. Edited by D. M. Shafer. Boston: Beacon Press, 104–21.

Muslow, Alun. 1997. *Deconstructing History*. New York: Routledge.

Nietzsche, Friederich. 1983. "On the Uses and Disadvantages of History for Life." In *Untimely Meditations*. Translated by R. J. Hollingdale. Cambridge, UK: Cambridge University Press, 57–124.

O'Brien, Tim. 1975. *If I Die in the Combat Zone*. New York: Random House.

———. 1979. "The Violent Vet." *Esquire* 92(6): 96–104.

———. 1990. *The Things They Carried*. New York: Broadway Books.

Olick, Jeffrey. 1999. "Collective Memory: The Two Cultures." *Sociological Theory* 17(3): 333–48.

Olick, Jeffrey, and Daniel Levy. 1997. "Collective Memory and Cultural Constraint: Holocaust Myth and Rationality in German Politics." *American Sociology Review* 62 (December): 921–36.

Olson, James, and Randy Roberts. 1990. *Where the Domino Fell: America and Vietnam, 1945–1990*. New York: St. Martin's Press.

Pellegrini, Robert, and Theodore Sarbin, eds. 2002. *Between Fathers and Sons: Critical Incidents in the Development of Men's Lives*. New York: Haworth Press.

Portelli, Alessandro. 1997. *The Battle of Valle Giulia: Oral History and the Art of Dialogue*. Madison: University of Wisconsin Press.

Prager, Jeffrey. 1998. *Presenting the Past: Psychoanalysis and the Sociology of Misremembering*. Cambridge: Harvard University Press.

Ramadanovic, Petar. 2001. "From Haunting to Trauma: Nietzsche's Active Forgetting and Blanchot's Writing of the Disaster." *Postmodern Culture*, 11(2): np.

Rosenheck, Robert, and Paul Nathan. 1985. "Secondary Traumatization in Children of Vietnam Veterans with Post-Traumatic Stress Disorder." *Hospital and Community Psychiatry* 36: 538–39.

Ruscio, Ayelet, Frank Weathers, Linda King, and Daniel King. 2002. "Male War-Zone Veterans' Perceived Relationships with their Children: The Importance of Emotional Numbing." *Journal of Traumatic Stress* 15: 352–60.

Santoli, Al, ed. 1981. *Everything We Had: An Oral History of the Vietnam War by Thirty-Three American Soldiers Who Fought It*. New York: Random House.

Sarbin, Theodore. 2002. "Sons and Fathers: The Storied Nature of Human Relationships." *Between Fathers and Sons*. R. Pellegrini and T. Sarbin. New York: Haworth Press, 11–26.

Sayer, Derek. 2004. *Going Down for Air: A Memoir in Search of a Subject*. Boulder, NC: Paradigm.

Schwartz, Barry. 2000. *Abraham Lincoln and the Forge of National Memory*. Chicago: University of Chicago Press.
Shafer, D. Michael, ed. 1990. *The Legacy: The Vietnam War in the American Imagination*. Boston, MA: Beacon Press.
Shay, Jonathan. 1994. *Achilles in Vietnam: Combat Trauma and the Undoing of Character*. New York: Antheneum Press.
———. 2002. *Odysseus in America*. New York: Scribner.
Showalter, Elaine. 1997. *Hystories: Hysterical Epidemics and Modern Media*. New York: Columbia University.
Silverman, Kaja. 1992. *Male Subjectivity at the Margins*. New York: Routledge.
Somers, Margaret, and Gloria Gibson. 1992. "Reclaiming the Epistemological 'Other': Narrative and the Social Constitution of Identity." In *Social Theory and the Politics of Identity*. Edited by C. Calhoun. Oxford: Blackwell.
Stacey, Judith. 1991. *Brave New Families: Stories of Domestic Upheaval in Late Twentieth Century America*. New York: Basic Books.
———. 1993. "Good Riddance to 'The Family': A Response to David Popenoe." *Journal of Marriage and the Family* 55(3): 545–7.
Stone, Oliver. 1986. *Platoon*. USA: 2 hours.
———. 1989. *Born on the Fourth of July*. USA: 2 hours 25 minutes.
———. 1993. *Heaven and Earth*. USA: 2 hours 20 minutes.
Sturken, Marita. 1997. *Tangled Memories: The Vietnam War, the AIDS Epidemic, and the Politics of Remembering*. Berkeley: University of California Press.
Toplin, R. B., ed. 2000. *Oliver Stone's USA: Film, History, and Controversy*. Lawrence: University of Kansas Press.
Vidali, Anna. 1996. "Political Identity and the Transmission of Trauma." *New Formations* 30 (Winter): 33–45.
Wagner-Pacifici, Robin, and Barry Schwartz. 1991. "The Vietnam Veterans Memorial: Commemorating a Difficult Past." *American Journal of Sociology* 97(2): 376–420.
Walker, Keith, ed. 1985. *A Piece of My Heart: The Stories of 26 American Women Who Served in Vietnam*. Novato, CA: Presidio Press.
Weber, Christina. 2001. "Conceptualizing a Vortical History: Narrative Negotiations of Vietnam Veterans." Department of Sociology, Buffalo, SUNY—University at Buffalo.
Williams, Raymond. 1977. *Marxism and Literature*. New York: Oxford University Press.
Zelizer, Barbie. 1995. "Reading the Past against the Grain: The Shape of Memory Studies." *Critical Studies on Mass Communication* (June): 214–39.
Zerubavel, Eviatar. 1996. "Social Memories: Steps to a Sociology of the Past." *Qualitative Sociology* 19(3): 283–9.

INDEX

Appy, Christian, 122, 213

Benjamin, Walter, 7, 11, 12, 19, 213
Bhabha, Homi, 166, 172, 191–2, 213
Bissell, Tom, 12–15, 83, 89, 159, 193–4, 197, 199–200, 213
Bordo, Susan, 59, 60, 213
Born on the Fourth of July, 47, 51–8, 69, 101, 104, 209, 215

Caruth, Cathy, 33, 37, 40, 42–4, 90, 91, 92, 95, 106, 114, 174, 214
crisis of articulation, 41–5, 83–7, 89–94, 100–8, 112–13, 119–20, 171–6, 189–90
crisis of survival, 42–4, 106–8, 174–5
crisis of truth, 42–4, 52, 89–92
Cvetkovich, Ann, 32–5, 206, 214

dominant fiction, 47–8, 50, 53–7, 59–63, 66–74, 76–8, 106–10, 114, 123–4, 127–8, 131, 134–5, 142–3, 146, 148–9, 153–4, 156–7, 173, 181, 191–2, 198–9, 207–8

Faludi, Susan, 48, 53, 54, 55, 57, 60, 71, 143
father
  heroic, 157, 158, 159, 160, 161, 162, 163, 165, 166, 167, 169, 171, 173

ideal, 121, 122, 123, 129, 130, 134, 161, 173, 177, 178, 179, 182, 184, 186, 187
new, 130, 131, 149, 210
traditional, 124–5, 127, 129–30
Felman, Shoshana, 7, 8, 11, 13, 93, 194, 214

gift, the, 5, 7, 9, 10, 11, 13, 14, 18, 34, 38, 40, 43, 44, 60, 89, 93, 106, 193, 194, 199
Gilberg, Gail Hosking, 98, 103, 104, 120, 129
Gordon, Avery, 20, 21, 22, 45, 140, 142, 147, 153, 156, 160, 190, 194, 195, 197, 201, 214
Griswold, Robert, 125, 130, 131

Hayslip, Le Ly, 78–80, 209
Herman, Judith, 36, 37
Hirsch, Marianne, 6, 205
historically traumatic event, 1, 12, 15, 32, 47, 61, 83, 119, 155–6, 158, 174, 191, 193
Holocaust, 33–5, 39, 205

intersubjective/intersubjectivity, 4, 6, 9, 13, 21, 30–2, 35, 39, 41–2, 84, 86–7, 116, 122, 149–50, 153–5, 159–60, 170–1, 193, 199

Karner, Tracey X., 77–8, 209
Kovic, Ron, 51–2, 55–8, 61, 69–78, 80–2, 126, 184, 197. See also *Born on the Fourth of July*
Kron, Lisa, 32–5, 206

Lessing, Doris, 35, 39

masculine subject, 16, 48–9, 52, 53–63, 65–76, 82, 114, 116, 122, 124–8, 130–1, 134–7, 139, 142, 145–6, 148–9, 156–60, 166, 170, 173, 190–1, 198, 199, 207–8, 209, 211
masculinity, 41, 53, 60, 62–3, 65–6, 73–4, 76, 84, 124, 125, 128, 130–1, 145, 150, 157, 166, 209, 210
 phallic, 54, 68, 75, 77–9, 102, 103, 108, 111, 114, 117, 122, 125–6, 144–6, 148, 184, 207
memory
 social, 19, 25, 27
 traumatic, 6, 8, 41, 42
monad. *See* social monad

O'Brien, Tim, 8, 9, 10, 11, 15–16, 17, 32, 43–4, 53, 62, 67, 158–9, 195–7, 208
Olick, Jeffrey, 25, 26, 27, 198, 206

phallic identification, 48–9, 52, 53–6, 59, 62–3, 68, 69–73, 76–81, 125, 142–4, 165–6, 171–3
Platoon, 51, 52, 53, 58, 61, 62–6, 69, 208
post-traumatic stress disorder (PTSD), 4, 5, 36, 40, 77, 127, 175, 203
Prager, Jeffrey, 9, 30, 31, 206

Silverman, Kaja, 54, 59, 60, 70, 71, 207
social monad, 6–7, 11–13, 15, 17–20, 22–3, 25–31, 33–8, 40–2, 45–6, 48, 50–1, 77, 83–4, 100, 105–8, 111, 122–3, 141–5, 153–5, 189–90, 193
Stone, Oliver, 15, 17, 47–9, 51–3, 58, 61, 63–4, 76, 197, 208, 209
Sturken, Marita, 28–9, 150, 206

trauma
 historical, 7, 89, 106–7, 113, 114, 137, 153, 190, 193, 194, 197
 intergenerational, 36, 41, 153, 180, 192
 narrative(s) of, 47, 153

Vietnam Memorial, 26, 28, 205–6. *See also* Wall, The
Vietnam Veteran, 1–2, 5–7, 13–19, 25–7, 30–2, 97, 101–5, 107–12, 126–9, 134–51, 161, 163–5, 169–70, 176–8, 180, 184, 189–91, 193, 206
 father, 121–3, 138–9, 149
 narrative, 15–19, 47–63, 69–70, 74, 76–9, 81–2, 84, 86, 108, 114, 144, 158, 193, 196, 199, 209
 representations of, 68–71, 138–9, 141–4, 159, 169, 172, 197
Vietnam War, 1–2, 6–7, 12–13, 18–23, 29–31, 35–8, 83–7, 105–6, 108–9, 135–7, 147–51, 193–4, 211

Wall, The, 28–30, 113

CPSIA information can be obtained at www.ICGtesting.com
Printed in the USA
LVOW01*1928021015

456708LV00012B/345/P